Hello! 365 Zucchini Recipes

(Zucchini Recipes - Volume 1)

Best Zucchini Cookbook Ever For Beginners

Ms. Fleming

Ms. Fruit

Content

CHAPTER 4: ZUCCHINI SOUP RECIPES

Introduction

***

Hi all,

Welcome to MrandMsCooking.com—a website created by a community of cooking enthusiasts with the goal of providing books for novice cooks featuring the best recipes, at the most affordable prices, and valuable gifts.

Hats off to you for believing and trying out "Hello! 365 Zucchini Recipes". I would like to congratulate you for taking the first step to a healthier life. I know that you are not just here to read about the different fruit and vegetable recipes, but also to learn on how to be healthy. Since all of us want to have good health and a meaningful life, I have written a variety of recipes for fruits and vegetables that you can prepare daily. In this series, I have made the process exciting for you and I'm sure that you will change the way you think about eating fruits and vegetables. Let this be a good start to a healthy life!

I. How nutritious are fruits and vegetables?

It's a known fact that fruits and vegetables contain a good amount of natural vitamins and minerals which are very essential to our health. They are not just a good source of energy and nutrients, but also helps us to prevent many dreaded diseases. Here are some of the nutrients that fruits and vegetables have and their corresponding benefits.

1. Vitamins and Minerals

These include antioxidants like Vitamins A, C, E and selenium. Most foods have the essential vitamins and minerals, but fruits and vegetables are excellent sources, which help the body improve its metabolic processes.

a. Vitamin A

- Benefits: Improves immunity, prevents cell damage from free radicals, enhances resistance to infection, maintains skin tissue and respiratory and gastrointestinal tracts

- Sources: apricots, carrots, greens, pumpkin, sweet potatoes, Swiss chard, watercress, and yellow squash

b. Vitamin C

- Benefits: Prevents cell damage from free radicals, promotes healthy gums, helps heal infections and bruising, improves immunity and resistance to disease, aids in iron absorption

- Sources: asparagus, avocados, cabbage, cantaloupe, citrus fruits, currants, green leafy vegetables, kiwi, mangos, papaya, parsley, peppers, pineapple, strawberries, and tomatoes

2. Phytonutrients

Certain phytochemicals have been studied and the results have been made well-known. Substances in plants are mostly antioxidants.

a. Lutein – found in dark green leafy vegetables; protects against some eye-related diseases

b. Lycopene – found in tomatoes; protection against prostate disease

c. Proanthocyanidins – found in cranberries; may prevent urinary tract infections

3. Fiber

Promotes a healthy digestive process by slowing down the absorption of carbohydrates and promotes satiety.

II. Why should I eat lots of fruits and vegetables?

These are some of the health benefits and why we should eat nutrient rich fruits and vegetables.

1. Good for the heart

Harvard studied and monitored the eating habits of around 100,000 men and women in the United States for 14 years. Based on the study, people who ate more fruits and vegetables had lower risk of heart disease and stroke compared to those who ate little or none at all in their daily diet. All types of fruits and vegetables have important contributions in protecting our overall health such as broccoli, cabbage, cauliflower, citrus fruits (including their juices), green leafy vegetables and a lot more.

One of the major risk factors for heart disease and stroke is high blood pressure. To lower blood pressure, a good diet is a great tool. Patients having a diet rich in fruits, vegetables, and dairy products (limited in saturated fat and total fat) have shown good results in lowering blood pressure. Thus, people with high blood pressure can use the diet provided by researchers to regulate their blood pressure.

2. Cancer prevention

Some fruits and vegetables have cancer fighting properties which can help protect the body from cancer. It has been reported by the World Cancer Research Fund and the American Institute for Cancer Research that some fruits and vegetables such as broccoli, cabbage, garlic, lettuce, onions, spinach and other leafy vegetables can protect the body against certain types of cancers, including esophagus, larynx, lung, mouth, stomach and throat cancer.

One good example is lycopene, which makes up the red color of tomatoes, can help protect men against prostate cancer. Increased consumption of tomato products and other foods containing lycopene, especially cooked tomato products, can reduce the occurrence of prostate cancer based on studies. Studies have shown that carotenoids like lycopene which are found in dark fruits and vegetables can protect the body against certain cancers like lung, mouth, throat, etc.

3. Aids digestion

Fiber is one of the great ingredients of fruits and vegetables. There are two types: soluble and insoluble fiber. Soluble fiber consists of pectin, pentozan and mucilaginous substance, which are found in rice bran, beans, peanut, apple peel, corn, white peony of grapefruits and oranges, grape peel and many others. Insoluble fiber, including cellulose and hemicellulose, are found in green fruits, vegetables, and bamboo shoots.

Soluble fiber is essential in lipid, glucid, and lipoprotein metabolism. It lessens the time it takes for food to remain in the digestive tract, making it less prone to food stress in terms of mass and biochemical aspects. On the other hand, insoluble fibers have shown evidence in preventing constipation and gastrointestinal cancers (especially colorectal cancer). When the insoluble fiber is in the intestine, it hatches and softens the stool, stimulates the intestinal walls, increases the motility of the intestines and promotes better bowel movements.

Fiber also absorbs toxins in the digestive system, heightens the immune system and activity of the gut bacteria, which in turn reduces the risk of gastrointestinal infection. The gut bacteria frequently affect the intestinal wall, restricts cell division, and prevents the development and growth of abnormal cysts on the intestinal wall. Additionally, fiber also provides an environment against oxidants when fermented in the intestines. Oxidants and toxins are in the colon during the processing of food metabolism.

4. Promotes good eyesight

Plenty of fruits and vegetables in your diet will provide the essential vitamins to your body and maintain good eyesight. Prevent macular degeneration of your eyes by consuming Vitamins A, C and E. Vitamin A helps to avoid night blindness, Vitamin C maintains eye health, while Vitamin E helps in preventing cataracts and delaying their growth.

Therefore, it is very clear that fruits and vegetables are vital in our daily diet. Anyone can reap the benefits by eating more fruits and vegetables. It is important to eat different kinds of fruits and vegetables to get all the nutrients your body needs. Consume 2 servings of fruit and 5 servings of vegetables each day to maintain a healthy lifestyle.

There are more recipes for fruits and vegetables in this series such as

- Beans And Peas
- Fruits
- Mushrooms
- Vegetables
- ...

You have reached the end of the article. Thank you for your support and for choosing "Hello! 365

Zucchini Recipes". Let this be an inspiration when preparing food in your kitchen. Please leave your story about cooking with fruits and vegetables in the comment sections below.

List of Abbreviations

C🙂🙂King LIST OF ABBREVIATIONS	
tbsp(s).	tablespoon(s)
tsp(s).	teaspoon(s)
c.	cup(s)
oz.	ounce(s)
lb(s).	pound(s)

Chapter 1: Zucchini Cookie Recipes

***

1. Chocolate Zucchini Cookies

""A unique touch of zucchini to these soft chocolate cookies.""
Serving: 48 | Prep: 15m | Ready in: 25m

Ingredients

- 1/2 cup butter flavored shortening
- 1/2 cup white sugar
- 1/2 cup brown sugar
- 1 egg
- 1 tsp. vanilla extract
- 2 1/4 cups all-purpose flour
- 1/3 cup unsweetened cocoa powder
- 1 tsp. baking soda
- 1/2 tsp. salt
- 1 3/4 cups grated zucchini

Direction

- Set oven to 175°C (350°F) and start preheating. Prepare cookie sheets by greasing.
- Beat brown sugar, white sugar and shortening in a medium bowl until the mixture is smooth. Blend in vanilla and egg. Mix together salt, baking soda, cocoa and flour; mix little by little into the beaten mixture. Fold grated zucchini into mixture. Scoop by rounded spoonfuls and place onto greased cookie sheets.
- Bake at 175°C (350°F) for 8-10 minutes. Let cool for 5 minutes on baking sheets then transfer to a wire rack to fully cool.

Nutrition Information

- Calories: 59 calories;
- Total Carbohydrate: 8.5 g
- Cholesterol: 4 mg
- Total Fat: 2.5 g
- Protein: 0.9 g
- Sodium: 53 mg

2. Frosted Zucchini Cookies

"Serve this garden-fresh zucchini with cream cheese frosting for your family and friends."
Serving: about 5 dozen. | Prep: 20m | Ready in: 35m

Ingredients

- 1/2 cup butter, softened
- 1 cup sugar
- 1 large egg
- 2 cups all-purpose flour
- 1 tsp. baking soda
- 1 tsp. ground cinnamon
- 1/2 tsp. salt
- 1/4 to 1/2 tsp. ground cloves, optional
- 1 cup finely shredded zucchini
- 1 cup raisins
- 1 cup chopped walnuts
- FROSTING:
- 1/4 cup butter, softened
- 3 oz. cream cheese, softened
- 1 tsp. vanilla extract
- 2 cups confectioners' sugar

Direction

- Cream sugar and butter in a large bowl until they are fluffy and light. Whisk in egg. If desired, mix cloves, salt, cinnamon, baking soda, and flour; add into the creamed mixture alternately with zucchini and whisk thoroughly after every addition. Stir in walnuts and raisins. Put a cover and store in the fridge for 2 hours.

- Add by heaping teaspoonfuls on slightly greased baking sheets, 2 inches apart. Bake at 375 degrees until brown lightly, for 12-15 minutes. Transfer to cool entirely on wire racks.
- Cream vanilla, cream cheese, and butter in a small bowl until they are fluffy. Whisk in confectioners' sugar gradually until smooth. Then frost the cooled cookies.

Nutrition Information

- Calories: 181 calories
- Total Carbohydrate: 26 g
- Cholesterol: 22 mg
- Total Fat: 8 g
- Fiber: 1 g
- Protein: 3 g
- Sodium: 139 mg

3. Peanut Butter Drops

"Super good!"
Serving: 48

Ingredients

- 2 cups white sugar
- 1/2 cup milk
- 3 tbsps. unsweetened cocoa powder
- 1/2 cup butter
- 1/2 cup peanut butter
- 3 cups quick cooking oats

Direction

- Use whisk to mix milk, cocoa and sugar in saucepan. Slice butter into mixture on low heat till all is melted and mixed.
- Put on rolling boil; boil for 2 1/2 minutes. To test: Put a spoonful of mixture into cup of cold water; if it makes a ball, it boiled for long enough, if not, it's not ready. This can take 3 minutes.
- Turn heat off; add peanut butter. Mix till combined. Use heavy spoon to mix oats in;

mix all together. By spoonfuls, drop onto waxed paper.

Nutrition Information

- Calories: 86 calories;
- Total Carbohydrate: 12.6 g
- Cholesterol: 5 mg
- Total Fat: 3.7 g
- Protein: 1.5 g
- Sodium: 27 mg

4. Zucchini Granola Cookies

"A fantastic cookies recipe to use plentiful of garden zucchini."
Serving: 6-1/2 dozen. | Prep: 10m | Ready in: 20m

Ingredients

- 3/4 cup butter, softened
- 1-1/2 cups packed brown sugar
- 1 large egg
- 1 tbsp. grated orange zest
- 1 tsp. vanilla extract
- 3-1/2 cups all-purpose flour
- 3 cups granola without raisins
- 1 tsp. baking soda
- 1 tsp. salt
- 3 cups shredded zucchini
- 1 package (10 to 12 oz.) semisweet chocolate or butterscotch chips

Direction

- Cream brown sugar and butter in a large bowl until they are fluffy and light. Whisk in vanilla, orange zest, and egg. Mix salt, baking soda, granola, and flour; then add into the creamed mixture and combine thoroughly.
- Stir in chips and zucchini.
- Add by tablespoonfuls on greased baking sheets, 2 inches apart. Bake at 350 degrees until brown lightly, for 8-10 minutes. Transfer onto wire racks and let cool.

Nutrition Information

- Calories: 177 calories
- Total Carbohydrate: 27 g
- Cholesterol: 15 mg
- Total Fat: 7 g
- Fiber: 2 g
- Protein: 4 g
- Sodium: 137 mg

5. Zucchini Raisin Cookies

"A wonderful recipe for a delicious zucchini."
Serving: 3 dozen. | Prep: 20m | Ready in: 35m

Ingredients

- 1/2 cup shortening
- 1 cup sugar
- 1 large egg
- 1 cup shredded peeled zucchini
- 2 cups all-purpose flour
- 1 tsp. baking soda
- 1 tsp. ground cinnamon
- 1/2 tsp. baking powder
- 1/2 tsp. salt
- 1/2 tsp. ground nutmeg
- 1/4 tsp. ground cloves
- 1 cup raisins

Direction

- Cream sugar and the shortening in a bowl. Add egg and whisk thoroughly. Add in zucchini and stir; then put aside. Mix cloves, nutmeg, salt, baking powder, cinnamon, baking soda, and flour. Then add into the zucchini mixture; stir until mix well. Add in raisins and stir. Add by rounded teaspoonfuls onto greased baking sheets, 2 inches apart. Bake at 375 degrees until golden brown, for 12-15 minutes. Let cool for 2 minutes on pans, then transfer onto a wire rack. Cookies will be cake-like.

Nutrition Information

- Calories: 172 calories
- Total Carbohydrate: 28 g
- Cholesterol: 12 mg
- Total Fat: 6 g
- Fiber: 1 g
- Protein: 2 g
- Sodium: 152 mg

Chapter 2: Zucchini Frittata Recipes

***

6. Chicken 'n' Ham Frittata

""This hearty egg dish is special and colorful enough to serve for holiday.""
Serving: 6 servings. | Prep: 15m | Ready in: 30m

Ingredients

- 1/2 cup chopped green onions
- 2 garlic cloves, minced
- 2 tbsps. canola oil
- 1-1/4 cups chopped yellow summer squash
- 1 cup chopped zucchini
- 1/2 cup chopped sweet yellow pepper
- 1/2 cup chopped sweet red pepper
- 1 tsp. minced fresh gingerroot
- 2 cups cubed cooked chicken breast
- 1 cup chopped deli ham
- 6 large eggs
- 3/4 cup mayonnaise
- 1/4 tsp. prepared horseradish
- 1/4 tsp. pepper
- 1 cup shredded Monterey Jack cheese

Direction

- In a large ovenproof skillet, sauté the garlic and onions in oil, 1 minute. Include in ginger, peppers, zucchini and yellow squash; cook while stirring till vegetables are crispy-tender, or for 8 minutes. Include in ham and chicken; cook for 1 more minute or till heated through. Take away from the heat.
- In a large bowl, beat pepper, horseradish, mayonnaise and eggs till blended. Pour into the skillet.
- Bake without a cover at 350° till eggs are totally set, or for 25-30 minutes. Top with cheese; cover and let stand till the cheese is melted, or for 5 minutes.

Nutrition Information

- Calories: 504 calories
- Total Carbohydrate: 5 g
- Cholesterol: 286 mg
- Total Fat: 40 g
- Fiber: 1 g
- Protein: 30 g
- Sodium: 669 mg

7. Full Garden Frittata

""*Made this recipe for someone that is conscious in health. Added a fresh mozzarella and leftover bruschetta topping to lighten it up. Served at breakfast. Well loved by everyone and pinned in my book of recipes.*""
Serving: 2 servings. | Prep: 25m | Ready in: 35m

Ingredients

- 4 large eggs
- 1/3 cup 2% milk
- 1/4 tsp. salt, divided
- 1/8 tsp. coarsely ground pepper
- 2 tsps. olive oil
- 1/2 medium zucchini, chopped
- 1/2 cup chopped baby portobello mushrooms
- 1/4 cup chopped onion
- 1 garlic clove, minced

- 2 tbsps. minced fresh basil
- 1 tsp. minced fresh oregano
- 1 tsp. minced fresh parsley
- Optional toppings: halved grape tomatoes, small fresh mozzarella cheese balls and thinly sliced fresh basil

Direction

- Prepare the oven by preheating to 375°F. Whisk together in a bowl 1/8 tsp. pepper and salt, milk and eggs. Heat oil over medium-high heat in an 8-inch oven proof skillet. Put onion, mushrooms and zucchini then stir and cook until softened. Add in the left salt, herbs and garlic; cook for 1 more minute. Put in the egg mixture. Place inside the preheated oven and bake for 10 to 15 minutes, without cover, or until the eggs are set. Slice into 4 wedges. Serve with toppings if you want.

Nutrition Information

- Calories: 227 calories
- Total Carbohydrate: 7 g
- Cholesterol: 375 mg
- Total Fat: 15 g
- Fiber: 1 g
- Protein: 15 g
- Sodium: 463 mg

8. Garden Cheddar Frittata

"*An easy to make and delicious frittata recipe.*"
Serving: 6 servings. | Prep: 30m | Ready in: 45m

Ingredients

- 2 small potatoes, peeled and cut into 1/2-inch cubes
- 8 large eggs, lightly beaten
- 2 tbsps. water
- 1/4 tsp. salt
- 1/8 tsp. garlic powder
- 1/8 tsp. chili powder
- 1/8 tsp. pepper

- 1 small zucchini, chopped
- 1/4 cup chopped onion
- 1 tbsp. butter
- 1 tbsp. olive oil
- 2 plum tomatoes, thinly sliced
- 1 cup shredded sharp cheddar cheese
- Minced chives and additional shredded cheddar cheese

Direction

- Set an oven to preheat to 425 degrees. In a small saucepan, put the potatoes and pour water to cover, then boil. Lower the heat, put cover and let it simmer for 5 minutes, then drain. Whisk the pepper, chili powder, garlic powder, salt, water and eggs in a big bowl, then put aside.
- Sauté the potatoes, onion and zucchini in oil and butter in a 10-inch cast iron or other ovenproof frying pan, until it becomes tender. Lower the heat. Pour 1 1/2 cups of the egg mixture into the frying pan. Lay out 1/2 of the tomatoes on top and sprinkle 1/2 cup of cheese on top. Put the leftover egg mixture and the tomatoes, then the cheese on top.
- Let it bake for 12 to 15 minutes without cover or until the eggs become fully set. Allow it to stand for 5 minutes. Sprinkle it with extra cheddar cheese and chives, then slice it into wedges.

Nutrition Information

- Calories: 251 calories
- Total Carbohydrate: 13 g
- Cholesterol: 307 mg
- Total Fat: 16 g
- Fiber: 2 g
- Protein: 14 g
- Sodium: 325 mg

9. Garlic Zucchini Frittata

"I usually serve dishes that both contrast and complement well with each. This quick savory egg dish can easily double. You may use a leftover chopped ham or taco meat in placed of bacon."
Serving: 4 servings. | Prep: 10m | Ready in: 25m

Ingredients

- 1 tbsp. butter
- 1 tbsp. finely chopped onion
- 4 garlic cloves, minced
- 1 medium zucchini, shredded
- 6 eggs, lightly beaten
- 1/4 tsp. ground mustard
- 4 bacon strips, cooked and crumbled
- 1/4 tsp. salt
- 1/8 tsp. pepper
- 1/4 cup shredded Swiss cheese
- 1/4 cup sliced green onions

Direction

- Place the butter in a 10-in. ovenproof skillet and melt over medium-high heat. Drop the garlic and onion; sauté for a minute. Mix in the zucchini and let it cook for 3 minutes or until softened.
- Beat the eggs and mustard in a big bowl. Pour the mixture in the skillet. Scatter the bacon and season with pepper and salt. As the eggs set, lift the edges while allowing the uncooked portion flow underneath. Let it cook for roughly 7 minutes until the eggs are almost set.
- Position the skillet under the broiler, 6 in. away from the heat source. Broil for 30-60 seconds or until the eggs are entirely set. Top it off with green onions and cheese. Broil for 30 seconds more or until the cheese has melt. Slice into wedges.

Nutrition Information

- Calories: 214 calories
- Total Carbohydrate: 4 g
- Cholesterol: 338 mg

- Total Fat: 15 g
- Fiber: 1 g
- Protein: 14 g
- Sodium: 393 mg

10. Gouda Turkey Frittata

"This frittata recipe is a great way to finish leftover turkey."
Serving: 6 servings. | Prep: 30m | Ready in: 35m

Ingredients

- 1 cup diced zucchini
- 2 shallots, finely chopped
- 1 tbsp. olive oil
- 1 tbsp. butter
- 4 eggs
- 2 tbsps. water
- 1 cup finely chopped cooked turkey
- 1-1/2 tsps. minced fresh tarragon
- 1/4 tsp. salt
- 1/4 tsp. pepper
- 1/2 cup shredded Gouda cheese

Direction

- In one 10-inch ovenproof skillet, sauté shallots and zucchini in oil and butter till they become softened.
- Mix water and eggs in a small-sized bowl; mix in seasonings and turkey. Add egg mixture to the skillet; keep it covered and let cook till eggs become almost set, about 8 to 10 minutes on medium-low heat.
- Uncover the skillet; drizzle with cheese. Broil 6 inches away from the heat source till eggs become totally set, about 2 to 3 minutes. Chop into wedges.

Nutrition Information

- Calories: 171 calories
- Total Carbohydrate: 3 g
- Cholesterol: 175 mg
- Total Fat: 11 g

- Fiber: 0 g
- Protein: 14 g
- Sodium: 256 mg

11. Italian Garden Frittata

"For a yummy breakfast or brunch, serve this beautiful frittata with melon slices."
Serving: 4 servings. | Prep: 15m | Ready in: 30m

Ingredients

- 4 large eggs
- 6 large egg whites
- 1/2 cup grated Romano cheese, divided
- 1 tbsp. minced fresh sage
- 1/2 tsp. salt
- 1/4 tsp. pepper
- 1 tsp. olive oil
- 1 small zucchini, sliced
- 2 green onions, chopped
- 2 plum tomatoes, thinly sliced

Direction

- Preheat broiler. In a big bowl, beat together 1/4 cup cheese, eggs, egg whites, sage, salt and pepper.
- Coat a 10-inch broiler-safe pan with cooking spray then pour oil to warm over medium-high heat. Toss in green onions and zucchini and stir-fry for 2 minutes. Turn heat down to medium-low. Stir in egg mixture and continue cooking, covered, for 4 to 7 minutes or until eggs are almost firm.
- Remove the cover and place tomatoes and the rest of the cheese on top. Broil 3 to 4 inches from heat for 2 to 3 minutes or until eggs have firmed up. Set aside for 5 minutes to cool then slice into wedges.

Nutrition Information

- Calories: 183 calories
- Total Carbohydrate: 4 g
- Cholesterol: 228 mg
- Total Fat: 11 g

- Fiber: 1 g
- Protein: 18 g
- Sodium: 655 mg

12. Italian Zucchini Mini Frittatas

"This mini frittata recipe is so fast for breakfast or even special events."
Serving: 6 servings. | Prep: 20m | Ready in: 35m

Ingredients

- 1 cup coarsely shredded yellow summer squash
- 1 cup coarsely shredded zucchini
- 1 cup chopped fresh mushrooms
- 2 tbsps. butter
- 1/2 tsp. salt
- 1/4 tsp. pepper
- 1/2 cup all-purpose flour
- 4 eggs, beaten
- 5 tbsps. chopped ripe olives, divided
- 2 tbsps. grated Parmesan cheese
- 1 tsp. dried basil
- 1/2 tsp. garlic salt
- 1 small onion, thinly sliced
- 1/2 cup diced grape tomatoes
- 1/2 cup shredded Monterey Jack cheese
- English muffins, split and toasted, optional

Direction

- Sauté mushrooms and squash with butter in a big nonstick skillet till soft. Use pepper and salt to season; put aside.
- Mix eggs and flour in a bowl till smooth. Mix in a quarter cup of olives and reserved veggies. Use cooking spray to coat 12 muffin cups; fill half full with egg mixture. Bake till set, about 6 to 8 minutes at 450 degrees.
- Mix garlic salt, basil, and Parmesan cheese; drizzle on top of the egg mixture. Mix the leftover olives, tomatoes and onion; scoop on the top. Drizzle with Monterey Jack cheese. Bake till melted cheese, about 5 minutes. Serve over English muffins if you want.

13. Mushroom Zucchini Fritatta

"This frittata is amazingly awesome with veggie flavor and its massive size. Perfect for lunch or even a late night supper."
Serving: 4 servings. | Prep: 20m | Ready in: 40m

Ingredients

- 1 large onion, chopped
- 2 medium zucchini, halved and thinly sliced
- 1 cup thinly sliced fresh mushrooms
- 4-1/2 tsps. butter
- 3 large eggs
- 1/3 cup fat-free milk
- 1 tsp. Dijon mustard
- 1/2 tsp. ground mustard
- 1/4 tsp. salt
- 1/4 tsp. pepper
- 1 cup shredded reduced-fat Swiss cheese
- 2 tbsps. dry bread crumbs

Direction

- In a large skillet, sauté mushrooms, zucchini, and onion in butter until softened. Drain. Pour cooked vegetables into an 8-inch square baking dish sprayed with cooking spray.
- Combine pepper, salt, mustards, milk, and eggs in a large bowl, whisk until incorporated; pour over the vegetable mixture. Top with bread crumbs and cheese.
- Uncover and bake for 18 to 22 minutes at 375° or until firm. Allow to stand for 5 minutes.

Nutrition Information

- Calories: 209 calories
- Total Carbohydrate: 13 g
- Cholesterol: 182 mg
- Total Fat: 10 g
- Fiber: 2 g
- Protein: 17 g
- Sodium: 391 mg

14. Pepperoni Frittata

"This frittata should be eaten with toast and fresh fruit."
Serving: 6 servings. | Prep: 5m | Ready in: 25m

Ingredients

- 1-1/4 cups chopped onions
- 2 to 3 tbsps. canola oil
- 1 cup sliced zucchini
- 1/2 cup small cauliflowerets
- 5 eggs, beaten
- 26 slices pepperoni
- 1/3 cup grated Parmesan cheese

Direction

- In one 10-inch ovenproof skillet, sauté the onions in oil till becoming soft. Put in eggs, cauliflower and zucchini. Keep it covered and cook over medium heat for 10 to 15 minutes till eggs become almost set.
- Arrange pepperoni on top of eggs. Broil 6 in. away from the heat for 2 minutes. Drizzle with Parmesan cheese; broil till the top becomes browned a bit and eggs become totally set, about 1 to 2 more minutes. Chop into wedges.

Nutrition Information

- Calories: 181 calories
- Total Carbohydrate: 5 g
- Cholesterol: 188 mg
- Total Fat: 14 g
- Fiber: 1 g
- Protein: 9 g
- Sodium: 299 mg

15. Ricotta & Cheddar Zucchini Frittata

"A beautiful dish that is great for both breakfast and dinner. Cheddar cheese makes it more cheesy and flavorful."
Serving: 4 servings. | Prep: 25m | Ready in: 50m

Ingredients

- 3 medium zucchini, thinly sliced
- 3 tbsps. whole wheat flour
- 2 tsps. olive oil
- 6 large egg whites
- 3 large eggs
- 1/2 cup reduced-fat ricotta cheese
- 1/2 cup shredded cheddar cheese, divided
- 1/3 cup plain yogurt
- 1 tbsp. dried parsley flakes
- 2 garlic cloves, minced
- 1/2 tsp. salt
- 1/4 tsp. white pepper
- 1/2 tsp. poppy seeds

Direction

- Toss to coat zucchini with flour. Sauté zucchini in oil in a large nonstick skillet coated with cooking spray until lightly browned and crisp-tender. Turn the heat off.
- Whisk pepper, salt, garlic, parsley, yogurt, 1/4 cup Cheddar cheese, ricotta cheese, eggs, and egg whites in a large bowl. Mix in zucchini. Pour mixture into a 9-inch pie plate coated with cooking spray. Sprinkle remaining cheddar cheese and poppy seeds on top.
- Bring to bake at 350° for 25 to 30 minutes or until a knife comes out clean when inserted in the center. Allow to stand for 5 minutes before cutting into smaller pieces.

Nutrition Information

- Calories: 238 calories
- Total Carbohydrate: 13 g
- Cholesterol: 185 mg
- Total Fat: 12 g
- Fiber: 3 g

- Protein: 19 g
- Sodium: 552 mg

16. Zucchini Ham Frittata

"A quick to make frittata."
Serving: 4 servings. | Prep: 10m | Ready in: 25m

Ingredients

- 4 cups finely chopped zucchini (3-4 medium)
- 1 small onion, chopped
- 4 large eggs
- 3/4 tsp. salt
- 1/8 tsp. pepper
- 1 cup shredded cheddar cheese
- 1 cup cubed fully cooked ham

Direction

- Mix together the onion and zucchini in a 9-inch microwave-safe pie plate. Microwave for 3 to 4 minutes on high with a cover or until it becomes tender, then drain.
- Whisk the pepper, salt and eggs in a bowl, then mix in the ham and cheese. Pour it on top of the zucchini mixture carefully. Microwave for 8 to 9 minutes at 70% power or until an inserted knife in the middle exits clean.

Nutrition Information

- Calories: 251 calories
- Total Carbohydrate: 7 g
- Cholesterol: 265 mg
- Total Fat: 15 g
- Fiber: 2 g
- Protein: 22 g
- Sodium: 1134 mg

17. Zucchini Tomato Frittata

""This dinner entrée is loaded with veggies.""
Serving: 4 servings. | Prep: 20m | Ready in: 35m

Ingredients

- 1/3 cup sun-dried tomatoes (not packed in oil)
- 1 cup boiling water
- 1-1/2 cups egg substitute
- 1/2 cup 2% cottage cheese
- 2 green onions, chopped
- 1/4 cup minced fresh basil or 1 tbsp. dried basil
- 1/8 tsp. crushed red pepper flakes
- 1 cup sliced zucchini
- 1 cup fresh broccoli florets
- 1 medium sweet red pepper, chopped
- 2 tsps. canola oil
- 2 tbsps. grated Parmesan cheese

Direction

- Put tomatoes into a small bowl. Pour in boiling water to cover; allow to sit for 5 minutes. Strain and set aside.
- In a large bowl, blend together the reserved tomatoes, pepper flakes, basil, onions, cottage cheese and egg substitute; set aside.
- Sauté red pepper, broccoli and zucchini together in a 10-in. ovenproof skillet with oil till tender. Lower the heat; transfer the reserved egg mixture on top. Cook with a cover till nearly set, for 4-6 minutes.
- Uncover the skillet. Sprinkle Parmesan cheese over. Allow to broil 3-4 in. from the heat source till the eggs are completely set, for 2-3 minutes. Allow to sit for 5 minutes. Cut into wedges.

Nutrition Information

- Calories: 138 calories
- Total Carbohydrate: 11 g
- Cholesterol: 6 mg
- Total Fat: 4 g
- Fiber: 3 g
- Protein: 15 g

- Sodium: 484 mg

Chapter 3: Zucchini Salad Recipes

***

18. 7 Vegetable Salad

"Italian dressing jazzed up with basil and chives sparks the flavor of this eye-catching salad. The blanched veggies in this colorful combination retain their crispness quite nicely."
Serving: 12 servings. | Prep: 30m | Ready in: 30m

Ingredients

- 1 cup cut fresh green beans
- 1 cup fresh sugar snap peas
- 1 cup sliced yellow summer squash
- 1 cup sliced zucchini
- 1/2 cup julienned onion
- 2 small tomatoes, seeded and chopped
- 1 cup coarsely grated carrots
- 2/3 cup reduced-fat Italian salad dressing
- 4 tsps. minced chives
- 2 tsps. dried basil

Direction

- Boil 2 in. of water in a saucepan. Put in onion, zucchini, yellow squash, peas and beans. Lower heat; cover up and let it simmer till veggies are tender-crisp or for 2 to 3 minutes. Drain off; wash in cold water and pat dry.
- Transfer veggies in a bowl; put in the leftover ingredients. Coat by lightly mixing. Keep chilled in refrigerator till serving.

Nutrition Information

- Calories: 47 calories
- Total Carbohydrate: 6 g
- Cholesterol: 0 mg
- Total Fat: 2 g
- Fiber: 2 g
- Protein: 1 g
- Sodium: 132 mg

19. Antipasto Tossed Salad

"This lettuce salad with lemon juice has homemade flair."
Serving: 16 servings. | Prep: 20m | Ready in: 20m

Ingredients

- 1-3/4 cups thinly sliced halved zucchini
- 1-1/2 cups fresh cauliflowerets
- 1/4 cup thinly sliced green onions
- 1 cup reduced-fat Italian salad dressing
- 1 tbsp. lemon juice
- 12 cups torn romaine
- 2 medium tomatoes, cut into wedges
- 4 large fresh mushrooms, thinly sliced
- 4 oz. sliced turkey salami, julienned
- 4 oz. reduced-fat provolone cheese, julienned
- 1 can (2-1/4 oz.) sliced ripe olives, drained
- 1 cup fat-free Italian croutons
- 1/4 cup shredded Parmesan cheese

Direction

- Mix onions, cauliflower and zucchini in a big bowl. Whisk the lemon juice and salad dressing; put on top of the veggies and coat by tossing. Keep it covered and let chill in the fridge for a minimum of 4 hours.
- Just prior to serve, in a serving bowl, mix together the olives, provolone, salami, mushrooms, tomatoes and romaine. Pour in marinated vegetables; coat by tossing. Put the croutons and Parmesan cheese on top.

Nutrition Information

- Calories: 86 calories

- Total Carbohydrate: 7 g
- Cholesterol: 12 mg
- Total Fat: 5 g
- Fiber: 1 g
- Protein: 6 g
- Sodium: 329 mg

20. Asian Linguine Salad

"With loads of vegetables and a delicious lemon-sesame oil dressing, this low-fat pasta toss offers guilt-free enjoyment."
Serving: 8 servings. | Prep: 20m | Ready in: 30m

Ingredients

- 8 oz. uncooked linguine
- 1/3 cup reduced-sodium soy sauce
- 1/4 cup water
- 2 tbsps. lemon juice
- 1-1/2 tsps. sesame oil
- 2 medium carrots, julienned
- 1/2 medium sweet red pepper, julienned
- 1-1/2 tsps. olive oil, divided
- 1/2 cup fresh snow peas
- 1 garlic clove, minced
- 1 small zucchini, julienned
- 1/2 cup canned bean sprouts
- 1 green onion, julienned

Direction

- Following the instruction on package, cook linguine; drain off and transfer into a big serving bowl. Mix the sesame oil, lemon juice, water and soy sauce in a small bowl. Keep chilled in the refrigerator a quarter cup for dressing. Put the leftover mixture on top of hot linguine; coat evenly by tossing.
- Stir-fry red pepper and carrots in three quarters tsp. of olive oil in a big nonstick skillet or wok coated with cooking spray for 2 minutes. Add garlic and snow peas; stir-fry 2 more minutes. Add to linguine.
- Stir-fry onion, bean sprouts and zucchini in leftover olive oil for 2 minutes; add to linguine

mixture. Keep it covered and let chill in the refrigerator for no less than 2 hours. Just prior to serving, put in dressing and coat by tossing.

Nutrition Information

- Calories: 141 calories
- Total Carbohydrate: 25 g
- Cholesterol: 0 mg
- Total Fat: 2 g
- Fiber: 2 g
- Protein: 5 g
- Sodium: 415 mg

21. Asparagus And Grape Tomato Salad

"This easy, fresh and flavorful salad recipe has created reputation at a church's cooking club."
Serving: 6 servings. | Prep: 10m | Ready in: 15m

Ingredients

- 1 lb. fresh asparagus, cut into 1-inch lengths
- 1 small zucchini, halved and sliced
- 1 cup grape or cherry tomatoes
- 1/4 cup sliced green onions
- 1/4 cup minced fresh parsley
- 3 tbsps. olive oil
- 2 tbsps. red wine vinegar
- 1 garlic clove, minced
- 1/4 tsp. seasoned salt
- 1/4 tsp. Dijon mustard
- 1/4 cup shredded Parmesan cheese, optional
- 2 tbsps. sunflower kernels, toasted, optional

Direction

- In a steamer basket, put asparagus and zucchini; place the basket into a saucepan with 1 in. of water. Boil the water then steam in 2 minutes with cover. Use cold water to rinse.
- Mix together parsley, onions, tomatoes, zucchini and asparagus in a large bowl.
- Stir in mustard, seasoned salt, garlic, vinegar and oil. Pour it onto the asparagus mixture so

that it can be fully coated. Top with a sprinkle of sunflower kernels and cheese (optional).

Nutrition Information

- Calories: 81 calories
- Total Carbohydrate: 4 g
- Cholesterol: 0 mg
- Total Fat: 7 g
- Fiber: 1 g
- Protein: 2 g
- Sodium: 78 mg

22. Asparagus Avocado Medley

"This pretty blend of garden-fresh vegetables and zesty herb dressing tastes as good as it looks!"
Serving: 7 servings. | Prep: 20m | Ready in: 20m

Ingredients

- 1 lb. fresh asparagus, trimmed and cut into 1-1/2-inch pieces
- 8 medium fresh mushrooms, sliced
- 1 large ripe avocado, peeled and cubed
- 1 medium zucchini, diced
- 1 large tomato, seeded and chopped
- 1 medium red onion, sliced
- 2 tbsps. lemon juice
- 2 tbsps. olive oil
- 1 tbsp. balsamic vinegar
- 1 tsp. Dijon mustard
- 1 garlic clove, minced
- 1/2 tsp. dried basil
- 1/2 tsp. dried thyme
- 1/4 tsp. salt
- 1/4 tsp. pepper

Direction

- In a microwave-safe dish, put 2 tbsp. of water and asparagus. Keep it covered and microwave on high heat till tender-crisp or for 2 to 4 minutes, mixing once; drain and let it cool off.

- Mix the onion, tomato, zucchini, avocado, mushrooms and asparagus in a big bowl then toss lightly. Mix the leftover ingredients in a tight-fitting lidded jar; shake the mixture well. Put on top of the salad and coat by slightly tossing. Keep it covered and let chill in the fridge till serving.

Nutrition Information

- Calories: 122 calories
- Total Carbohydrate: 11 g
- Cholesterol: 0 mg
- Total Fat: 9 g
- Fiber: 4 g
- Protein: 4 g
- Sodium: 111 mg

23. Baby Kale Salad With Avocado-lime Dressing

"We pull a bunch of ingredients from our garden when we make this salad of greens, zucchini and sweet onion. The yogurt dressing layers on big lime flavor."
Serving: 4 servings (3/4 cup dressing). | Prep: 20m | Ready in: 20m

Ingredients

- 6 cups baby kale salad blend
- 1 cup julienned zucchini
- 1/2 cup thinly sliced sweet onion
- 1/2 cup fat-free plain yogurt
- 2 tbsps. lime juice
- 1 garlic clove, minced
- 1/4 tsp. salt
- 1/8 tsp. pepper
- 1/2 medium ripe avocado, peeled
- 3 green onions, chopped
- 2 tbsps. minced fresh parsley

Direction

- Mix sweet onion, zucchini and salad blend in a big bowl. Add the leftover ingredients into blender; cover up and process in the blender until smooth in consistency. Separate salad mixture between 4 dishes; Sprinkle with dressing.

Nutrition Information

- Calories: 74 calories
- Total Carbohydrate: 10 g
- Cholesterol: 1 mg
- Total Fat: 3 g
- Fiber: 4 g
- Protein: 4 g
- Sodium: 197 mg

24. Bait And Tackle Salad

"This fresh veggies with chopped zucchini, yellow squash and tomato bobbers served alongside cilantro, sweet tangy vinaigrette."
Serving: 6 servings. | Prep: 15m | Ready in: 15m

Ingredients

- 2 cups grape or cherry tomatoes
- 2 small zucchini, coarsely chopped
- 2 small yellow summer squash, coarsely chopped
- 2 tbsps. minced fresh cilantro
- 5 tbsps. white wine vinegar
- 3 tbsps. sugar
- 1 tsp. Dijon mustard
- 1/4 tsp. salt
- 1/8 tsp. pepper
- 2 tbsps. olive oil

Direction

- Mix cilantro, yellow squash, zucchini and tomatoes in a big bowl. Mix the pepper, salt, mustard, sugar and vinegar in a blender. During process, slowly put in oil. Sprinkle on top of veggies; coat by tossing. Keep it covered and chilled in the fridge refrigerator for no less than 20 minutes.

25. Balsamic Grilled Vegetable And Barley Salad

"The glaze in this recipe will surprise you with how well it complements grilled veggies. Barley makes a really great accompaniment to this amazingly delicious salad."
Serving: 9 servings. | Prep: 25m | Ready in: 35m

Ingredients

- 2 tbsps. olive oil
- 1/4 tsp. salt
- 1-1/4 cups balsamic vinegar, divided
- 3 medium yellow summer squash, quartered and cut into 1-inch slices
- 3 medium zucchini, quartered and cut into 1-inch slices
- 2 cups grape tomatoes, halved
- 1 tbsp. brown sugar
- 1 tbsp. honey
- 2 fresh thyme sprigs
- 1 fresh rosemary sprig
- 1/2 tsp. garlic powder
- 1-3/4 cups reduced-sodium chicken broth
- 1 cup quick-cooking barley
- 2 tbsps. minced fresh basil or 2 tsps. dried basil

Direction

- Mix the salt, 1/4 cup of vinegar and oil together in a big Ziplock plastic bag. Put in the zucchini, tomatoes and yellow squash then seal the Ziplock bag and turn to coat the vegetables with the marinade. Keep in the fridge for up to 4 hours.
- Mix the thyme, rosemary, remaining vinegar, honey, garlic powder and brown sugar together in a small saucepan. Let it boil and cook the mixture until half of the liquid has evaporated. Throw away the rosemary and thyme then put the glaze mixture aside.
- Put broth in a big saucepan and let it boil. Mix in the barley. Lower the heat then cover the pan and let it simmer for 10-12 minutes until the barley has softened.

- While the barley is simmering, drain the marinated vegetables and throw away the marinade mixture. Put the marinated vegetables in a grill basket or a grill wok. Put it on an open grill and let it grill for 8-12 minutes on medium heat until the vegetables has softened, stir the vegetables from time to time and use a brush to occasionally baste the vegetables with the glaze.
- Take the barley from the heat and let it sit for 5 minutes. Place the cooked barley in a big serving bowl. Put in the basil and grilled vegetables and mix until well-coated. Serve the salad while warm along with a slotted spoon.

Nutrition Information

- Calories: 145 calories
- Total Carbohydrate: 29 g
- Cholesterol: 0 mg
- Total Fat: 2 g
- Fiber: 5 g
- Protein: 5 g
- Sodium: 154 mg

26. Black Bean Bow Tie Salad

"This wonderful salad which contains beans combining with cilantro and lime dressing is perfect for potlucks and family get-togethers."
Serving: 10 servings. | Prep: 15m | Ready in: 15m

Ingredients

- 8 oz. uncooked bow tie pasta
- 2/3 cup reduced-sodium chicken broth or vegetable broth
- 3 garlic cloves, sliced
- 1 can (15 oz.) black beans, rinsed and drained, divided
- 1/2 cup fresh cilantro
- 3 tbsps. lime juice
- 2 tbsps. olive oil
- 1 tbsp. tomato paste
- 1-1/2 tsps. dried oregano

- 3/4 tsp. salt
- 1 medium zucchini, cut in half lengthwise and sliced
- 1 medium sweet red pepper, chopped
- 1 medium green pepper, chopped
- 1/3 cup chopped red onion

Direction

- Cook the pasta following the directions on package. Use cold water to rinse then drain, put it aside. Put garlic and broth into a small saucepan and let it boil. Lower the heat; let it simmer while uncovered until garlic is tender or for about 5 minutes. Let it cool slightly.
- Put everything in a food processor, and then add salt, oregano, tomato paste, oil, lime juice, cilantro and a quarter cup of black beans. Process with a cover until it smoothens.
- Pour everything into a large serving bowl. Add the remaining beans, onion, peppers, zucchini and pasta; stir well and gently toss for coating. Put it in the fridge until served.

Nutrition Information

- Calories: 159 calories
- Total Carbohydrate: 26 g
- Cholesterol: 0 mg
- Total Fat: 4 g
- Fiber: 4 g
- Protein: 6 g
- Sodium: 352 mg

27. Black Bean Spinach Salad

"A salad of black beans, walnuts and spinach served with no meat."
Serving: 4 servings. | Prep: 15m | Ready in: 15m

Ingredients

- 4 cups fresh baby spinach
- 1 can (15 oz.) black beans, rinsed and drained
- 1 cup chopped sweet yellow pepper
- 2 medium tomatoes, cut into wedges
- 1 cup shredded zucchini

- 1 cup shredded cheddar cheese
- 1/2 cup chopped walnuts, toasted
- Salad dressing of your choice

Direction

- Mix pepper, beans and spinach in a big salad bowl. Add zucchini and tomatoes on top; drizzle with walnuts and cheese. Serve alongside salad dressing.

Nutrition Information

- Calories: 322 calories
- Total Carbohydrate: 25 g
- Cholesterol: 33 mg
- Total Fat: 18 g
- Fiber: 7 g
- Protein: 17 g
- Sodium: 419 mg

28. Bow Tie Garden Pasta

"Super fun and easy to make pasta."
Serving: 14 servings. | Prep: 15m | Ready in: 15m

Ingredients

- 1 cup Italian salad dressing
- 2 tbsps. olive oil
- 1 cup packed fresh basil leaves
- 2 tbsps. grated Parmesan cheese
- 2 tbsps. chopped walnuts
- 1 tbsp. minced garlic
- 2 cups quartered fresh mushrooms
- 1 cup fresh broccoli florets
- 1 cup fresh cauliflowerets
- 1 medium onion, julienned
- 1 small green pepper, julienned
- 1 small zucchini, sliced
- 1 yellow summer squash, sliced
- 3 carrots, julienned
- 1 can (14 oz.) water-packed artichoke hearts, rinsed, drained and quartered
- 4 cups cooked multicolor cheese-filled tortellini

- 2 cups cooked bow tie pasta

Direction

- Mix first 6 ingredients in a blender, process until smooth on high. Sauté vegetables in 1/2 cup of salad dressing mixture in a big skillet until crisp-tender for about 3 to 3 1/2 minutes. Add pasta. Drizzle the rest of the dressing while tossing until coated. Serve cold or warm.

29. Broccoli-cauliflower Cashew Salad

"A summertime refreshing, healthy and low carb salad. You can add chicken or shrimp with cooked pasta."
Serving: 3 servings. | Prep: 20m | Ready in: 20m

Ingredients

- 2/3 cup fresh cauliflowerets
- 2/3 cup fresh broccoli florets
- 1/2 cup chopped zucchini
- 1/3 cup canned garbanzo beans or chickpeas, rinsed and drained
- 1/4 cup chopped celery
- 3 tbsps. chopped red onion
- 2 tbsps. plain yogurt
- 2 tbsps. reduced-fat mayonnaise
- 1/8 tsp. celery seed
- 1/8 tsp. salt
- 1/8 tsp. pepper
- 3 tbsps. chopped cashews

Direction

- Mix the initial 6 ingredients in a big bowl. Mix pepper, salt, celery seed, mayonnaise, and yogurt in a small bowl. Put on top of broccoli mixture and coat by tossing.
- Keep it covered and let chill in the fridge for 2 hours or till chilled. Just prior to serving, mix in cashews.

Nutrition Information

- Calories: 135 calories

- Total Carbohydrate: 13 g
- Cholesterol: 5 mg
- Total Fat: 8 g
- Fiber: 3 g
- Protein: 4 g
- Sodium: 296 mg

30. Butter Bean Tomato Salad

"This simple salad is for summer barbecues."
Serving: 5-6 servings. | Prep: 20m | Ready in: 20m

Ingredients

- 1 can (16 oz.) butter beans, rinsed and drained
- 1 pint cherry tomatoes, halved
- 1 small red onion, chopped
- 1/2 cup diced yellow summer squash
- 1/2 cup diced zucchini
- 1/4 cup minced fresh cilantro
- DRESSING:
- 3 tbsps. olive oil
- 2 tbsps. lemon juice
- 1 tsp. ground cumin
- 1/4 tsp. salt

Direction

- Mix cilantro, zucchini, yellow squash, onion, tomatoes, and beans in a big bowl. Combine the dressing ingredients in a small bowl. Sprinkle on top of salad; coat by lightly stirring. Keep it covered and let chill till serving.

Nutrition Information

- Calories: 121 calories
- Total Carbohydrate: 15 g
- Cholesterol: 0 mg
- Total Fat: 7 g
- Fiber: 4 g
- Protein: 4 g
- Sodium: 356 mg

31. Calico Corn Salad

" "Recipes that can be prepared in advance are best for people with little time spare like me. I always try to make new dishes; my friends and family are my tasters!" "
Serving: 8-10 servings. | Prep: 10m | Ready in: 10m

Ingredients

- 2 packages (16 oz. each) frozen corn, thawed
- 4 small zucchini, finely chopped
- 1 large sweet red pepper, finely chopped
- 2 cans (4 oz. each) chopped green chilies, drained
- 1 medium onion, chopped
- 2/3 cup olive oil
- 1/4 cup fresh lime juice
- 2 tbsps. cider vinegar
- 2 to 2-1/2 tsps. ground cumin
- 1-1/2 tsps. salt
- 1 tsp. pepper
- 1/2 tsp. garlic salt

Direction

- Add onion, chilies, red pepper, zucchini, corn in a large bowl and mix.
- Mix together other ingredients in a tight-fitting-lid jar and shake thoroughly. Pour it slightly onto the salad and mix gently. Let it chilled overnight or for several hours.

Nutrition Information

- Calories: 191 calories
- Total Carbohydrate: 15 g
- Cholesterol: 0 mg
- Total Fat: 15 g
- Fiber: 3 g
- Protein: 2 g
- Sodium: 494 mg

32. Calico Tomato Salad

""This easy and flavorful salad recipe is our family traditional dish for years.""
Serving: about 8 servings. | Prep: 15m | Ready in: 15m

Ingredients

- 5 medium tomatoes
- 1 small zucchini
- 1 small sweet yellow pepper
- 1/4 cup cider vinegar
- 2 tbsps. olive oil
- 2 tbsps. minced fresh parsley
- 2 tsps. sugar
- 1/2 tsp. salt, optional
- 1/2 tsp. dried basil
- 1/4 tsp. dried marjoram
- 1/8 tsp. pepper

Direction

- Finely slice yellow pepper, zucchini and tomatoes to 1/2 inch pieces and transfer them into a large bowl. Add other ingredients to a tight-fitting-lid jar and mix thoroughly. Combine the mixture with vegetable and stir. It is ready for immediate serving.

Nutrition Information

- Calories: 49 calories
- Total Carbohydrate: 5 g
- Cholesterol: 0 mg
- Total Fat: 3 g
- Fiber: 0 g
- Protein: 1 g
- Sodium: 4 mg

33. Cauliflower Zucchini Toss

"I appreciate make-ahead recipes like this that keep me out of the kitchen."
Serving: 14-16 servings. | Prep: 20m | Ready in: 20m

Ingredients

- 2 cups cauliflowerets
- 2 cups sliced zucchini
- 1/2 cup sliced green onions
- 1/2 cup halved pitted ripe olives
- 1/3 cup vegetable oil
- 1/4 cup orange juice
- 2 tbsps. cider vinegar
- 1 tsp. dried tarragon
- 1 tsp. grated orange zest
- 1/2 tsp. salt
- 1/4 to 1/2 tsp. pepper
- 8 cups torn salad greens

Direction

- In a saucepan, pour water to cover 1 in.; put in cauliflower. Boil. Lower heat; keep it covered and let simmer till tender-crisp or for 5 to 8 minutes. Wash under cold water; drain off and transfer into a big bowl. Put in olives, onions and zucchini; toss.
- Mix pepper, salt, orange peel, tarragon, vinegar, orange juice and oil in a tight-fitting lidded jar; shake the mixture well.
- Put on top of cauliflower mixture and coat by tossing. Keep it covered and let chill in the fridge for 2 hours. Just prior to serving, use salad greens to toss.

Nutrition Information

- Calories: 58 calories
- Total Carbohydrate: 3 g
- Cholesterol: 0 mg
- Total Fat: 5 g
- Fiber: 1 g
- Protein: 1 g
- Sodium: 116 mg

34. Celebration Antipasto

"This simple recipe is a delightful combination of vegetables that is tumbled together with a dressing that is specially flavored. It's an exciting and delectable addition to many meals."
Serving: 16 servings. | Prep: 10m | Ready in: 10m

Ingredients

- 1 medium cucumber, halved and sliced
- 1 medium zucchini, julienned
- 1 medium carrot, julienned
- 1 medium red onion, sliced
- 1 cup fresh broccoli florets
- 1 cup fresh cauliflowerets
- 1 can (2-1/4 oz.) sliced ripe olives, drained, optional
- 1/2 cup olive oil
- 1/4 cup white wine vinegar
- 1 tsp. dried oregano
- 1/2 tsp. ground mustard
- 1/4 tsp. garlic powder
- 1/4 tsp. salt, optional
- 1/8 tsp. pepper
- 1/8 tsp. celery salt

Direction

- Mix the vegetables together in a bowl and if you prefer, you can also throw in some olives. Beat the oil, vinegar and seasonings in a small bowl. Pour over vegetables and toss then leave it to chill for 3 hours. Serve it in a bowl that has been lined with lettuce and have a slotted spoon to go with it.

Nutrition Information

- Calories: 72 calories
- Total Carbohydrate: 2 g
- Cholesterol: 0 mg
- Total Fat: 7 g
- Fiber: 0 g
- Protein: 1 g
- Sodium: 10 mg

35. Colorful Bean & Barley With Almonds Salad

"Jazz up any table setting with this tasty combination of colorful veggies, beans and nuts."
Serving: 4 servings. | Prep: 10m | Ready in: 25m

Ingredients

- 2 cups vegetable broth
- 1 cup quick-cooking pearl barley
- 1 (15-oz.) can kidney beans, rinsed and drained
- 1 large red bell pepper, diced
- 3/4 cup diced zucchini
- 1/2 cup slivered California almonds, roasted*
- 1/3 cup diced scallions
- 2 tbsps. extra virgin olive oil
- 1 tbsp. balsamic vinegar
- Salt and pepper

Direction

- Boil vegetable broth in a medium-sized pot. Mix in barley.
- Cover up and lower heat; let it simmer till softened or for 10-12 minutes. At the same time, in a big salad bowl, add scallions, almonds, zucchini, bell pepper, and kidney beans.
- Add cooked barley to a colander then wash under cold water for cooling off and avoid sticking.
- On a salad bowl, place drained and cooled barley. Season pepper, salt, vinegar and oil to taste, and toss well.

Nutrition Information

- Calories: 488 calories
- Total Carbohydrate: 72 g
- Cholesterol: 0 mg
- Total Fat: 16 g
- Fiber: 18 g
- Protein: 19 g
- Sodium: 687 mg

36. Colorful Linguine Salad

"This tasty and summer-fit pasta recipe can be made as for the need of reducing high-fat food."
Serving: 4 servings. | Prep: 15m | Ready in: 15m

Ingredients

- 1 medium zucchini, thinly sliced
- 1/2 cup julienned carrots
- 1/2 cup fresh or frozen pea pods
- 3 cups cooked linguine
- 3/4 cup julienned sweet red pepper
- DRESSING:
- 3 tbsps. white wine vinegar
- 2 tbsps. olive oil
- 2 tsps. Dijon mustard
- 1 garlic clove, minced
- 1 tsp. sugar
- 1 tsp. dried thyme, optional
- 1/2 tsp. salt
- 1/4 tsp. white pepper

Direction

- In a steamer basket, put in carrots and zucchini; place the basket into a saucepan with 1 in. of water. Boil the water; steam in 2 to 3 minutes with cover. Put pea pods in and continue steaming for another 1 minute. Take the vegetable out and put them into a large bowl. Put in red pepper and linguine.
- Combine the ingredients for dressing in a small bowl and whisk well. Pour the dressing onto the linguine mixture and toss for coating. Put in the fridge while covering in 1 hour or until served.

Nutrition Information

- Calories: 252 calories
- Total Carbohydrate: 39 g
- Cholesterol: 0 mg
- Total Fat: 8 g
- Fiber: 4 g
- Protein: 7 g
- Sodium: 466 mg

37. Colorful Papaya Panzanella

"I like to combine fruits with vegetables with homemade croutons to create pizzazzy (my new favorite word) side dishes."
Serving: 16 servings (1 cup each). | Prep: 20m | Ready in: 35m

Ingredients

- 1 loaf whole wheat boule or sourdough bread (1 lb.), cut into 1-in. cubes
- 1 cup balsamic vinaigrette, divided
- 4 cups torn mixed salad greens
- 2 medium zucchini, cubed
- 2 medium yellow zucchini, cubed
- 2 cups cubed peeled ripe papaya
- 2 cups grape tomatoes
- 8 thin slices sweet onion, quartered

Direction

- Mix two thirds cup of vinaigrette and bread cubes in a big bowl. Place on baking sheets. Bake for 14 to 16 minutes or till lightly browned in color at 375 degrees, stirring once in a while. Let it cool off to room temperature.
- Mix bread, onion, tomatoes, papaya, zucchini, and salad greens in a big bowl. Sprinkle with leftover dressing. Serve right away.

38. Colorful Summer Veggie Salad

"A very delicious salad with no lettuce and is lightly dressed."
Serving: 12 servings. | Prep: 30m | Ready in: 30m

Ingredients

- 1 cup thinly sliced carrots
- 1 cup fresh green beans, cut into 2-inch pieces
- 1 cup fresh sugar snap peas
- 1 cup thinly sliced zucchini
- 1 cup thinly sliced yellow summer squash
- 1/2 cup thinly sliced green onions

- 1/2 cup chopped sweet red pepper
- 1 can (2-1/4 oz.) sliced ripe olives, drained
- DRESSING:
- 6 tbsps. olive oil
- 4-1/2 tsps. lemon juice
- 1 tbsp. red wine vinegar
- 1 tbsp. minced fresh parsley
- 1-1/2 tsps. sugar
- 1 garlic clove, minced
- 1/8 tsp. salt
- Dash pepper
- 1/4 cup shredded Parmesan cheese, optional

Direction

- Boil 4 in. of water in a big saucepan. Put in peas, beans and carrots; cook for 4 minutes. Drain off and wash under cold water. Transfer into a bowl; put in olives, red pepper, onions, summer squash and zucchini.
- Mix pepper, salt, garlic, sugar, parsley, vinegar, lemon juice and oil in a tight-fitting lidded jar; shake the mixture well. Put on top of vegetable mixture and coat by tossing. Keep chilled in the refrigerator for maximum 60 minutes. Just prior to serving, drizzle with Parmesan cheese if you want.

39. Colorful Tortellini Salad

"This is a recipe for a real Mediterranean entreé with no meat but still high in quality. It can also be served as side dish with the perfect combination of zucchini, onion and sweet pepper together with a tart vinaigrette dressing."
Serving: 7 servings. | Prep: 10m | Ready in: 25m

Ingredients

- 1 package (19 oz.) frozen cheese tortellini
- 1-1/2 cups julienned zucchini
- 1-1/2 cups julienned yellow summer squash
- 1 cup sliced fresh mushrooms
- 1 tbsp. olive oil
- 1 tbsp. minced garlic
- 3/4 tsp. Italian seasoning
- 1/4 tsp. pepper

- 1 cup julienned sweet red pepper
- 1/2 cup sliced red onion, halved
- 1 cup balsamic vinaigrette

Direction

- Cook tortellini following the direction on the package. At the same time, in a large skillet, sauté mushrooms, yellow squash and zucchini in oil until they turn crisp-tender. Add pepper, Italian seasoning and garlic; stir well. Continue cooking for another 1 minutes or until the garlic is tender enough.
- Drain the tortellini and use cold water to rinse. Transfer it to a large bowl and combine it with onion, red pepper and squash mixture. Pour vinaigrette slightly on top and stir so that it can be fully coated. Refrigerate or enjoy right away. Use a slotted spoon for easier serve.

Nutrition Information

- Calories: 261 calories
- Total Carbohydrate: 30 g
- Cholesterol: 12 mg
- Total Fat: 13 g
- Fiber: 2 g
- Protein: 8 g
- Sodium: 486 mg

40. Contest-winning Colorful Coleslaw

"Give your coleslaw a fresh and fruity flavor by using raspberry vinegar. Double the recipe for when you're cooking for a bigger crowd."
Serving: 9 servings. | Prep: 20m | Ready in: 20m

Ingredients

- 7 cups shredded cabbage
- 1 cup cherry tomatoes, halved
- 1/2 cup chopped fresh broccoli
- 1/2 cup chopped zucchini
- 1/4 cup chopped red onion
- 1/4 cup chopped sweet red pepper

- 1/2 cup white wine vinegar
- 1/2 cup canola oil
- 1/3 cup sugar
- 2 tsps. Dijon mustard
- 1 tsp. salt
- 1 tsp. celery seed
- 1 tsp. mustard seed
- 1 tsp. raspberry vinegar

Direction

- In a big bowl, mix the first six ingredients together. In a small bowl, combine the rest of the ingredients then pour over the salad. Toss well until coated. Cover bowl and store in the refrigerator for at least four hours, stirring once in a while.

Nutrition Information

- Calories: 169 calories
- Total Carbohydrate: 14 g
- Cholesterol: 0 mg
- Total Fat: 13 g
- Fiber: 2 g
- Protein: 1 g
- Sodium: 303 mg

41. Creepy-crawly Pasta Salad

"Unlike the traditional mayonnaise or Italian dressing for pasta salad, the dressing with sweet and sour taste brings about a striking flavor!"
Serving: 12 servings (3/4 cup each) | Prep: 20m | Ready in: 35m

Ingredients

- 8 oz. uncooked fusilli or other spiral pasta
- 1 medium zucchini, julienned
- 1 cup fresh cauliflower florets
- 1 cup cherry tomatoes, halved
- 1 small green pepper, chopped
- 1/2 cup chopped red onion
- 1 cup colossal ripe olives, halved
- 3/4 cup pimiento-stuffed olives

- DRESSING:
- 1/4 cup ketchup
- 2 tbsps. sugar
- 2 tbsps. white vinegar
- 1 garlic clove, peeled
- 1 tsp. paprika
- 1/4 tsp. salt
- 1/2 small onion, cut into wedges
- 1/4 cup canola oil

Direction

- Cook pasta following the directions on package. Drain well; use cold water to rinse. Drain thoroughly. Put the drained pasta into a large bowl. Put in olives and vegetables.
- In a blender, add the first seven ingredients for dressing. Blend with cover until well combined. Pour in oil gradually and steadily while blending; continue blending until it turns into thick mixture. Pour it onto salad and stir well to coat. Put it into refrigerator for a minimum of 2 hours with cover, then serve.

Nutrition Information

- Calories: 162 calories
- Total Carbohydrate: 22 g
- Cholesterol: 0 mg
- Total Fat: 7 g
- Fiber: 2 g
- Protein: 3 g
- Sodium: 380 mg

42. Crisp Side Salad

"A crunchy combination of colorful salad fixings contains a hint of sweetness."
Serving: 4 servings. | Prep: 10m | Ready in: 10m

Ingredients

- 1/4 cup olive oil
- 2 tbsps. cider vinegar
- 4 tsps. sugar
- 1/2 tsp. salt

- 1/4 tsp. pepper
- 4 cups torn salad greens
- 3/4 cup sliced zucchini
- 2 medium carrots, sliced
- 2 celery ribs, sliced
- 2 green onions, sliced
- 1/4 cup seasoned croutons
- 1 tbsp. whole almonds, toasted
- 1 tbsp. sesame seeds, toasted

Direction

- Whisk pepper, salt, sugar, vinegar and oil in a tight-fitting lidded jar; shake the mixture well.
- Mix onions, celery, carrots, zucchini and greens in a big salad bowl. Use dressing to sprinkle and coat by tossing. Place sesame seeds, almonds and croutons on top.

Nutrition Information

- Calories: 204 calories
- Total Carbohydrate: 14 g
- Cholesterol: 0 mg
- Total Fat: 16 g
- Fiber: 4 g
- Protein: 3 g
- Sodium: 382 mg

43. Crisp Tomato Zucchini Salad

"This salad recipe is Tomato Zucchini Salad served with tasty Dijon-tarragon vinaigrette."
Serving: 8 servings. | Prep: 15m | Ready in: 20m

Ingredients

- 2 cups water
- 4 small zucchini, thinly sliced
- 1/8 tsp. salt
- 2 small tomatoes, cut into wedges
- 2 slices red onion, separated into rings
- VINAIGRETTE:
- 3 tbsps. olive oil
- 1 tbsp. balsamic vinegar
- 1 tbsp. Dijon mustard

- 1 tbsp. minced fresh tarragon
- 1/2 tsp. salt
- 1/2 tsp. hot pepper sauce
- 1 garlic clove, minced
- 1 tbsp. minced fresh parsley

Direction

- Boil water in a big saucepan. Put in zucchini; cover up and let boil for 2-3 minutes. Drain and right away add zucchini into ice water. Drain off and pat dry. Place in a big serving bowl; drizzle with salt. Add the onion and tomatoes.
- Mix garlic, hot pepper sauce, salt, mustard, tarragon, vinegar, and oil in tight-fitting lidded jar; shake the mixture well. Put on top of veggies and coat by tossing lightly. Drizzle with parsley. Keep chilled in the fridge till serving.

Nutrition Information

- Calories: 63 calories
- Total Carbohydrate: 4 g
- Cholesterol: 0 mg
- Total Fat: 5 g
- Fiber: 1 g
- Protein: 1 g
- Sodium: 238 mg

44. Crunchy Asian Coleslaw

"This flavor-packed twist on traditional creamy coleslaw makes a perfect complement to the Thai shrimp. The light, tangy vinaigrette enhances the fresh flavors of the veggies."
Serving: 2 servings. | Prep: 15m | Ready in: 15m

Ingredients

- 1 cup shredded Chinese or napa cabbage
- 1/2 cup sliced water chestnuts, chopped
- 1/2 small zucchini, julienned
- 2 tbsps. chopped green pepper
- 4-1/2 tsps. rice vinegar
- 1 tsp. sugar
- 1 tsp. sesame seeds, toasted

- 1 tsp. reduced-sodium soy sauce
- 1/2 tsp. sesame oil
- Dash crushed red pepper flakes

Direction

- Mix green pepper, zucchini, water chestnuts, and cabbage in a small bowl. Mix the leftover ingredients in a small bowl. Sprinkle on top of salad; coat by mixing. Let chill in the fridge for no less than 60 minutes.

Nutrition Information

- Calories: 65 calories
- Total Carbohydrate: 11 g
- Cholesterol: 0 mg
- Total Fat: 2 g
- Fiber: 2 g
- Protein: 2 g
- Sodium: 120 mg

45. Crunchy Vegetable Salad

"This is a kid-friendly yet delicious and nice-looking recipe to be your favorite: crunchy vegetable salad."
Serving: 6 servings. | Prep: 10m | Ready in: 10m

Ingredients

- 2 cups cauliflowerets
- 2 cups broccoli florets
- 2 carrots, thinly sliced
- 1 small zucchini, sliced
- 1 small red onion, sliced
- 1 to 1-1/2 cups Italian salad dressing

Direction

- Mix all ingredients together in a large bowl and stir well to coat. Put it in the refrigerator until ready to serve.

Nutrition Information

- Calories: 176 calories
- Total Carbohydrate: 9 g
- Cholesterol: 0 mg

- Total Fat: 15 g
- Fiber: 3 g
- Protein: 2 g
- Sodium: 698 mg

46. Family Picnic Salad

"This salad is for annual family reunion, Italian dressing or other type can be used instead."
Serving: 10 servings. | Prep: 20m | Ready in: 20m

Ingredients

- 1 can (16 oz.) kidney beans, rinsed and drained
- 2 cans (7 oz. each) white or shoepeg corn, drained
- 1 large zucchini, chopped
- 1 medium cucumber, chopped
- 1 large tomato, chopped
- 1 large green pepper, chopped
- 1 medium red onion, chopped
- 6 green onions, chopped
- 1 can (3.8 oz.) sliced ripe olives, drained
- 1 cup Catalina salad dressing
- 1-1/2 cups shredded cheddar cheese
- 1-1/2 cups corn chips

Direction

- Mix the initial 9 ingredients in a big salad bowl. Sprinkle with dressing and coat by tossing. Mix in corn chips and cheese. Serve right away.

47. Farmers Market Orzo Salad

"Orzo works really great with lemony vinaigrette, cheeses (like feta, smoked Gouda or mozzarella) and vegetables."
Serving: 8 servings. | Prep: 25m | Ready in: 35m

Ingredients

- 1 package (16 oz.) orzo pasta
- 2 small yellow summer squash, halved lengthwise

- 1 medium zucchini, halved lengthwise
- 1 medium red onion, quartered
- 8 tbsps. olive oil, divided
- 1/2 tsp. salt, divided
- 1/4 tsp. pepper, divided
- 3 tbsps. lemon juice
- 8 oz. smoked mozzarella cheese, cut into 1/4-inch cubes
- 1-1/2 cups grape tomatoes, halved lengthwise
- 1/2 cup chopped fresh basil
- 1/2 cup pine nuts, toasted

Direction

- Follow the package instructions in cooking the orzo then drain once cooked. Use a brush to coat the onion, yellow squash and zucchini with 2 tbsps. of oil then season it with 1/8 tsp. of pepper and 1/4 tsp. of salt. Put the seasoned vegetables on a grill on medium heat then cover and grill or put the vegetables in a broiler and let it broil 4 inches away from the heat for 10-12 minutes until the vegetables are soft and a little bit burnt, turn the vegetables once to cook evenly. Let it cool down a bit. Slice the vegetables into pieces 1 inch in thickness.
- Combine the remaining oil and lemon juice together in a small bowl and beat until well-mixed. Mix the grilled vegetables, basil, tomatoes, remaining pepper and salt, cooked orzo and mozzarella together in a big bowl. Pour in the dressing and mix well until coated. Top it off with pine nuts.

Nutrition Information

- Calories: 291 calories
- Total Carbohydrate: 7 g
- Cholesterol: 25 mg
- Total Fat: 27 g
- Fiber: 2 g
- Protein: 9 g
- Sodium: 274 mg

48. Fast Marinated Salad

"A very chilled pasta salad with sweet corn, zucchini and tomatoes lightly dressed with dill week, olive oil and tarragon vinegar."
Serving: 7 servings, 1 cup per serving. | Prep: 10m | Ready in: 10m

Ingredients

- 3-1/4 cups fresh whole kernel corn, cooked and drained
- 2 cups cherry tomatoes, halved
- 1-1/2 cups cooked rigatoni or cooked large tube pasta
- 1 medium zucchini, halved lengthwise and thinly sliced
- 1/2 cup pitted ripe olives
- 1/3 cup tarragon vinegar
- 2 tbsps. olive oil
- 1-1/2 tsps. dill weed
- 1 tsp. salt
- 1/2 tsp. ground mustard
- 1/4 tsp. garlic powder
- 1/4 tsp. pepper

Direction

- Mix olives, zucchini, rigatoni, tomatoes and corn in a big bowl.
- Combine together pepper, garlic powder, mustard, salt, dill, oil and vinegar in a small bowl. Put on top of corn mixture; coat by tossing. Keep it covered and let chill in the refrigerator for no less than 2 hours.

Nutrition Information

- Calories: 166 calories
- Total Carbohydrate: 28 g
- Cholesterol: 0 mg
- Total Fat: 6 g
- Fiber: 4 g
- Protein: 4 g
- Sodium: 429 mg

49. Fiesta Chopped Salad

"Cut and toss the avocado garnish in lemon juice just before serving to prevent discoloration. Then sprinkle it over the top without tossing, or the salad will be mushy."
Serving: Makes 6 servings

Ingredients

- 1 red bell pepper, cored, seeded and cut into 1/2-inch dice
- 1 yellow bell pepper, cored, seeded and cut into 1/2-inch dice
- 1 green bell pepper, cored, seeded and cut into 1/2-inch dice
- 1 ripe tomato, seeded and cut into 1/2-inch dice
- 1 small zucchini, cut into 1/4-inch dice
- 2 scallions (3 inches of green left on), thinly sliced on diagonal
- 1/2 hothouse (seedless) cucumber, unpeeled, cut into 1/2-inch dice
- 2 tbsps. chopped fresh flat-leaf parsley leaves
- 2 tbsps. olive oil
- 1 tbsp. red-wine vinegar
- 1/2 tsp. sugar
- Salt and freshly ground black pepper, to taste
- 1 avocado, cut into 1/4-inch dice, tossed with 1 tbsp. of fresh lemon juice (for garnish)

Direction

- To make preparation:
- 1. In a bowl, mix the parsley, cucumber, scallions, zucchini, tomato and peppers.
- 2. In a small bowl, combine pepper, salt, sugar, vinegar and olive oil. Put on top of the salad and toss well. Correct the seasonings. Just prior to serving, drizzle the salad with the avocado.

50. Fresh Garden Salad

"A yummy salad that only takes 10 minutes!"
Serving: 2 servings. | Prep: 10m | Ready in: 10m

Ingredients

- 1/2 small zucchini, cut into 1/4-inch slices
- 1/2 small yellow summer squash, cut into 1/4-inch slices
- 1/2 small sweet red pepper, cut into 1-inch pieces
- 1 thin slice sweet onion, quartered
- 1/4 cup poppy seed salad dressing

Direction

- Mix onion, red pepper, yellow squash, and zucchini in a small bowl. Drizzle dressing then toss well to coat.

Nutrition Information

- Calories: 70 calories
- Total Carbohydrate: 15 g
- Cholesterol: 5 mg
- Total Fat: 0 g
- Fiber: 1 g
- Protein: 2 g
- Sodium: 85 mg

51. Garden Bow Tie Salad

"Add diced tomatoes and sliced mushrooms before serving if you want."
Serving: 24 servings (3/4 cup each). | Prep: 30m | Ready in: 40m

Ingredients

- 1 medium cucumber
- 1 medium yellow summer squash
- 1 medium zucchini
- 1 medium sweet red pepper
- 1 medium green pepper

- 4 cups fresh broccoli florets
- 3 cups fresh cauliflowerets
- 1 small red onion, finely chopped
- 2 packages Italian salad dressing mix
- 4-1/2 cups uncooked bow tie pasta
- 1/4 cup olive oil
- 1/4 cup red wine vinegar
- 3/4 tsp. salt
- 1/2 tsp. pepper

Direction

- Wash the first 5 ingredients without drying. Chop then put in a big bowl. Add the rest of the vegetables. Sprinkle dry dressing mix and toss to coat. Keep in fridge for 4-6 hours or overnight, covered.
- Cook pasta following package directions. Drain then rinse under cold water. Add to vegetable mixture. Whisk the remaining ingredients in a small bowl. Add into salad and toss to coat.

Nutrition Information

- Calories: 89 calories
- Total Carbohydrate: 14 g
- Cholesterol: 0 mg
- Total Fat: 3 g
- Fiber: 2 g
- Protein: 3 g
- Sodium: 296 mg

52. Garden Chickpea Salad

"You can add cooked and sliced lamb or chicken if you want."
Serving: 2 servings. | Prep: 25m | Ready in: 25m

Ingredients

- 1/2 tsp. cumin seeds
- 1/4 cup chopped tomato
- 1/4 cup lemon juice
- 1/4 cup olive oil
- 1 garlic clove, minced

- 1/4 tsp. salt
- 1/4 tsp. cayenne pepper
- SALAD:
- 3/4 cup canned garbanzo beans or chickpeas, rinsed and drained
- 1 medium carrot, julienned
- 1 small zucchini, julienned
- 2 green onions, thinly sliced
- 1/2 cup coarsely chopped fresh parsley
- 1/4 cup thinly sliced radishes
- 1/4 cup crumbled feta cheese
- 3 tbsps. chopped walnuts
- 3 cups spring mix salad greens

Direction

- Dressing: toast cumin seeds in a small, dry skillet on medium heat, stirring frequently, until aromatic. Place in a small bowl. Mix in cayenne pepper, salt, garlic, oil, lemon juice, and tomato.
- Combine walnuts, cheese, radishes, parsley, green onions, zucchini, carrot, and chickpeas in a bowl. Mix in 1/3 cup of dressing.
- Distribute greens on two plates to serve. Top with chickpea mixture. Drizzle with leftover dressing.

Nutrition Information

- Calories: 492 calories
- Total Carbohydrate: 30 g
- Cholesterol: 8 mg
- Total Fat: 38 g
- Fiber: 9 g
- Protein: 12 g
- Sodium: 619 mg

53. Garden Fresh Summer Vegetable Salad

"You can use whatever veggies you want in this salad recipe."
Serving: 6 servings. | Prep: 15m | Ready in: 15m

Ingredients

- 1 cup fresh cauliflowerets
- 1 cup fresh baby carrots
- 1 cup sliced red onion
- 1 cup halved grape tomatoes
- 1 cup chopped zucchini
- 3 tbsps. cider vinegar
- 2 tbsps. olive oil
- 1 tsp. dill weed
- 1/2 tsp. salt
- 1/2 tsp. ground mustard
- 1/4 to 1/2 tsp. garlic powder
- 1/4 tsp. pepper

Direction

- Mix zucchini, tomatoes, onion, carrots, and cauliflower in a big bowl. Mix the rest of the ingredients in a small bowl. Pour on vegetables while tossing to coat.
- Cover and keep in fridge for a minimum of 2 hours, occasionally stirring. Serve using a slotted spoon.

Nutrition Information

- Calories: 75 calories
- Total Carbohydrate: 8 g
- Cholesterol: 0 mg
- Total Fat: 5 g
- Fiber: 2 g
- Protein: 1 g
- Sodium: 226 mg

54. Garden Pesto Pasta Salad

"I love using veggies that are in season for pasta salads."
Serving: 10 servings. | Prep: 15m | Ready in: 15m

Ingredients

- 3 cups uncooked spiral pasta (about 9 oz.)
- 1/2 cup prepared pesto
- 3 tbsps. white wine vinegar
- 1 tbsp. lemon juice
- 1/2 tsp. salt
- 1/4 tsp. pepper
- 1/4 cup olive oil
- 1 medium zucchini, halved and sliced
- 1 medium sweet red pepper, chopped
- 1 medium tomato, seeded and chopped
- 1 small red onion, halved and thinly sliced
- 1/2 cup grated Parmesan cheese

Direction

- Cook pasta following package directions then drain. Rinse under cold water; drain well.
- As it cooks, mix seasonings, lemon juice, vinegar, and pesto. Slowly whisk in oil until it's blended.
- Mix pasta and vegetables. Drizzle the pesto dressing while tossing to coat. Keep in fridge for an hour, covered, until cold. Serve with some parmesan cheese.

Nutrition Information

- Calories: 217 calories
- Total Carbohydrate: 23 g
- Cholesterol: 3 mg
- Total Fat: 11 g
- Fiber: 2 g
- Protein: 6 g
- Sodium: 339 mg

55. Garden Vegetable Pasta Salad

"Start your day with this colorful and tasty garden vegetable pasta salad!"
Serving: 4 servings | Prep: 20m | Ready in: 20m

Ingredients

- 1-3/4 cups farfalle (bow-tie pasta) , uncooked
- 2 cups cut-up fresh asparagus spears (1 inch lengths)
- 1/4 cup KRAFT Classic Ranch Dressing
- 1/4 cup KRAFT Real Mayo Mayonnaise
- 1/2 cup finely chopped red onion s
- 2 cups halved cherry tomatoes
- 1/4 cup KRAFT Grated Parmesan Cheese
- 1/4 cup chopped fresh basil

Direction

- Follow packaging directions to cook pasta, don't add salt and put asparagus into boiling water for the last 3 minutes.
- While waiting, in a big bowl, combine mayo and dressing. Stir in the onions and toss in tomatoes, basil, cheese, and pasta mixture; stir lightly.
- Serve immediately or keep in the refrigerator with cover until time to serve.

Nutrition Information

- Calories: 430
- Total Carbohydrate: 52 g
- Cholesterol: 15 mg
- Total Fat: 19 g
- Fiber: 5 g
- Protein: 13 g
- Sodium: 360 mg
- Sugar: 8 g
- Saturated Fat: 4 g

56. Garden Vegetable Potato Salad

"This salad tastes so fresh and crispy!"
Serving: 12 servings | Prep: 20m | Ready in: 20m

Ingredients

- 1/2 lb. fresh green beans, cut into 1-inch pieces
- 2 medium carrots, sliced 1/8 inch thick
- 1 medium zucchini, sliced 1/4 inch thick
- 6 medium potatoes (about 2 lbs.), cooked and peeled
- 1/3 cup mayonnaise
- 1/3 cup plain yogurt
- 1 tbsp. lemon juice
- 1/2 cup finely chopped onion
- 2 tbsps. minced fresh parsley
- 1-1/2 tsps. minced fresh dill
- 3/4 tsp. salt
- 1/4 tsp. pepper

Direction

- Parboil carrots and beans in a big kettle for 5 minutes. Add zucchini then cook for about 2 minutes. Drain then rinse under cold water. Allow to cool and place in a big bowl. Cube potatoes to 1/2-inch and add to vegetables. Mix remaining ingredients in a small bowl. Pour on salad while tossing to coat. Cover and chill for a minimum of an hour before serving.

57. Garden Vegetable Salad

"Crisp and refreshing light garden salad."
Serving: 2 servings. | Prep: 15m | Ready in: 15m

Ingredients

- 1/3 cup sliced zucchini
- 1/3 cup sliced fresh mushrooms
- 1 small tomato, sliced
- 1/3 cup sliced green pepper
- 1/3 cup sliced celery
- 1/3 cup sliced green onions with tops
- 1/2 tsp. chopped fresh basil
- DRESSING:

- 1/4 cup olive oil
- 2 tbsps. red wine vinegar
- 1/4 tsp. dried oregano
- 1/8 tsp. garlic powder
- 1/8 tsp. salt
- 1/8 tsp. pepper

Direction

- In a salad bowl, combine all the vegetables. Whisk dressing ingredients in a small bowl. Pour on salad then toss until coated.

Nutrition Information

- Calories: 272 calories
- Total Carbohydrate: 7 g
- Cholesterol: 0 mg
- Total Fat: 27 g
- Fiber: 2 g
- Protein: 2 g
- Sodium: 173 mg

58. Grandma's Sweet-sour Veggies

"A big bowl of fresh veggies for a summer meal is our favorite."
Serving: 12-14 servings. | Prep: 20m | Ready in: 20m

Ingredients

- 3 cups cauliflowerets
- 3 cups broccoli florets
- 2 medium carrots, thinly sliced
- 1 medium zucchini, quartered and thinly sliced
- 1 small red onion, julienned
- 3/4 cup cider vinegar
- 1/4 cup sugar
- 1/2 tsp. salt, optional
- 2 tbsps. vegetable oil
- Sunflower kernels, optional

Direction

- Mix onion, zucchini, carrots, broccoli and cauliflower in a bowl; put aside. On medium heat, boil sugar, vinegar and salt if you want in a saucepan. Take off the heat; mix in oil. Put on top of vegetables and coat by tossing. Keep it covered and let chilled in the fridge overnight. Just prior to serving, drizzle with sunflower kernels if you want.

Nutrition Information

- Calories: 60 calories
- Total Carbohydrate: 10 g
- Cholesterol: 0 mg
- Total Fat: 2 g
- Fiber: 0 g
- Protein: 1 g
- Sodium: 17 mg

59. Great Garden Veggies

"Veggies are fantastic with grilled fish, chicken, etc."
Serving: 4 servings. | Prep: 15m | Ready in: 15m

Ingredients

- 1 medium zucchini, cut into 1/4-inch slices
- 1 medium yellow summer squash, cut into 1/4-inch slices
- 1/4 cup sliced onion
- 1 tbsp. butter
- 1 medium tomato, cut into wedges
- 1/4 tsp. salt
- 1/4 tsp. garlic salt
- 1/4 tsp. dried basil
- 1/4 tsp. pepper
- 2 tbsps. grated Parmesan cheese

Direction

- Sauté onion, yellow squash, and zucchini in butter in a big skillet until crisp-tender. Add pepper, basil, garlic salt, salt, and tomato. Cook until heated through for another 2-3 minutes. Sprinkle parmesan cheese on top.

Nutrition Information

- Calories: 64 calories

- Total Carbohydrate: 6 g
- Cholesterol: 10 mg
- Total Fat: 4 g
- Fiber: 2 g
- Protein: 3 g
- Sodium: 342 mg

60. Grilled Corn Pasta Salad

"Combine sweet corn, zucchini, and tomatoes to make this perfect and colorful salad. This dish is better when served on warm weather. Coat the fresh ingredients with oil, mild basil vinegar, and other seasonings and herbs."
Serving: 8 servings. | Prep: 20m | Ready in: 45m

Ingredients

- 4 large ears sweet corn in husks
- 1-1/2 cups uncooked penne pasta
- 2 cups cherry tomatoes
- 1 medium zucchini, thinly sliced
- 1 can (2-1/4 oz.) sliced ripe olives, drained
- 1/3 cup white wine vinegar
- 2 tbsps. olive oil
- 1 tbsp. minced fresh basil or 1 tsp. dried basil
- 1 tsp. sugar
- 1 tsp. salt
- 1/2 tsp. ground mustard
- 1/4 tsp. garlic powder
- 1/4 tsp. pepper

Direction

- Peel corn husks carefully up to 1-inch of the bottom of the corn. Remove the silk and rewrap the corn with husks. Tie the husks and corn together with kitchen string and place it inside the stockpot. Cover the corn with cold water and soak for at least 20 minutes. Drain it well.
- Cover the corn and grill over medium heat, turning it occasionally until tender, for about 25-30 minutes.
- Cook the pasta following the package directions. Rinse the cooked pasta with cold water and drain. Remove the kernels from the

cobs once cool enough to handle and put it in a large bowl. Add olives, tomatoes, pasta, and zucchini into the bowl.
- Mix all the remaining ingredients in a small bowl. Pour the mixture all over the salad, tossing it well to coat the salad. Cover the bowl and place it inside the refrigerator before serving.

Nutrition Information

- Calories: 164 calories
- Total Carbohydrate: 27 g
- Cholesterol: 0 mg
- Total Fat: 6 g
- Fiber: 3 g
- Protein: 5 g
- Sodium: 382 mg

61. Grilled Vegetable Orzo Salad

"It's picnic time! Add this orzo salad dish to your picnic for a refreshing flavor."
Serving: 8 servings. | Prep: 35m | Ready in: 45m

Ingredients

- 1-1/4 cups uncooked orzo pasta
- 1/2 lb. fresh asparagus, trimmed
- 1 medium zucchini, cut lengthwise into 1/2-inch slices
- 1 medium sweet yellow or red pepper, halved
- 1 large portobello mushroom, stem removed
- 1/2 medium red onion, halved
- DRESSING:
- 1/3 cup olive oil
- 1/4 cup balsamic vinegar
- 3 tbsps. lemon juice
- 4 garlic cloves, minced
- 1 tsp. lemon-pepper seasoning
- SALAD:
- 1 cup grape tomatoes, halved
- 1 tbsp. minced fresh parsley
- 1 tbsp. minced fresh basil
- 1/2 tsp. salt
- 1/4 tsp. pepper

- 1 cup (4 oz.) crumbled feta cheese

Direction

- Follow packaging instructions to cook the orzo. In a big bowl, add vegetables. Beat the dressing ingredients in a small-sized bowl; toss with the vegetables until coated.
- Take out the vegetables and reserve dressing. On medium heat, grill with cover the pepper, mushroom, and onion for 5 to 10 minutes until tender, flipping occasionally. For 3 to 4 minutes, grill with cover the zucchini and asparagus until cooked to the desired doneness, flipping occasionally.
- Let vegetables cool enough to handle; slice into bite-size pieces. Mix together tomatoes, pepper, basil, reserved dressing, parsley, cooked orzo, salt, and grilled vegetables in a big bowl; tossing until blended. Keep in refrigerator until cold or eat at room temperature. Add in cheese just before serving.

Nutrition Information

- Calories: 260 calories
- Total Carbohydrate: 30 g
- Cholesterol: 8 mg
- Total Fat: 12 g
- Fiber: 2 g
- Protein: 8 g
- Sodium: 352 mg

62. Grilled Vegetable Ranch Salad

"Combine some of your garden goodies to make this quick and easy salad. Serve with grilled salmon or burgers and hotdogs."
Serving: 6 servings (1 cup dressing). | Prep: 20m | Ready in: 30m

Ingredients

- 1 yellow summer squash
- 1 medium zucchini
- 1 small red onion
- 1 small eggplant
- 1 small sweet red pepper
- 2 tsps. olive oil
- 2 tsps. balsamic vinegar
- 2 tsps. reduced-sodium soy sauce
- 1/2 tsp. dried oregano
- 1/4 tsp. dried rosemary, crushed
- 1/3 cup sour cream
- 1/3 cup mayonnaise
- 1/4 cup 2% milk
- 4 tsps. ranch salad dressing mix
- 1/2 tsp. garlic salt
- 1/4 tsp. pepper
- 6 cups spring mix salad greens

Direction

- Cut zucchini, red onion, and squash. Slice red pepper into 1-inch pieces and cube eggplant. Transfer into a big bowl and stir in vinegar, rosemary, soy sauce, oil, and oregano, tossing until coated.
- Place into a grill wok or basket. On medium heat, grill with cover until tender, stir once, 10 to 12 minutes.
- Beat mayonnaise, garlic salt, milk, sour cream, pepper, and dressing mix in a small sized bowl. Distribute salad greens onto 6 plates and add the grilled vegetables on top. Serve with dressing.

Nutrition Information

- Calories: 194 calories
- Total Carbohydrate: 14 g
- Cholesterol: 14 mg
- Total Fat: 14 g
- Fiber: 5 g
- Protein: 4 g
- Sodium: 766 mg

63. Grilled Vegetable Salad With Poppy Seed Dressing

"A fresh and tasty salad inspired by Italian cuisine. Enjoy the combination of sweet and sour flavors."
Serving: 2 servings. | Prep: 15m | Ready in: 25m

Ingredients

- 2 tbsps. canola oil
- 1 tbsp. cider vinegar
- 2 tsps. sugar
- 1/2 tsp. grated onion
- 1/2 tsp. poppy seeds
- 1/4 tsp. ground mustard
- Dash salt
- SALAD:
- 1 small zucchini, cut into 3/4-inch pieces
- 1 small sweet yellow pepper, cut into 1-inch pieces
- 2/3 cup cherry tomatoes
- 2 tsps. olive oil
- 1/4 tsp. salt
- 1/8 tsp. freshly ground pepper
- 2 tsps. minced fresh basil
- 2 tsps. minced fresh parsley
- 1 tsp. minced fresh thyme

Direction

- Beat first seven ingredients in a small sized bowl until combined. Keep in refrigerator until ready to use.
- Mix yellow pepper, tomatoes, and zucchini in a big bowl. Stir in pepper, oil, and salt until coated. Place onto open grill basket or grill wok and transfer to grill rack. On medium-high heat, grill with a cover, stir occasionally, 10 to 12 minutes until vegetables are tender and crispy.
- Prepare a serving bowl and place in the vegetables. Season with herbs and serve with dressing.

Nutrition Information

- Calories: 219 calories
- Total Carbohydrate: 11 g
- Cholesterol: 0 mg
- Total Fat: 19 g
- Fiber: 2 g
- Protein: 2 g
- Sodium: 378 mg

64. Harvest Layered Salad

"This variation is topped with a tasty vinegar-and-oil dressing instead of a mayonnaise topping like the usual version of layered salad."
Serving: 10-14 servings. | Prep: 20m | Ready in: 20m

Ingredients

- 2-1/2 cups shredded carrots
- 2-1/2 cups sliced fresh mushrooms
- 2-1/2 cups shredded cabbage
- 2-1/2 cups sliced zucchini
- 1 small red onion, thinly sliced
- 1 cup shredded Colby or cheddar cheese
- DRESSING:
- 1/4 cup vegetable oil
- 2 tbsps. red wine vinegar
- 1/8 tsp. ground mustard
- 1/8 tsp. sugar
- 1/8 tsp. garlic salt
- 1/8 tsp. pepper

Direction

- Layer the initial 6 ingredients following the listed order in a 3-1/2 quart bowl. In a jar with a tight-fitting lid, mix all the dressing ingredients then shake well. Spread over the salad then immediately serve.

Nutrition Information

- Calories: 86 calories
- Total Carbohydrate: 5 g
- Cholesterol: 8 mg
- Total Fat: 7 g
- Fiber: 1 g
- Protein: 3 g
- Sodium: 75 mg

65. Hearty Chicken And Rice Salad

"A salad recipe I learned from a party then modified it a bit."
Serving: 6-8 servings. | Prep: 10m | Ready in: 10m

Ingredients

- 2 cups cooked rice
- 1 medium carrot, chopped
- 1 small zucchini, chopped
- 1 celery rib, thinly sliced
- 1/2 cup cubed cooked chicken
- 1/2 cup cubed fully cooked ham
- 1/2 cup cubed Swiss cheese
- 2 hard-boiled large eggs, chopped
- 2 tbsps. mayonnaise
- 1 tbsp. minced fresh parsley
- 1 tbsp. lemon juice
- 1 tbsp. olive oil
- 1/2 tsp. salt
- 1/8 tsp. pepper

Direction

- Mix all ingredients in a big bowl. Keep it covered and let chill in the fridge for 4 hours or overnight.

Nutrition Information

- Calories: 179 calories
- Total Carbohydrate: 13 g
- Cholesterol: 74 mg
- Total Fat: 10 g
- Fiber: 1 g
- Protein: 9 g
- Sodium: 331 mg

66. Hearty Tortellini Salad

"This salad's a family favorite-especially at summer picnics-and unbelievably easy."
Serving: 12 servings. | Prep: 10m | Ready in: 20m

Ingredients

- 1 package (19 oz.) frozen cheese tortellini
- 1 cup grape tomatoes, halved
- 1 cup chopped zucchini
- 1 cup chopped yellow summer squash
- 4 oz. provolone cheese, cubed
- 1 package (3-1/2 oz.) sliced pepperoni
- 1/2 cup prepared pesto
- 1/8 tsp. salt
- 1/8 tsp. pepper

Direction

- Based on the instructions on the package, cook tortellini.
- At the same time, mix the leftover ingredients in a big bowl. Drain tortellini off and wash under cold water. Pour to vegetable mixture and coat by tossing. Keep it covered and let chill in the fridge till serving.

Nutrition Information

- Calories: 220 calories
- Total Carbohydrate: 14 g
- Cholesterol: 24 mg
- Total Fat: 14 g
- Fiber: 1 g
- Protein: 10 g
- Sodium: 457 mg

67. Heavenly Zucchini Salad

"We always have an overabundance of zucchini in our garden, so I came up with this tasty recipe to use some of the bounty."
Serving: 6-8 servings. | Prep: 20m | Ready in: 20m

Ingredients

- 2 medium zucchini, diced
- 1 cup chopped red onion
- 1 cup chopped sweet red pepper
- 1/2 cup chopped green pepper
- 3 small sweet pickles, chopped
- 1/4 cup peanuts, chopped
- SALAD DRESSING:
- 3/4 cup cider vinegar
- 1/4 cup vegetable oil
- 2/3 cup sugar
- 1/2 tsp. salt
- 1/4 tsp. pepper

Direction

- Combine the initial 6 ingredients in a big bowl. Mix the salad dressing ingredients in a tight-fitting lidded jar then shake the mixture well. Put on top of salad and coat by tossing. Keep it covered and let chill in the refrigerator for no less than 60 minutes. Use a slotted spoon to serve.

68. Heirloom Tomato & Zucchini Salad

"Those with gardens can make full use of veggies and fresh herbs. It is juicy with tomato wedges."
Serving: 12 servings (1 cup each). | Prep: 25m | Ready in: 25m

Ingredients

- 7 large heirloom tomatoes (about 2-1/2 lbs.), cut into wedges
- 3 medium zucchini, halved lengthwise and thinly sliced
- 2 medium sweet yellow peppers, thinly sliced

- 1/3 cup cider vinegar
- 3 tbsps. olive oil
- 1 tbsp. sugar
- 1-1/2 tsps. salt
- 1 tbsp. each minced fresh basil, parsley and tarragon

Direction

- Mix together peppers, zucchini and tomatoes in a large bowl. Mix salt, sugar, oil and vinegar in a small bowl; whisk well until everything is well-combined. Mix in herbs.
- Pour the dressing slightly on salad just before serving. Stir gently to coat.

Nutrition Information

- Calories: 68 calories
- Total Carbohydrate: 8 g
- Cholesterol: 0 mg
- Total Fat: 4 g
- Fiber: 2 g
- Protein: 2 g
- Sodium: 306 mg

69. Herb Garden Zucchini

"Great side dish for steak or grilled chicken."
Serving: 6 servings plus 1 cup leftover dressing. | Prep: 20m | Ready in: 20m

Ingredients

- 3 large zucchini, thinly sliced
- 1 tsp. salt
- 1/2 cup olive oil
- 1/4 cup fresh basil leaves
- 1/4 cup packed fresh parsley sprigs
- 1/4 cup minced fresh rosemary
- 1/4 cup fresh thyme
- 1/4 cup lemon juice
- 3 tbsps. honey
- 2 tbsps. Dijon mustard
- 4 garlic cloves, peeled

Direction

- Put zucchini in a colander above a plate. Sprinkle salt then toss. Let it stand for half an hour. Rinse, drain well, then pat dry.
- In a food processor, put garlic, mustard, honey, lemon juice, herbs, and oil. Cover then process until it's smooth. Place zucchini in a big bowl. Drizzle 1/4 cup of dressing on zucchini. Toss until coated. Cover then keep the rest of the dressing in fridge for a maximum of 2 days.

Nutrition Information

- Calories: 68 calories
- Total Carbohydrate: 8 g
- Cholesterol: 0 mg
- Total Fat: 4 g
- Fiber: 2 g
- Protein: 2 g
- Sodium: 434 mg

70. Italian Dressing Pasta Salad

"A great make-ahead dish will herbs, veggies is hearty enough for a light meal."
Serving: 36 servings. | Prep: 40m | Ready in: 60m

Ingredients

- 2 packages (12 oz. each) tricolor spiral pasta
- 2 packages (16 oz. each) frozen California-blend vegetables, thawed
- 2 pints grape tomatoes
- 1 large zucchini, halved and thinly sliced
- 1 large yellow summer squash, quartered and thinly sliced
- 1 large red onion, finely chopped
- 1 block (8 oz.) cheddar cheese, cubed
- 1 block (8 oz.) Monterey Jack cheese, cubed
- 2 packages (4 oz. each) crumbled tomato and basil feta cheese
- 1 bottle (16 oz.) Italian salad dressing
- 3 tbsps. minced fresh parsley
- 1 tbsp. minced fresh basil

- 1 tsp. Italian seasoning
- 1 tsp. seasoned salt
- 1/2 tsp. pepper
- 1 can (3.8 oz.) sliced ripe olives, drained
- Grated Romano cheese, optional

Direction

- Following the instructions on the package, cook pasta. Wash under cold water; drain well. Mix pasta, cheeses, onion, yellow squash, zucchini, tomatoes and California vegetables in 2 big bowls.
- Mix the pepper, seasoned salt, Italian seasoning, basil, parsley and salad dressing in a small bowl. Put on top of pasta mixture; coat by tossing. Mix in olives. Keep it covered and let chill in the refrigerator for 8 hours or overnight.
- Mix prior to serving. Serve with Romano cheese if you want.

Nutrition Information

- Calories: 157 calories
- Total Carbohydrate: 11 g
- Cholesterol: 15 mg
- Total Fat: 10 g
- Fiber: 1 g
- Protein: 5 g
- Sodium: 405 mg

71. Italian Fresh Vegetable Salad

"Garden-fresh veggies are a hit at community potlucks. I carry the dressing in a mason jar to add just before serving."
Serving: 20 servings (1 cup each). | Prep: 25m | Ready in: 25m

Ingredients

- SALAD:
- 1 bunch romaine, torn
- 4 cups fresh baby spinach
- 2 cups grape tomatoes

- 1 can (14 oz.) water-packed artichoke hearts, rinsed, drained and quartered
- 1 medium zucchini, thinly sliced
- 1 small green pepper, sliced
- 1 small sweet red pepper, sliced
- 1 cup thinly sliced fresh mushrooms
- 1 cup thinly sliced red onion
- 1 cup shredded part-skim mozzarella cheese
- 1/2 cup sliced pepperoncini
- 1 can (2-1/4 oz.) sliced ripe olives, drained
- VINAIGRETTE:
- 2/3 cup canola oil
- 1/2 cup red wine vinegar
- 1/4 cup minced fresh basil
- 1-1/2 tsps. garlic powder
- 1-1/2 tsps. ground mustard
- 1 tsp. honey
- 1/2 tsp. salt

Direction

- Mix the salad ingredients in a big bowl. Combine the vinaigrette ingredients in a small bowl.
- Just prior to serving, add three quarters cup of vinaigrette on top of salad; coat by tossing. Keep chilled in the refrigerator the leftover vinaigrette for another time.

Nutrition Information

- Calories: 84 calories
- Total Carbohydrate: 5 g
- Cholesterol: 3 mg
- Total Fat: 6 g
- Fiber: 1 g
- Protein: 3 g
- Sodium: 149 mg

72. Italian Garden Salad

"Add grilled chicken to this if you want."
Serving: 4 servings | Prep: 10m | Ready in: 10m

Ingredients

- 1 pkg. (10 oz.) torn mixed salad greens
- 1 small red pepper , cut into strips
- 1 small zucchini , sliced
- 1/2 cup sliced red onion s
- 1/2 cup pitted black olives
- 1/2 cup KRAFT Sun Dried Tomato Vinaigrette Dressing

Direction

- Toss greens with olives and vegetables in a big bowl.
- Add dressing and lightly mix.

Nutrition Information

- Calories: 100
- Total Carbohydrate: 10 g
- Cholesterol: 0 mg
- Total Fat: 6 g
- Fiber: 3 g
- Protein: 2 g
- Sodium: 500 mg
- Sugar: 5 g
- Saturated Fat: 1 g

73. Italian Salad Bowl

"You can add your family's favorite veggies in this salad."
Serving: 4 servings. | Prep: 15m | Ready in: 15m

Ingredients

- 1 bunch leaf lettuce, torn into bite-size pieces
- 8 cherry tomatoes, halved
- 8 fresh mushrooms, sliced
- 4 radishes, sliced
- 1 small zucchini, thinly sliced
- 1/2 yellow, red or green pepper, thinly sliced
- 1/4 cup shredded mozzarella cheese

- Italian salad dressing to taste

Direction

- Mix all ingredients together in a big salad bowl. Serve right away.

Nutrition Information

- Calories: 57 calories
- Total Carbohydrate: 7 g
- Cholesterol: 5 mg
- Total Fat: 2 g
- Fiber: 2 g
- Protein: 4 g
- Sodium: 52 mg

74. Italian Spaghetti Salad Recipe

"An attractive, fresh-tasting salad can be made 1 day ahead in a big bowl."
Serving: 16 servings. | Prep: 20m | Ready in: 20m

Ingredients

- 1 package (16 oz.) thin spaghetti, halved
- 3 medium tomatoes, diced
- 3 small zucchini, diced
- 1 large cucumber, halved, seeded and diced
- 1 medium green pepper, diced
- 1 medium sweet red pepper, diced
- 1 bottle (8 oz.) Italian salad dressing
- 2 tbsps. grated parmesan cheese
- 1-1/2 tsps. sesame seeds
- 1-1/2 tsps. poppy seeds
- 1/2 tsp. paprika
- 1/4 tsp. celery seed
- 1/8 tsp. garlic powder

Direction

- Following the instruction on package, cook spaghetti; drain off water and wash under cold water. Transfer into a big bowl; put in peppers, cucumber, zucchini and tomatoes.

- Mix the leftover ingredients; put on top of salad and coat by tossing. Keep it covered and let chill in the fridge for at least 2 hours.

Nutrition Information

- Calories: 137 calories
- Total Carbohydrate: 27 g
- Cholesterol: 1 mg
- Total Fat: 1 g
- Fiber: 0 g
- Protein: 5 g
- Sodium: 150 mg

75. Italian Summer Squash Salad

"This recipe is perfect for abundant squash."
Serving: 2 servings. | Prep: 10m | Ready in: 10m

Ingredients

- 2 cups torn Boston lettuce
- 1/3 cup thinly sliced zucchini
- 1/3 cup thinly sliced yellow summer squash
- 3 radishes, sliced
- 1/4 cup reduced-fat Italian salad dressing

Direction

- Mix together radishes, yellow squash, zucchini and lettuce in a bowl. Drizzle the dressing and serve.

Nutrition Information

- Calories: 67 calories
- Total Carbohydrate: 5 g
- Cholesterol: 0 mg
- Total Fat: 5 g
- Fiber: 2 g
- Protein: 2 g
- Sodium: 233 mg

76. Italian Tortellini Salad

"This original recipe included flavors that family and friends love to eat. Served warm or chilled"
Serving: 6 servings. | Prep: 10m | Ready in: 30m

Ingredients

- 1 lb. ground beef
- 1 envelope Italian salad dressing mix
- 1/4 cup water
- 1 package (19 oz.) frozen cheese tortellini, cooked and drained
- 3 to 4 plum tomatoes, chopped
- 1 medium zucchini, chopped
- 1 cup shredded mozzarella cheese
- 2 tbsps. olive oil
- 2 tbsps. red wine vinegar

Direction

- On medium heat, cook beef in a big skillet until not pink anymore; drain off. Add water and salad dressing mix. Boil. Lower heat; let it simmer while uncovered, for 3 minutes.
- Mix beef mixture, cheese, zucchini, tomatoes, and tortellini in a big bowl. Mix vinegar and oil; put on top of salad and coat by tossing. Keep chilled if you want.

77. Italian Tuna Pasta Salad

"An Italian recipe for potluck suppers or picnics."
Serving: 2 servings. | Prep: 10m | Ready in: 10m

Ingredients

- 1-1/2 cups cooked small shell pasta
- 1 cup shredded carrot
- 1 cup shredded zucchini
- 1 can (6 oz.) light water-packed tuna, drained
- 6 tbsps. creamy Italian salad dressing
- Lettuce leaf, optional

Direction

- Mix salad dressing, tuna, zucchini, carrots and pasta in a big bowl. Keep it covered and let chill in the fridge for 2 hours or overnight. Serve in a bowl lined with lettuce if you want.

Nutrition Information

- Calories: 418 calories
- Total Carbohydrate: 35 g
- Cholesterol: 26 mg
- Total Fat: 18 g
- Fiber: 4 g
- Protein: 27 g
- Sodium: 684 mg

78. Italian Zucchini Salad

"This dressing is of multi-use, either for marinating meats or for other types of salad."
Serving: 12 servings. | Prep: 20m | Ready in: 20m

Ingredients

- 2 lbs. zucchini
- 1/2 cup water
- 2 tsps. seasoned salt
- 12 large ripe pitted olives
- 2/3 cup olive oil
- 1/2 cup white wine vinegar
- 1 tsp. salt
- 1/2 tsp. paprika
- 1/2 tsp. pepper
- 1/2 tsp. sugar
- 1/4 tsp. basil leaves
- 1 clove garlic
- 1 avocado
- Pimientoor red pepper strips

Direction

- Wash zucchini and chop off its ends. Cut into 3/4 in. slices. Mix together water and salt. In a saucepan, pour salted water over zucchini. Cook until they turn crisp-tender. Drain and set them aside.

- Cut each olive into 4 pieces and stir them into the zucchini mixture. Mix together basil, sugar, pepper, paprika, salt, vinegar and oil. Use toothpick to spear garlic; put into the dressing. In a bowl, combine the dressing and the zucchini mixture, toss gently to coat. Let it chilled overnight.
- Remove the garlic. Peel avocado and slice it some hours before serving. Stir them in the salad. Use pimiento or red pepper for garnish.

Nutrition Information

- Calories: 167 calories
- Total Carbohydrate: 5 g
- Cholesterol: 0 mg
- Total Fat: 17 g
- Fiber: 0 g
- Protein: 1 g
- Sodium: 469 mg

79. Lemony Zucchini Ribbons

"Shave fresh zucchini and combine it with lemon juice for a fabulous salad. Top with feta or goat cheese and it is ready for you to dig in."
Serving: 4 servings. | Prep: 15m | Ready in: 15m

Ingredients

- 1 tbsp. olive oil
- 1/2 tsp. grated lemon zest
- 1 tbsp. lemon juice
- 1/2 tsp. salt
- 1/4 tsp. pepper
- 3 medium zucchini
- 1/3 cup crumbled goat or feta cheese

Direction

- Combine the first 5 ingredients for dressing in a small bowl. Shave zucchini with a vegetable peeler in lengthways so that it is cut into thin slices. Put the slices on a plate for serving.
- Pour the dressing slightly onto the vegetables and stir lightly until coated well. Sprinkle cheese on top.

Nutrition Information

- Calories: 83 calories
- Total Carbohydrate: 5 g
- Cholesterol: 12 mg
- Total Fat: 6 g
- Fiber: 2 g
- Protein: 3 g
- Sodium: 352 mg

80. Macaroni Salad With Basil Dressing

" "We overdid the zucchini and tomato plants when my hubby and I planned our first garden. I was wondering what else I could try to do with all those veggies. So my sister and I ended up with this perfect tasting recipe. I still prepare this common dish up until today." "
Serving: 10 servings. | Prep: 10m | Ready in: 10m

Ingredients

- 1 cup loosely packed fresh basil leaves
- 3 garlic cloves
- 1/2 tsp. pepper
- 1/2 tsp. salt, optional
- 2/3 cup olive oil
- 1 tbsp. red wine vinegar
- 3 medium tomatoes, seeded and diced
- 2 to 3 medium zucchini, cut into 1/4-inch slices
- 7 to 8 oz. elbow macaroni, cooked and drained
- 2 cups shredded cheddar cheese or part-skim mozzarella cheese

Direction

- Mix together the pepper, garlic, basil and salt if wished, in a blender container or food processor. Pulse until finely chopped. Stir in vinegar and oil and pulse until well combined. Reserve. Mix cheese, macaroni, zucchini and tomatoes in a 4-qt.salad bowl then lightly toss. Put all of the dressing over the mixture and mix to coat. Keep in the refrigerator, covered, for at least 2 hours or overnight.

Nutrition Information

- Calories: 273 calories
- Total Carbohydrate: 21 g
- Cholesterol: 12 mg
- Total Fat: 18 g
- Fiber: 0 g
- Protein: 10 g
- Sodium: 126 mg

81. Marinated Vegetable Salad

"This mixture of veggies is marinated by celery seed dressing."
Serving: 4

Ingredients

- 3/4 cup white sugar
- 1 tsp. celery seed
- 1/2 tsp. ground black pepper
- 1 cup distilled white vinegar
- 1/4 cup canola oil
- 1 tsp. salt
- 2 cups cucumbers, peeled and thinly sliced
- 1 onion, sliced into thin rings
- 2 cups thinly sliced carrots
- 1/2 cup chopped celery

Direction

- In a screw-top jar, mix salt, oil, vinegar, black pepper, celery seeds and sugar. Shake the mixture well to combine.
- In a big bowl, mix veggies. Put dressing on top of veggies then mix lightly. Keep it covered, and let chill in the fridge for a few hours or overnight.

Nutrition Information

- Calories: 319 calories;
- Total Carbohydrate: 48.4 g
- Cholesterol: 0 mg
- Total Fat: 14.5 g
- Protein: 1.5 g
- Sodium: 639 mg

82. Marinated Veggie Salad

"If you want dish that can be made ahead, this is the right recipe for you as you need to marinate overnight."
Serving: 12 servings. | Prep: 15m | Ready in: 15m

Ingredients

- 1 pint cherry tomatoes, halved
- 1 medium zucchini, cubed
- 1 medium yellow summer squash, cubed
- 1 medium cucumber, cubed
- 1 each medium sweet yellow, red and green pepper, cut into 1-inch pieces
- 1 can (6 oz.) pitted ripe olives, drained
- 1 small red onion, chopped
- 1/2 to 3/4 cup Italian salad dressing

Direction

- Mix together all ingredients and stir to coat in a serving bowl. Put into refrigerator overnight with cover.

Nutrition Information

- Calories: 77 calories
- Total Carbohydrate: 7 g
- Cholesterol: 0 mg
- Total Fat: 5 g
- Fiber: 2 g
- Protein: 1 g
- Sodium: 296 mg

83. Marinated Zucchini Salad

"Meet the Cook: This recipe has been passed down for generations in my family - it helps to use up the late-summer squash from the garden, and it'll keep for several days in the refrigerator."
Serving: 8 servings. | Prep: 10m | Ready in: 10m

Ingredients

- 6 small zucchini (about 1-1/2 lbs.), thinly sliced
- 1/2 cup chopped green pepper
- 1/2 cup diced celery
- 1/2 cup diced onion
- 1 jar (2 oz.) diced pimientos, drained
- 2/3 cup vinegar
- 1/3 cup vegetable oil
- 1/2 cup sugar
- 3 tbsps. white wine vinegar
- 1/2 tsp. salt
- 1/2 tsp. pepper

Direction

- In a medium bowl, mix pimientos, onion, celery, green pepper and zucchini; put aside. Mix the leftover ingredients in a jar; tightly cover then vigorously shake. Put marinade on top of the veggies then lightly mix. Keep it covered and chilled for 8 hours or overnight. Use a slotted spoon to serve.

Nutrition Information

- Calories: 152 calories
- Total Carbohydrate: 18 g
- Cholesterol: 0 mg
- Total Fat: 9 g
- Fiber: 2 g
- Protein: 1 g
- Sodium: 158 mg

84. Mediterranean Pasta Salad

"A simple pasta salad filled with the flavors of the sunny Mediterranean."
Serving: 2 | Prep: 10m | Ready in: 25m

Ingredients

- 1 cup macaroni
- 2 oz. roasted red bell peppers, diced
- 1/4 cup sliced black olives
- 1/4 cup crumbled feta cheese
- 1 tbsp. olive oil
- 1 tbsp. minced garlic
- 1 tsp. lemon juice
- salt and pepper to taste

Direction

- In a cup or small bowl, whisk sliced garlic and olive oil. Reserve.
- Cook pasta until al dente in a big pot of boiling water. Drain off the water.
- Place pasta into a medium mixing bowl, and put in feta cheese, olives and roasted red peppers. Toss with lemon juice and olive oil mixture. Sprinkle pepper and salt to season. Serve right away.

Nutrition Information

- Calories: 340 calories;
- Total Carbohydrate: 44.2 g
- Cholesterol: 17 mg
- Total Fat: 13.6 g
- Protein: 10.3 g
- Sodium: 472 mg

85. Mimi's Lentil Medley

"My husband really like this recipe."
Serving: 8 servings. | Prep: 15m | Ready in: 40m

Ingredients

- 1 cup dried lentils, rinsed
- 2 cups water

- 2 cups sliced fresh mushrooms
- 1 medium cucumber, cubed
- 1 medium zucchini, cubed
- 1 small red onion, chopped
- 1/2 cup chopped soft sun-dried tomato halves (not packed in oil)
- 1/2 cup rice vinegar
- 1/4 cup minced fresh mint
- 3 tbsps. olive oil
- 2 tsps. honey
- 1 tsp. dried basil
- 1 tsp. dried oregano
- 4 cups fresh baby spinach, chopped
- 1 cup (4 oz.) crumbled feta cheese
- 4 bacon strips, cooked and crumbled, optional

Direction

- Put lentils in a small saucepan. Pour in water; boil. Lower heat; let it simmer while covered till soft or for 20 to 25 minutes. Drain off and wash under cold water.
- Place in a big bowl. Put in tomatoes, onion, zucchini, cucumber and mushrooms. Combine oregano, basil, honey, oil, mint, and vinegar in a small bowl. Sprinkle on top of lentil mixture; coat by tossing. Put in cheese, spinach and bacon if you want; combine by tossing.

Nutrition Information

- Calories: 225 calories
- Total Carbohydrate: 29 g
- Cholesterol: 8 mg
- Total Fat: 8 g
- Fiber: 5 g
- Protein: 10 g
- Sodium: 404 mg

86. Minted Zucchini Salad

"This recipe can be prepared in 45 minutes or less."
Serving: Serves 4

Ingredients

- 1 tomato
- 1 1/2 tbsps. fresh lemon juice
- 3 tbsps. extra-virgin
- olive oil
- 1/3 cup packed fresh mint leaves
- 1/4 cup packed fresh flat-leafed parsley leaves
- 3 medium zucchini (about 1 lb. total)
- Garnish: fresh mint sprigs

Direction

- To prepare: Chop tomato into 1/4-inch dice and place in a small bowl. Mix pepper, salt, oil, and lemon juice to taste in another small bowl.
- Finely chop parsley and mint in a food processor. Use shredding disk instead of chopping blade and shred zucchini over herbs. Pour mixture into a big bowl. Sprinkle 3/4 vinaigrette on top of zucchini and mix with pepper and salt to taste. Drain off any juices from diced tomato and mix tomato with leftover vinaigrette and add pepper and salt to taste. Separate zucchini salad between four dishes, mounding it, and make an indentation in the middle of every mound. Use tomatoes to fill indentations and use mint to garnish.

87. Mostaccioli Veggie Salad

"The mix of pasta, zucchini, summer squash, cucumber, sweet peppers and black olives is coated with a light vinaigrette. Any pasta can be substituted for the mostaccioli."
Serving: 10 servings. | Prep: 20m | Ready in: 20m

Ingredients

- 3 cups uncooked mostaccioli
- 1 medium cucumber, thinly sliced

- 1 small yellow summer squash, quartered and sliced
- 1 small zucchini, halved and sliced
- 1/2 cup diced sweet red pepper
- 1/2 cup diced green pepper
- 1/2 cup sliced ripe olives
- 3 to 4 green onions, chopped
- DRESSING:
- 1/3 cup sugar
- 1/3 cup white wine vinegar
- 1/3 cup canola oil
- 1-1/2 tsps. prepared mustard
- 3/4 tsp. dried minced onion
- 3/4 tsp. garlic powder
- 1/2 tsp. salt
- 1/2 tsp. pepper

Direction

- Following the instructions on package, cook pasta. Drain off and wash under cold water. Put in a big bowl; put in onions, olives, peppers, zucchini, summer squash and cucumbers.
- Combine dressing ingredients in a small bowl. Put on top of pasta mixture; coat by tossing. Keep it covered and let chill in the fridge for 8 hours or overnight. Toss another time prior to serving. Use a slotted spoon to serve.

88. Pesto Pasta Salad

"A creamy pesto sauce turns this simple pasta salad into a delightful dinner plus with broccoli to pasta cooking water for a vivid shade of green and a bit soften."
Serving: 5 | Prep: 20m | Ready in: 20m

Ingredients

- 8 oz. whole-wheat fusilli (about 3 cups)
- 1 cup small broccoli florets
- 2 cups packed fresh basil leaves
- ¼ cup pine nuts, toasted
- ¼ cup grated Parmesan cheese
- 2 tbsps. mayonnaise
- 2 tbsps. extra-virgin olive oil

- 2 tbsps. lemon juice
- 1 large clove garlic, quartered
- ¾ tsp. salt
- ½ tsp. ground pepper
- 1 cup quartered cherry tomatoes

Direction

- Boil water in a large saucepan. Following instruction on package, add and cook fusilli. Mix in broccoli 1 minute before done cooking pasta. Cook for 1 minute, then drain off and wash in cold running water to stop the cooking process.
- At the same time, in a mini food processor, add pepper, salt, garlic, lemon juice, oil, mayonnaise, Parmesan, pine nuts and basil. Run the processor until nearly smooth in consistency. Put in a big bowl. Add the broccoli and pasta, alongside tomatoes. Coat by tossing.

Nutrition Information

- Calories: 317 calories;
- Total Carbohydrate: 38 g
- Cholesterol: 6 mg
- Total Fat: 16 g
- Fiber: 5 g
- Protein: 8 g
- Sodium: 474 mg
- Sugar: 1 g
- Saturated Fat: 2 g

89. Picnic Pasta Salad

"This salad is served with small amount of mayonnaise allows it to keep much better than the traditional pasta salad."
Serving: 12

Ingredients

- 1 lb. seashell pasta
- 1 cup chopped mushrooms
- 1 cup chopped cucumber
- 1 cup chopped broccoli

- 1 cup white sugar
- 3/4 cup vegetable oil
- 1/4 cup prepared mustard
- 2 tbsps. mayonnaise
- 1/4 cup distilled white vinegar
- 1/4 cup shredded Cheddar cheese
- salt to taste
- ground black pepper to taste

Direction

- In large pot of boiling salted water, cook pasta until al dente. Wash under cool water. Drain well.
- At the same time, in a large bowl, mix shredded Cheddar cheese, vinegar, mayonnaise, mustard, oil, sugar, and chopped vegetables. Use pepper and salt to season to taste. Mix them well. Mix in pasta. Keep in the refrigerator for 2 to 4 hours prior to serving.

Nutrition Information

- Calories: 356 calories;
- Total Carbohydrate: 45.5 g
- Cholesterol: 3 mg
- Total Fat: 17.5 g
- Protein: 6.3 g
- Sodium: 92 mg

90. Picnic Salad Skewers

"A chilled salad with homemade vinaigrette of sliced zucchini, cherry tomatoes, crisp peppers and tender potatoes."
Serving: 8 servings. | Prep: 15m | Ready in: 30m

Ingredients

- 8 unpeeled small red potatoes
- 8 fresh pearl onions
- 1 tbsp. water
- 1 medium sweet red pepper, cut into 1-inch pieces
- 1 medium green pepper, cut into 1-inch pieces
- 16 cherry tomatoes

- 1 small zucchini, cut into 1/4-inch slices
- VINAIGRETTE:
- 2/3 cup olive oil
- 1/3 cup red wine vinegar
- 2 garlic cloves, minced
- 1 tbsp. dried oregano
- 1 tsp. salt
- 1/4 tsp. pepper
- 4 oz. crumbled feta cheese, optional

Direction

- Put potatoes with water to cover in a saucepan; boil. Cook till softened or for 10 to 13 minutes; drain off. Transfer water and onions into a microwave-safe bowl. Cover up and microwave till tender-crisp or for one to one and a half minutes on high heat; drain off.
- Alternately thread zucchini, tomatoes, pepper, onions and potatoes on wooden/metal skewers. Add into a big resealable plastic bag or big shallow plastic container.
- Combine pepper, salt, oregano, garlic, vinegar and oil in a bowl. Put on top of vegetable skewers. Let it marinate for at least 60 minutes, flipping often. Drizzle with feta cheese if you want.

91. Picnic Zucchini Bean Salad

"An easy-to-pack-up salad for picnic in hot weather."
Serving: 5 cups. | Prep: 10m | Ready in: 10m

Ingredients

- 3 small zucchini, sliced
- 3/4 cup chopped green pepper
- 1/2 cup chopped onion
- 1 can (15-1/2 oz.) kidney beans, rinsed and drained
- 1/4 cup vegetable oil
- 3 tbsps. vinegar
- 1-1/2 tsps. garlic salt
- 1/4 tsp. pepper

Direction

- Mix all ingredients in a bowl. Keep it covered and let chill in the refrigerator no less than 4 hours, stirring once in a while.

Nutrition Information

- Calories: 140 calories
- Total Carbohydrate: 14 g
- Cholesterol: 0 mg
- Total Fat: 8 g
- Fiber: 4 g
- Protein: 5 g
- Sodium: 491 mg

92. Pom-pom Potato Salad

"This delightful potato salad is perfect for a pregame tail party, sport gatherings or football supper when served with sandwich, especially for football fans!"
Serving: 18 servings. | Prep: 15m | Ready in: 15m

Ingredients

- 3 lbs. red potatoes, cooked and cubed
- 1 cup sweet pickle or zucchini relish
- 1/4 cup chopped celery
- 3/4 tsp. onion salt
- 1/2 tsp. garlic salt
- 1/2 tsp. celery seed
- 1/2 tsp. pepper
- 4 hard-boiled large eggs
- 1 cup (8 oz.) sour cream
- 1/2 cup mayonnaise
- 1 tbsp. cider vinegar
- 1 tsp. prepared mustard
- Additional hard-boiled large eggs, cut into wedges

Direction

- Add the first seven ingredients and mix them together in a large bowl. Cut the eggs into halves and separate yolks and whites. Cut the whites into small pieces and put them into the potato mixture.

- Mash egg yolks in a small bowl. Whisk in mustard, vinegar, mayonnaise, sour cream. Pour the dressing onto the potato mixture and toss so that it can be fully coated. Put it in the refrigerator until serving. Use egg wedges for garnish.

Nutrition Information

- Calories: 160 calories
- Total Carbohydrate: 18 g
- Cholesterol: 58 mg
- Total Fat: 8 g
- Fiber: 1 g
- Protein: 3 g
- Sodium: 299 mg

93. Quick Italian Salad

"Toss in every veggie you love and the results for this recipe will be fantastic."
Serving: 1-1/2 cups dressing. | Prep: 20m | Ready in: 20m

Ingredients

- Salad greens
- Sliced tomatoes, zucchini, mushrooms and green pepper or vegetables of your choice
- 1 cup canola oil
- 1/2 cup white wine vinegar
- 1 garlic clove, minced
- 2 tbsps. minced fresh parsley
- 1 tbsp. grated Parmesan cheese
- 1-1/2 tsps. dried basil
- 1 tsp. dried oregano
- 1/2 tsp. pepper

Direction

- On separate salad dishes or in a salad bowl, arrange vegetables and greens. Mix all leftover ingredients in a tight-fitting lidded jar; shake the mixture well. Serve on top of salad.

Nutrition Information

- Calories: 167 calories
- Total Carbohydrate: 1 g
- Cholesterol: 0 mg
- Total Fat: 18 g
- Fiber: 0 g
- Protein: 0 g
- Sodium: 8 mg

94. Quinoa With Roasted Veggies And Feta

"A salad recipe of roasted medley of veggies with fluffy quinoa and super nutritious grain."
Serving: 8 servings. | Prep: 25m | Ready in: 60m

Ingredients

- 3 medium carrots
- 2 small zucchini
- 2 medium sweet red peppers, chopped
- 1 medium sweet onion, chopped
- 1 tbsp. olive oil
- 2 garlic cloves, minced
- 1 tsp. dried oregano
- 1/2 tsp. pepper
- 1/4 tsp. salt
- 1 can (15-1/4 oz.) whole kernel corn, drained
- 2 cups reduced-sodium chicken broth
- 1 cup quinoa, rinsed
- 1/4 cup minced fresh parsley
- 1/4 cup minced fresh basil or 1 tbsp. dried basil
- 1/2 cup crumbled feta cheese
- Lemon wedges

Direction

- Halve zucchini and carrots into half-in. slices; put in a big bowl. Put in salt, pepper, oregano, garlic, oil, onion and peppers; coat by tossing. Place on a 15x10x1-in. baking pan coated with cooking spray.

- Bake for 10 minutes at 400 degrees. Mix in corn; bake till veggies are soft for 25 to 30 minutes more. Put aside to let it cool.
- At the same time, boil broth in a small saucepan. Put in quinoa. Lower heat; keep it covered and let simmer till liquid is absorbed for 12 to 15 minutes. Take off the heat; use a fork to fluff.
- Place quinoa in a big bowl; mix in the basil, parsley and veggies. Drizzle with cheese; serve alongside lemon.

Nutrition Information

- Calories: 193 calories
- Total Carbohydrate: 30 g
- Cholesterol: 4 mg
- Total Fat: 5 g
- Fiber: 5 g
- Protein: 7 g
- Sodium: 460 mg

95. Ribbon Salad With Orange Vinaigrette

"Zucchini, cucumbers and carrots are peeled into "ribbons" for this citrusy salad, served best for parties and special occasions."
Serving: 8 servings. | Prep: 30m | Ready in: 30m

Ingredients

- 1 medium zucchini
- 1 medium cucumber
- 1 medium carrot
- 3 medium oranges
- 3 cups fresh baby spinach
- 4 green onions, finely chopped
- 1/2 cup chopped walnuts
- 1/2 tsp. salt
- 1/2 tsp. pepper
- 1/2 cup golden raisins, optional
- VINAIGRETTE:
- 1/4 cup olive oil
- 4 tsps. white wine vinegar

- 1 tbsp. finely chopped green onion
- 2 tsps. honey
- 1/4 tsp. salt
- 1/4 tsp. pepper

Direction

- Shave carrot, cucumber, zucchini lengthwise into very thin strips using a vegetable peeler.
- Finely grate enough peel from oranges to have 2 tbsp. orange peel. Halve an orange crosswise; squeeze juice from orange to measure half a cup. Store the juice and peel for making vinaigrette. From the top and bottom of leftover oranges, cut a thin slice; let oranges stand upright on a cutting board. Trim off peel and outer membrane from orange using a knife. Slice along the membrane of each segment to remove fruit.
- Mix pepper, salt, walnuts, green onions, orange sections and spinach and, if you want, raisins in a big bowl. Put in vegetable ribbons; mix by gently tossing. Whisk vinaigrette ingredients in a small bowl. Put in reserved orange juice and peel then mix till blended. Sprinkle half of the vinaigrette on top of salad; coat by tossing. Serve with leftover vinaigrette.

Nutrition Information

- Calories: 162 calories
- Total Carbohydrate: 14 g
- Cholesterol: 0 mg
- Total Fat: 12 g
- Fiber: 2 g
- Protein: 3 g
- Sodium: 240 mg

96. Roasted Pepper Spinach Salad

"This recipe of a wonderful and fresh salad is made by combining sliced veggies with spinach and dressed with elegant red wine vinaigrette."
Serving: 2 servings. | Prep: 15m | Ready in: 25m

Ingredients

- 1 medium sweet red pepper
- 1/3 cup thinly sliced fresh mushrooms
- 1/2 small zucchini, julienned
- 1/4 cup red wine vinaigrette
- 2 cups fresh baby spinach

Direction

- Place the red pepper 4 in. from the heat and broil in 2 minutes until the skin starts to blister. Use tongs to rotate the pepper a quarter turn. Repeat the broiling and rotating process for each quarter with tongs so that all quarters are blackened-blistered. Transfer the pepper to a bowl right away. Set it aside for 15 to 20 minutes with cover.
- Peel off and remove pepper seeds, stem and charred skin. Cut pepper into fine slices and put them into a bowl. Put in vinaigrette, zucchini and mushrooms; set aside for at least 10 minutes to marinate. In a serving bowl, put spinach then stir in vegetables and make sure that it is fully coated.

Nutrition Information

- Calories: 45 calories
- Total Carbohydrate: 9 g
- Cholesterol: 0 mg
- Total Fat: 0 g
- Fiber: 2 g
- Protein: 2 g
- Sodium: 436 mg

97. Roasted Veggie Pasta Salad

"A tasty meatless entry with oven-roasted veggies, pasta and dressing."
Serving: 8 servings. | Prep: 20m | Ready in: 50m

Ingredients

- 1 small butternut squash, peeled and cut into 1-inch pieces
- 2 cups water
- 1 medium eggplant, cut into 1-inch pieces
- 1 large zucchini, cut into 1-inch pieces
- 1 medium sweet red pepper, cut into 1-inch pieces
- 1 medium red onion, cut into 1-inch pieces
- 1/2 cup olive oil
- 1 tsp. dried marjoram
- 1 package (16 oz.) tricolor spiral pasta
- 1/2 cup Italian salad dressing
- 1/4 cup minced fresh basil
- 1 tsp. salt
- 1/2 tsp. pepper

Direction

- In a microwave-safe bowl, put in water and squash. Cover it up and cook till soft for 10 minutes; drain off the water.
- On a 15x10x1 in. baking pan that is greased, arrange onion, red pepper, zucchini, eggplant and squash. Mix marjoram and oil in a small bowl till combined. Sprinkle on top of veggies.
- Bake, while uncovered, for 30 minutes till soft at 450 degrees. At the same time, cook pasta based on the instruction on package; drain off.
- Mix roasted vegetables and pasta in a big bowl. Combine in pepper, salt, basil, and salad dressing. Serve at room temperature or warm.

Nutrition Information

- Calories: 461 calories
- Total Carbohydrate: 62 g
- Cholesterol: 0 mg
- Total Fat: 20 g
- Fiber: 8 g
- Protein: 10 g

- Sodium: 560 mg

98. Sesame Chicken Couscous Salad

"A perfect summer salad with chicken and mixed veggies is so crunchy and fresh-tasting."
Serving: 4 servings. | Prep: 20m | Ready in: 20m

Ingredients

- 1-1/2 cups reduced-sodium chicken broth
- 3 tsps. reduced-sodium soy sauce, divided
- 2 tsps. sesame oil, divided
- 1 cup uncooked couscous
- 2 green onions, sliced
- 1-1/2 cups fresh or frozen sugar snap peas
- 3/4 cup fresh broccoli florets
- 1-1/2 cups cubed cooked chicken
- 1 large sweet red pepper, chopped
- 3/4 cup diced zucchini
- 2 tbsps. cider vinegar
- 1 tbsp. thawed apple juice concentrate
- 1 tbsp. water
- 2 tsps. canola oil
- 1/2 tsp. ground ginger
- 1/4 tsp. pepper
- 2 tbsps. slivered almonds, toasted
- 2 tsps. sesame seeds, toasted

Direction

- Mix 1 tsp. sesame oil, 1 tsp. soy sauce and broth in a saucepan; boil. Mix in couscous. Keep it covered and take off the heat. Let rest for 5 minutes. Use a fork to fluff. Mix in green onions. Keep it covered and chilled in the fridge till chilled.
- In a steamer basket in a saucepan over 1 in. of water, add pea pods; boil. Keep it covered and let it steam for 60 seconds. Put in broccoli; keep it covered and let steam 2 minutes longer or till tender-crisp. Wash under cold water; drain off. Place in a serving bowl; put in zucchini, red pepper and chicken.

- Mix sesame oil, leftover soy sauce, pepper, ginger, canola oil, water, apple juice concentrate and vinegar in a tight-fitting lidded jar. Shake the mixture well. Put on top of chicken mixture and coat by tossing. Keep it covered and let chill in the refrigerator till chilled or for half an hour. Serve on top of couscous. Drizzle with sesame seeds and almonds.

Nutrition Information

- Calories: 382 calories
- Total Carbohydrate: 45 g
- Cholesterol: 45 mg
- Total Fat: 9 g
- Fiber: 6 g
- Protein: 26 g
- Sodium: 451 mg

99. Southwestern Veggie Salad

"A quick-cook and bright veggies look pretty on a buffet table."
Serving: 5 servings. | Prep: 15m | Ready in: 15m

Ingredients

- 2 cups whole kernel corn
- 1 small zucchini, sliced 1/4 inch thick
- 1 ripe avocado, peeled and chopped
- 1/4 cup thinly sliced radishes
- Bibb or Boston lettuce leaves, optional
- 2 to 3 medium tomatoes, sliced
- DRESSING:
- 3 tbsps. ketchup
- 2 tbsps. cider vinegar
- 1 tbsp. canola oil
- 1 tbsp. minced fresh cilantro
- 1/2 tsp. garlic powder
- 1/4 tsp. salt
- 1/4 tsp. chili powder

Direction

- Mix the radishes, avocado, zucchini and corn in a big bowl. Arrange lettuce and tomatoes if you want on a serving plate. Mix the dressing ingredients in a small bowl. Put on top of corn mixture; coat by tossing lightly. Scoop on top of tomatoes.

Nutrition Information

- Calories: 185 calories
- Total Carbohydrate: 26 g
- Cholesterol: 0 mg
- Total Fat: 10 g
- Fiber: 5 g
- Protein: 4 g
- Sodium: 249 mg

100. Spring Greek Pasta Salad

"This recipe is light when combining rotini pasta with sweet peppers, zucchini and cucumber; and a main dish when served with grilled chicken."
Serving: 16 servings (3/4 cup each). | Prep: 15m | Ready in: 30m

Ingredients

- 4 cups veggie rotini or other spiral pasta (about 12 oz.)
- VINAIGRETTE:
- 1/4 cup olive oil
- 3 tbsps. lemon juice
- 2 tbsps. balsamic vinegar
- 1 tbsp. water
- 3 garlic cloves, minced
- 1 tsp. salt
- 1/4 tsp. pepper
- 3 tbsps. minced fresh oregano or 1 tbsp. dried oregano
- SALAD:
- 3 large tomatoes, seeded and chopped
- 1 medium sweet red pepper, chopped
- 1 small cucumber, seeded and chopped
- 1 small zucchini, chopped

- 1 small red onion, halved and thinly sliced
- 1/3 cup sliced pitted Greek olives, optional
- 1 cup (4 oz.) crumbled feta cheese

Direction

- Cook pasta following the directions on package. Drain well; use cold water to rinse. Drain thoroughly.
- Mix pepper, salt, garlic, water, vinegar, lemon juice and oil together in a small bowl until combined. Add oregano and stir.
- Mix together vegetables, pasta and olive oil if desired in a large bowl. Add cheese and vinaigrette, stir well to combine. Put it into the refrigerator with cover until serving.

Nutrition Information

- Calories: 142 calories
- Total Carbohydrate: 20 g
- Cholesterol: 4 mg
- Total Fat: 5 g
- Fiber: 2 g
- Protein: 5 g
- Sodium: 219 mg

101. Springtime Pasta Salad

"Prior to serving the next day, add a bit of water then toss again if you make this 1 night before."
Serving: 8 | Prep: 15m | Ready in: 2h25m

Ingredients

- 2 cups spiral veggie pasta
- 1 cucumber - peeled, seeded, and chopped
- 1/2 cup sliced black olives
- 1/4 cup chopped red onion
- 1/2 cup mayonnaise
- 1/4 cup sour cream
- 1 1/4 tsps. dill weed
- 1/2 tsp. salt
- 1/2 tsp. dry mustard
- 1/4 tsp. garlic salt

Direction

- Boil a big pot of lightly salted water. Cook pasta for 8 minutes at a boil until tender yet firm to chew. Drain. Rinse pasta in cold water until its cool. Drain. Put pasta in a big bowl.
- In a bowl, mix garlic salt, dry mustard, salt, dill, sour cream, mayonnaise, red onion, black olives and cucumber. Put on paste. Evenly coat by gently mixing/
- Use plastic wrap to cover the bowl. Keep in fridge for 2 hours prior to serving.

Nutrition Information

- Calories: 134 calories;
- Total Carbohydrate: 14.7 g
- Cholesterol: 7 mg
- Total Fat: 7.7 g
- Protein: 2.5 g
- Sodium: 392 mg

102. Squash Salad

"This is a thin zucchini and yellow squash with little seeds."
Serving: Makes 4 servings

Ingredients

- 2 each small zucchini and yellow squash, ends trimmed
- 2 tbsps. red-wine vinegar
- 1 tbsp. Dijon mustard
- 3 tbsps. extra-virgin olive oil
- 1 large bunch arugula, trimmed, washed, and patted dry
- 1 large ripe tomato, cored
- 2 tbsps. chopped flat-leaf parsley

Direction

- 1. Slice squash and zucchini diagonally into thin slices. Transfer into a bowl.
- 2. Make the dressing: In a bowl, whisk together pepper, salt, vinegar, and mustard. Gradually sprinkle in oil while whisking

continuously until the resulting mixture is thickened. Mix with the squash; allow to stand for ten minutes.

- 3. In a salad bowl, put the arugula. Slice tomato lengthwise in half and then slice into very thin wedges. Spread them atop the greens.
- 4. Before you serve, scoop the dressing and squash on top of arugula. Sprinkle with the parsley and add pepper and salt to taste. Serve right away and toss at the table.

103. Summer Squash Salad

"This recipe is best fit for a feast with eye-catching colors of zucchini and yellow squash topped with mint leaves and hazelnuts."
Serving: 4 servings, 3/4 cup each | Prep: 15m | Ready in: 15m

Ingredients

- 1 yellow squash , ends trimmed
- 1 zucchini , ends trimmed
- 1/4 cup KRAFT Zesty Italian Dressing
- 1/4 cup hazelnuts
- 2 Tbsp. chopped fresh mint

Direction

- 1. Cut zucchini and squash into thin slices using vegetable peeler.
- 2. In each of 4 salad plates, drizzle 1 tbsp. of dressing and put vegetables on top.
- 3. Top with a sprinkle of mint and nuts.

Nutrition Information

- Calories: 100
- Total Carbohydrate: 6 g
- Cholesterol: 0 mg
- Total Fat: 8 g
- Fiber: 2 g
- Protein: 2 g
- Sodium: 160 mg
- Sugar: 3 g
- Saturated Fat: 1 g

104. Summer Squash Slaw

""Red pepper, squash and zucchini – a delicious bowl to freshen you right up!""
Serving: 10 servings. | Prep: 15m | Ready in: 15m

Ingredients

- 2 small yellow summer squash, julienned
- 2 small zucchini, julienned
- 1 small sweet red pepper, julienned
- 1/3 cup sliced onion
- 3 tbsps. vegetable oil
- 2 tbsps. cider or white wine vinegar
- 1 tbsp. mayonnaise
- 1 tsp. sugar
- 1/2 tsp. dill weed
- 1/2 tsp. garlic salt
- 1/4 tsp. celery salt
- 1/4 tsp. pepper

Direction

- Mix onion, red pepper, zucchini and squash together in a big bowl. Mix the rest of the ingredients together thoroughly in a small bowl then empty it out into the big bowl. Finish off by coating everything through tossing and keeping it in the fridge, covered. Use a slotted spoon to serve.

Nutrition Information

- Calories: 52 calories
- Total Carbohydrate: 4 g
- Cholesterol: 0 mg
- Total Fat: 4 g
- Fiber: 0 g
- Protein: 1 g
- Sodium: 140 mg

105. Summer Squash Toss

"This squash salad dressed with vinegar and oil dressing can beat the summer heat!"
Serving: 4 servings. | Prep: 10m | Ready in: 10m

Ingredients

- 1 medium yellow summer squash, julienned
- 1 medium zucchin, julienned
- 1 medium tomato, julienned
- 3 tbsps. olive oil
- 3 tbsps. cider vinegar
- 4 tsps. sugar
- 1/2 tsp. dried basil
- 1/4 tsp. dried thyme
- 1/8 tsp. salt
- Dash pepper

Direction

- Mix together tomato, zucchini and squash in a serving bowl. Mix together other ingredients in a small bowl. Pour it slightly on the vegetables.

Nutrition Information

- Calories: 132 calories
- Total Carbohydrate: 10 g
- Cholesterol: 0 mg
- Total Fat: 10 g
- Fiber: 2 g
- Protein: 2 g
- Sodium: 80 mg

106. Sweet & Sour Squash Salad

"This salad goes over really well with all ages, and it's a good way to get kids to eat summer squash."
Serving: 6 servings. | Prep: 20m | Ready in: 20m

Ingredients

- 3/4 cup sugar
- 1/2 cup cider vinegar
- 1/4 cup olive oil
- 2 tbsps. ranch salad dressing mix
- 1/4 to 1/2 tsp. pepper
- 1/8 tsp. salt
- 2 medium zucchini, thinly sliced
- 2 medium yellow summer squash, thinly sliced
- 2 celery ribs, chopped
- 1 cup chopped red onion
- 1/2 cup chopped green pepper
- 1/2 cup chopped sweet red pepper

Direction

- To make dressing, combine initial 6 ingredients till dissolves sugar. Transfer veggies into a big bowl; toss with dressing.
- Chill in the refrigerator, while covered, till cold. Use a slotted spoon to serve.

Nutrition Information

- Calories: 241 calories
- Total Carbohydrate: 38 g
- Cholesterol: 0 mg
- Total Fat: 10 g
- Fiber: 2 g
- Protein: 2 g
- Sodium: 703 mg

107. Sweet And Sour Zucchini

"This is a wonderful and loved recipe for potlucks and good for travel. We can make full use of abundant source of summer zucchini and have a prolific dish."
Serving: 6-8 servings. | Prep: 10m | Ready in: 10m

Ingredients

- 3/4 cup sugar
- 1 tsp. salt
- 1/2 tsp. pepper
- 1/3 cup vegetable oil
- 2/3 cup cider vinegar
- 2 tbsps. white wine vinegar
- 5 cups thinly sliced zucchini
- 1 small onion, chopped

- 1/2 cup chopped green pepper
- 1/2 cup chopped celery

Direction

- Mix together the first six ingredients in a large bowl, combine well. Add vegetables and stir. Put it in the refrigerator with cover overnight or in some hours.

Nutrition Information

- Calories: 174 calories
- Total Carbohydrate: 24 g
- Cholesterol: 0 mg
- Total Fat: 9 g
- Fiber: 1 g
- Protein: 1 g
- Sodium: 305 mg

108. Sweet Pepper Wild Rice Salad

"A wild rice salad that's packed with health and fun flavors in every bite."
Serving: 8 servings. | Prep: 20m | Ready in: 01h20m

Ingredients

- 1/2 cup uncooked wild rice
- 1 can (14-1/2 oz.) reduced-sodium chicken broth or vegetable broth, divided
- 1-1/4 cups water, divided
- 3/4 cup uncooked long grain rice
- 1 medium sweet red pepper, chopped
- 1 medium sweet yellow pepper, chopped
- 1 medium zucchini, chopped
- 2 tbsps. olive oil, divided
- 4 green onions, chopped
- 1/2 tsp. salt
- 1/4 tsp. pepper
- 2 tbsps. lemon juice

Direction

- Mix half cup of water, 1 cup broth and wild rice in a small saucepan. Boil. Lower heat; keep it covered and let simmer till rice is soft for 50 to 60 minutes.
- At the same time, mix water, leftover broth and long grain rice in a large saucepan. Boil. Lower heat; cover up and let it simmer till rice is soft for 15 to 18 minutes.
- Sauté the zucchini and pepper in 1 tbsp. oil for 3 minutes in a big nonstick skillet. Put in onions; sauté till veggies are soft for 1 to 2 more minutes. Place in a big bowl.
- Drain wild rice if needed; mix into vegetable mixture. Mix in white rice. Use salt and pepper to drizzle. Sprinkle with leftover oil and lemon juice; coat by tossing. Serve at room temperature or warm.

Nutrition Information

- Calories: 154 calories
- Total Carbohydrate: 26 g
- Cholesterol: 0 mg
- Total Fat: 4 g
- Fiber: 2 g
- Protein: 4 g
- Sodium: 287 mg

109. Sweet-sour Zucchini Salad

"A make-ahead mixture with flavorful marinade and cucumbers can be served as salad or condiment."
Serving: 10 servings. | Prep: 15m | Ready in: 15m

Ingredients

- 1/2 cup cider vinegar
- 4-1/2 tsps. dried minced onion
- 7 small zucchini, thinly sliced
- 1/2 cup chopped celery
- 1/4 cup chopped green pepper
- 1/4 cup chopped sweet red pepper
- DRESSING:
- 3/4 cup sugar
- 2/3 cup cider vinegar
- 1/3 cup canola oil
- 1 tsp. salt, optional
- 1 tsp. pepper

Direction

- Mix onion and vinegar in a big bowl. Put in peppers, celery and zucchini.
- Mix dressing ingredients in a tight-fitting lidded jar; shake the mixture well. Put on top of veggies and lightly mix. Keep it covered and let chill in the fridge for 8 hours or overnight. Use a slotted spoon to serve.

Nutrition Information

- Calories: 113 calories
- Total Carbohydrate: 10 g
- Cholesterol: 0 mg
- Total Fat: 7 g
- Fiber: 0 g
- Protein: 1 g
- Sodium: 9 mg

110. Thai Beef Noodle Salad

"I served this salad to our passengers and crew, and it always received compliments, best chilled overnight."
Serving: 8 servings. | Prep: 30m | Ready in: 30m

Ingredients

- 1/2 cup reduced-sodium soy sauce
- 1/2 cup rice vinegar
- 3 tbsps. orange juice
- 3 tbsps. canola oil
- 1 tbsp. sesame oil
- 2 garlic cloves, minced
- 2 tsps. ground ginger
- 1 tsp. peanut butter
- 3/4 tsp. salt
- 1/2 tsp. cayenne pepper
- 12 oz. uncooked spaghetti
- 1 cup fresh broccoli florets
- 1 cup fresh or frozen snow peas, thawed
- 1 cup julienned sweet red pepper
- 1 cup julienned zucchini
- 1/2 cup thinly sliced celery
- 1 lb. boneless beef sirloin steak, cooked and cut into thin strips
- 2 tbsps. sesame seeds, toasted

Direction

- To make dressing, in a blender, mix the initial ten ingredients; keep it covered up and run the blender till blended.
- Based on the instruction on package, cook spaghetti; drain off and transfer into a big bowl. Put in the cooked beef, celery, zucchini, red pepper, peas, and broccoli. Pour in dressing and coat by tossing.
- Keep it covered and let chill in the refrigerator for no less than 2 hours. Just prior to serving, drizzle with sesame seeds.

Nutrition Information

- Calories: 367 calories
- Total Carbohydrate: 36 g
- Cholesterol: 50 mg
- Total Fat: 13 g
- Fiber: 3 g
- Protein: 25 g
- Sodium: 880 mg

111. Tomato Zucchini Platter

"If making this pretty vegetable salad for a potluck, make sure you use a platter with raised sides to prevent it from spilling when transporting it."
Serving: 6 servings. | Prep: 20m | Ready in: 25m

Ingredients

- 4 medium zucchini, cut into 1/4-inch slices
- 3 medium tomatoes, cut into 1/4-inch slices
- 1/3 cup vegetable oil
- 3 tbsps. white vinegar
- 1-1/2 tsps. lemon juice
- 1 tsp. sugar
- 1/2 tsp. salt
- 1/2 tsp. ground mustard
- 1/2 tsp. dried oregano
- 1/4 tsp. coarsely ground pepper
- Pitted ripe olives

Direction

- In a big skillet, pour in 1 in. of water and zucchini; boil. Lower heat; keep it covered and let it simmer till tender-crisp or for 2 to 3 minutes. Drain off and pat dry. Arrange tomatoes and zucchini in alternating circles on a serving platter.
- Mix pepper, oregano, mustard, salt, sugar, lemon juice, vinegar and oil in tight-fitting lidded jar; shake the mixture well. Sprinkle on top of tomatoes and zucchini. Keep it covered and let chill in the fridge for no less than 2 hours. Add olives in middle of veggies.

Nutrition Information

- Calories: 146 calories
- Total Carbohydrate: 8 g
- Cholesterol: 0 mg
- Total Fat: 13 g
- Fiber: 2 g
- Protein: 2 g
- Sodium: 207 mg

112. Tomato Zucchini Salad

"What is more special than a plain green salad yet easier to make than this?"
Serving: 1 serving. | Prep: 10m | Ready in: 10m

Ingredients

- 1 cup torn salad greens
- 1/2 small tomato, cut into wedges
- 1/4 cup thinly sliced zucchini
- 1 tbsp. mayonnaise
- 1 tbsp. French salad dressing
- 1 tsp. toasted wheat germ
- 1/4 tsp. sugar
- 1/4 tsp. vinegar

Direction

- In a plate or a salad bowl, mix together zucchini, tomato and greens. Mix together other ingredients then pour it over the salad.

Nutrition Information

- Calories: 107 calories
- Total Carbohydrate: 14 g
- Cholesterol: 0 mg
- Total Fat: 6 g
- Fiber: 0 g
- Protein: 2 g
- Sodium: 279 mg

113. Tortellini Vegetable Salad

"A quick and wonderfully colorful salad for luncheons or light suppers."
Serving: 6-8 servings. | Prep: 5m | Ready in: 15m

Ingredients

- 1 package (9 oz.) refrigerated cheese- or meat-filled tortellini
- 1 bottle (8 oz.) Italian dressing
- 2 tbsps. Dijon mustard
- 1 cup fresh broccoli florets
- 1 cup sliced fresh mushrooms
- 1 cup cherry tomato halves
- 1 cup sliced zucchini
- 1/2 cup sliced pitted ripe olives

Direction

- Based on the instructions on package, cook tortellini; drain off and wash under cold water.
- Mix mustard and Italian dressing in a big bowl. Put in tortellini, olives and vegetables; coat by tossing. Keep it covered and let chill in the fridge till chilled.

Nutrition Information

- Calories: 221 calories
- Total Carbohydrate: 19 g
- Cholesterol: 14 mg
- Total Fat: 14 g
- Fiber: 2 g
- Protein: 6 g
- Sodium: 742 mg

114. Tossed Eggplant Salad

"This recipe will turn into a hit when the ingredients and a little dressing are mixed together to make eye-catching salad."
Serving: 8 servings (2/3 cup dressing). | Prep: 15m | Ready in: 30m

Ingredients

- 2 heads Bibb or Boston lettuce, torn
- 1 small bunch romaine, torn
- 2 large tomatoes, chopped
- 1 large sweet onion, thinly sliced
- 1 small green pepper, julienned
- 2 medium zucchini, thinly sliced
- 1 small eggplant, peeled and cubed
- 3 tbsps. olive oil
- DRESSING:
- 2 tbsps. egg substitute
- 1 tbsp. Dijon mustard
- 1 tsp. ground mustard
- 1/4 tsp. garlic salt
- 1/4 tsp. dried basil
- 1/4 tsp. dried oregano
- 1/2 cup olive oil
- 1 tbsp. rice vinegar

Direction

- Mix together the first five ingredients in a large bowl. Sauté eggplant and zucchini with oil in a large skillet until they turn tender. Mix them together with the lettuce mixture.
- Mix together oregano, basil, garlic salt, ground mustard, Dijon mustard and egg substitute in a blender. Process with cover until smooth or for 30 seconds. Pour in oil gradually and steadily while processing. Add vinegar and stir. Serve with salad.

Nutrition Information

- Calories: 215 calories
- Total Carbohydrate: 10 g
- Cholesterol: 0 mg
- Total Fat: 19 g
- Fiber: 4 g
- Protein: 3 g
- Sodium: 124 mg

115. Tossed Italian Salad

"This Tossed Italian Salad is the combination of romaine lettuce with fresh veggies, like red onions, tomatoes, mushrooms and zucchini."
Serving: 6 servings | Prep: 10m | Ready in: 10m

Ingredients

- 10 cups loosely packed torn romaine lettuce
- 2 cups sliced fresh mushrooms
- 2 plum tomatoes, chopped
- 1 small zucchini, sliced
- 1/4 cup chopped red onions
- 1/4 cup chopped fresh basil
- 3/4 cup KRAFT Lite House Italian Dressing

Direction

- 1. In a big bowl, toss lettuce with all leftover ingredients without dressing.
- 2. Put in dressing just prior to serving; stir gently.

Nutrition Information

- Calories: 60
- Total Carbohydrate: 10 g
- Cholesterol: 0 mg
- Total Fat: 1.5 g
- Fiber: 3 g
- Protein: 2 g
- Sodium: 290 mg
- Sugar: 5 g
- Saturated Fat: 0 g

116. Tossed Salad With Cilantro Vinaigrette

"This is not a salad that you'll see everywhere...with its unique mix of veggies that tossed with romaine."
Serving: 16 servings (3/4 cup each). | Prep: 25m | Ready in: 25m

Ingredients

- 1/3 cup olive oil
- 1/4 cup minced fresh cilantro
- 1/4 cup lime juice
- 1/8 tsp. salt
- 8 cups torn romaine
- 1 medium zucchini, chopped
- 1 medium cucumber, chopped
- 1 medium sweet yellow pepper, chopped
- 5 to 10 radishes, sliced

Direction

- Combine salt, lime juice, cilantro and oil in a small bowl.
- Mix radishes, yellow pepper, cucumber, zucchini and romaine in a big bowl. Sprinkle with dressing; coat by tossing. Serve right away.

Nutrition Information

- Calories: 53 calories
- Total Carbohydrate: 3 g
- Cholesterol: 0 mg
- Total Fat: 5 g
- Fiber: 1 g
- Protein: 1 g
- Sodium: 23 mg

117. Tossed Salad With Pine Nut Dressing

"This salad is made with veggies dressed with pine nut dressing, all of which are homemade."
Serving: 2 servings. | Prep: 25m | Ready in: 25m

Ingredients

- 2 cups torn romaine
- 1/4 cup seasoned salad croutons
- 1/4 cup shredded red cabbage
- 3 tbsps. shredded carrot
- 3 tbsps. shredded zucchini
- Dash pepper
- DRESSING:
- 3 tbsps. pine nuts
- 3 tbsps. water
- 4-1/2 tsps. cider vinegar
- 1 tbsp. lemon juice
- 1/2 cup packed fresh parsley sprigs
- 3 garlic cloves, peeled and halved
- 1/2 tsp. dried basil
- 1/8 tsp. salt
- 1/4 cup olive oil

Direction

- Mix the first six ingredients together in a small salad bowl. In a blender, put pine nuts and grind with a cover until the nuts are finely ground. Add salt, basil, garlic, parsley, lemon juice, vinegar and water; cover and continue processing until blended. Pour in oil gradually and steadily while blending.
- Pour the dressing into a small bowl or pitcher. Enjoy with salad. The leftover dressing can be reserved in the fridge for up to 3 days.

Nutrition Information

- Calories: 205 calories
- Total Carbohydrate: 10 g
- Cholesterol: 0 mg
- Total Fat: 18 g
- Fiber: 3 g
- Protein: 4 g
- Sodium: 154 mg

118. Tossed Salad With Vinaigrette

"A crisp salad with tangy dressing and garden-fresh ingredients."
Serving: 8 servings. | Prep: 15m | Ready in: 15m

Ingredients

- 6 cups mixed greens
- 1 large tomato, cut into wedges
- 1 small zucchini, sliced
- 6 fresh mushrooms, quartered
- DRESSING:
- 3 tbsps. white wine vinegar
- 2 tbsps. vegetable oil
- 2 to 3 drops hot pepper sauce
- 2 to 2-1/2 tsps. sugar
- 1/4 tsp. garlic powder
- 1/4 tsp. salt

Direction

- Mix the veggies and greens together in a big bowl. In a tight-fitting lidded jar, mix the dressing ingredients together; shake the mixture well. Put on top of the salad and toss. Serve right away.

Nutrition Information

- Calories: 53 calories
- Total Carbohydrate: 5 g
- Cholesterol: 0 mg
- Total Fat: 4 g
- Fiber: 1 g
- Protein: 1 g
- Sodium: 87 mg

119. Vegetable Garden Pasta Salad

"A colorful salad even kids love."
Serving: 4 servings. | Prep: 30m | Ready in: 30m

Ingredients

- 2 cups uncooked spiral pasta
- 1 cup fresh broccoli florets
- 1/4 cup sliced carrots
- 1/4 cup chopped green pepper
- 1/4 cup chopped sweet red pepper
- 1/4 cup sliced zucchini
- 1/2 cup ranch salad dressing
- 1 tbsp. Dijon mustard

Direction

- Cook pasta following package directions. As it cooks, mix zucchini, peppers, carrots, and broccoli in a big bowl.
- Drain then rinse pasta under cold water. Add to vegetables. Mix mustard and salad dressing. Pour on pasta mixture while tossing to coat. Keep in fridge until serving time.

Nutrition Information

- Calories: 239 calories
- Total Carbohydrate: 49 g
- Cholesterol: 0 mg
- Total Fat: 1 g
- Fiber: 0 g
- Protein: 7 g
- Sodium: 414 mg

120. Vegetable Pasta Salad

"This pasta salad is made from onions, tomatoes, cauliflower, carrots and broccoli to give it the best level of crunchiness."
Serving: Makes 12 servings, 2/3 cup each. | Prep: 20m | Ready in: 20m

Ingredients

- 3 cups rotini pasta , cooked

- 1 cup small broccoli florets
- 4 carrot s (about 1/2 lb.), thinly sliced
- 1 cup small cauliflower florets
- 1 tomato , chopped
- 1/2 cup chopped red onion s
- 3/4 cup MIRACLE WHIP Dressing

Direction

- Add all ingredients and mix together.

Nutrition Information

- Calories: 130
- Total Carbohydrate: 22 g
- Cholesterol: 5 mg
- Total Fat: 3.5 g
- Fiber: 2 g
- Protein: 3 g
- Sodium: 140 mg
- Sugar: 4 g
- Saturated Fat: 0.5 g

121. Vegetable Stack-up Salad

"This colorful salad is great for family reunions or church get-togethers because it can be prepared the night before, just sprinkle on the cheese and bacon right before serving."
Serving: 10-12 servings. | Prep: 10m | Ready in: 10m

Ingredients

- 4 cups shredded salad greens
- 1 small green pepper, chopped
- 1 can (11 oz.) Mexicorn, drained
- 2 small zucchini, sliced
- 2 cups chopped fresh tomatoes
- 1 cup sliced celery
- 2 cups Miracle Whip
- 2 cups shredded cheddar cheese
- 6 bacon strips, cooked and crumbled

Direction

- Layer salad greens, green pepper, corn, zucchini, tomatoes and celery in a two and a half qt. glass serving bowl. Arrange Miracle

Whip on top of them; seal to edges of bowl. Keep it covered and let chill in the fridge for a few hours or overnight. Just prior to serving, drizzle with bacon and cheese.

Nutrition Information

- Calories: 393 calories
- Total Carbohydrate: 9 g
- Cholesterol: 38 mg
- Total Fat: 37 g
- Fiber: 2 g
- Protein: 7 g
- Sodium: 531 mg

122. Veggie Barley Salad

"This salad is often fixed with basil-flavored vinegar for summertime. Best taste when chilled the most."
Serving: 6 servings. | Prep: 15m | Ready in: 30m

Ingredients

- 1-1/4 cups reduced-sodium chicken broth or vegetable broth
- 3/4 cup water
- 1 cup quick-cooking barley
- 1 medium tomato, seeded and chopped
- 1 small zucchini, halved and thinly sliced
- 1 small sweet yellow pepper, chopped
- 2 tbsps. minced fresh parsley
- DRESSING:
- 3 tbsps. olive oil
- 2 tbsps. white wine vinegar
- 1 tbsp. water
- 1 tbsp. lemon juice
- 1 tbsp. minced fresh basil
- 1/2 tsp. salt
- 1/4 tsp. pepper
- 1/4 cup slivered almonds, toasted

Direction

- Boil barley, water and broth in a small saucepan. Lower heat; keep it covered and let simmer till barley is soft for 10 to 12 minutes. Take off the heat; let rest for 5 minutes.

- Mix the parsley, yellow pepper, zucchini and tomato in a big bowl. Mix in barley. Combine pepper, salt, basil, lemon juice, water, vinegar and oil in a small bowl. Put on top of barley mixture; coat by tossing. Keep it covered and let chill in the refrigerator for no less than 3 hours. Just prior to serving, mix in almonds.

Nutrition Information

- Calories: 211 calories
- Total Carbohydrate: 27 g
- Cholesterol: 0 mg
- Total Fat: 10 g
- Fiber: 7 g
- Protein: 6 g
- Sodium: 334 mg

123. Veggie Bean Salad

"A colorful blend of hearty beans and crunchy vegetables is what brings folks back for seconds after they try this salad."
Serving: 18-20 servings. | Prep: 15m | Ready in: 15m

Ingredients

- 2 cans (16 oz. each) kidney beans, rinsed and drained
- 2 cans (15 oz. each) garbanzo beans or chickpeas, rinsed and drained
- 2 medium carrots, grated
- 1 small zucchini, diced
- 5 medium radishes, sliced
- 2/3 cup olive oil
- 1/3 cup red wine vinegar
- 1 tsp. Italian seasoning
- 1/2 tsp. salt
- 1/2 tsp. garlic powder
- 1/2 tsp. onion powder
- 1/2 cup shredded Swiss cheese

Direction

- Mix the initial 6 ingredients in a bowl. Mix onion powder, garlic powder, salt, Italian seasoning, vinegar, and oil in a small bowl; stir the mixture well. Put on top of vegetable mixture and coat by tossing. Keep it covered and chilled in the refrigerator for no less than 2 hours. Put cheese on top. Use a slotted spoon to serve.

Nutrition Information

- Calories: 118 calories
- Total Carbohydrate: 8 g
- Cholesterol: 2 mg
- Total Fat: 8 g
- Fiber: 2 g
- Protein: 3 g
- Sodium: 133 mg

124. Veggie Pasta Salad

"This flexible and good-for-health recipe can be adjusted as for your taste by replacing normal pasta with low-carb or whole-grains ones, or simply differ the vegetables. Be careful when you cut hot peppers and don't let it touch your eyes!"
Serving: 8 | Prep: 20m | Ready in: 2h30m

Ingredients

- 1 (8 oz.) package pasta spirals
- 1/4 cup diced sweet onion
- 1 green bell pepper, seeded and minced
- 1/2 fresh hot chile pepper, seeded and minced
- 2 tomatoes, seeded and chopped
- 1 cucumber, seeded and chopped
- 1/4 cup olive oil
- 1/4 cup tomato sauce
- 1/4 cup lime juice
- 3 tbsps. red wine vinegar
- 1 tsp. garlic powder
- 1 tsp. salt
- ground black pepper to taste

Direction

- In a large pot, pour in water and a little salt. Bring it to a boil. Put in the pasta spirals in the boiling water and cook for about 8 minutes until it gets tender but still firm when bitten. Drain. Use cold water to rinse the pasta to cool, drain.
- In a large bowl, combine cucumber, tomatoes, chile pepper, green bell pepper, sweet onion and the drained pasta.
- In a separate bowl, add black pepper, salt, garlic powder, red wine vinegar, lime juice, tomato sauce and olive oil. Whisk well. Pour it slightly over the pasta mixture and toss to coat.
- Put in the refrigerator for 2 hours for chilling. Stir when served.

Nutrition Information

- Calories: 190 calories;
- Total Carbohydrate: 27.1 g
- Cholesterol: 0 mg
- Total Fat: 7.4 g
- Protein: 4.7 g
- Sodium: 336 mg

125. Walnut Romaine Salad

"This is a crunchy salad recipe with oil dressing and zippy vinegar."
Serving: 12 servings. | Prep: 10m | Ready in: 10m

Ingredients

- 1 small bunch romaine, torn
- 1 small zucchini, chopped
- 1 cup seasoned salad croutons
- 1/4 cup chopped walnuts
- 6 tbsps. olive oil
- 2 tbsps. red wine vinegar
- 2 tbsps. Dijon mustard
- 2 tbsps. honey
- 1 garlic clove, minced
- Dash pepper

Direction

- Mix together walnuts, croutons, zucchini and the romaine in a large bowl. Combine pepper, garlic, honey, mustard, vinegar and oil in a small bowl; whisk until it smoothens. Use salad as side dish.

Nutrition Information

- Calories: 112 calories
- Total Carbohydrate: 7 g
- Cholesterol: 0 mg
- Total Fat: 9 g
- Fiber: 1 g
- Protein: 2 g
- Sodium: 108 mg

126. Zesty Gazpacho Salad

"A salad recipe for summertime."
Serving: 8-10 servings. | Prep: 10m | Ready in: 10m

Ingredients

- 2 medium zucchini
- 2 medium tomatoes, chopped
- 1 small ripe avocado, chopped
- 1 cup fresh or frozen corn, thawed
- 1/2 cup thinly sliced green onions
- 1/2 cup picante sauce
- 2 tbsps. minced fresh parsley
- 2 tbsps. lemon juice
- 1 tbsp. vegetable oil
- 3/4 tsp. garlic salt
- 1/4 tsp. ground cumin

Direction

- Mix the initial 5 ingredients in a big bowl. Mix the leftover ingredients in a small bowl. Put on top of zucchini mixture; coat by tossing. Keep it covered and let chilled in the refrigerator for no less than 4 hours.

Nutrition Information

- Calories: 75 calories

- Total Carbohydrate: 8 g
- Cholesterol: 0 mg
- Total Fat: 5 g
- Fiber: 2 g
- Protein: 2 g
- Sodium: 198 mg

127. Zesty Tomato Zucchini Toss

"Everyone loves the flavor of tangy salad with grilled meat."
Serving: 10-12 servings. | Prep: 10m | Ready in: 10m

Ingredients

- 6 medium fresh tomatoes, sliced
- 3 medium zucchini, sliced
- 1 medium red onion, sliced into rings
- 1/4 cup minced fresh parsley
- DRESSING:
- 2/3 cup vegetable oil
- 1/2 cup white wine vinegar
- 2 tsps. minced fresh basil
- 1 tsp. salt
- 1/2 tsp. pepper
- 1/4 tsp. garlic powder

Direction

- Layer tomatoes, zucchini, onion and parsley in a big bowl. Combine dressing ingredients; put on top of the veggies. Let it chill down prior to serving.

Nutrition Information

- Calories: 137 calories
- Total Carbohydrate: 7 g
- Cholesterol: 0 mg
- Total Fat: 12 g
- Fiber: 2 g
- Protein: 1 g
- Sodium: 206 mg

128. Zucchini "linguine" Salad

"This idea came to me from a recipe I saw for zucchini cut into noodle-like strips and dressed with a creamy sauce."
Serving: 6 servings. | Prep: 30m | Ready in: 30m

Ingredients

- 5 medium zucchini
- 3/4 tsp. salt, divided
- 1 large sweet red pepper, julienned
- 1 large tomato, seeded and cut into thin strips
- 1/2 cup thinly sliced sweet onion
- 3 tbsps. olive oil
- 2 tbsps. cider vinegar
- 1/4 cup minced fresh parsley
- 1-1/2 tsps. minced fresh oregano or 1/2 tsp. dried oregano
- 1/4 tsp. pepper
- Shredded Parmesan cheese, optional

Direction

- Chop off the ends all of the zucchini. Slice the zucchini lengthwise into thin strips using a vegetable peeler or a cheese slicer. Slice zucchini like peeling carrot on every side, till the seeds can be seen. Get rid of seeded portion or reserve for another use. Slice zucchini strips into 1/4-in. widths.
- Put in a strainer; drizzle with half tsp. of salt and coat by lightly tossing. Let it rest for 15 minutes. Shake strainer lightly. On paper towels, drain off the zucchini and pat dry.
- Put in a big bowl; add the onion, tomato and red pepper. Combine the leftover salt, pepper, oregano, parsley, vinegar and oil in a small bowl. Put on top of zucchini mixture coat by tossing. Keep it covered and let chill in the fridge for at least half an hour prior to serving. Drizzle with cheese if you want.

Nutrition Information

- Calories: 100 calories
- Total Carbohydrate: 9 g
- Cholesterol: 0 mg
- Total Fat: 7 g

- Fiber: 3 g
- Protein: 2 g
- Sodium: 254 mg

129. Zucchini Apple Salad

"A salad of red apples and fresh, green zucchini."
Serving: 6 servings. | Prep: 15m | Ready in: 15m

Ingredients

- 2 medium red apples, chopped
- 2 small zucchini, chopped
- 1/2 cup coarsely chopped walnuts
- 2/3 cup Italian salad dressing

Direction

- Mix walnuts, zucchini and apples in a big bowl. Put in salad dressing; coat by tossing.

Nutrition Information

- Calories: 114 calories
- Total Carbohydrate: 13 g
- Cholesterol: 1 mg
- Total Fat: 6 g
- Fiber: 2 g
- Protein: 3 g
- Sodium: 383 mg

130. Zucchini Bean Salad

"A fun combination of good-for-you ingredients makes up Zucchini Bean Salad with tangy and fresh-tasting vinaigrette light coating."
Serving: 6 servings. | Prep: 20m | Ready in: 30m

Ingredients

- 1 cup cut fresh green beans
- 1 can (16 oz.) kidney beans, rinsed and drained
- 1-1/2 cups thinly sliced halved zucchini
- 1 medium green pepper, julienned
- 3 green onions, thinly sliced

- 3 tbsps. cider vinegar
- 2 tbsps. canola oil
- 3/4 tsp. sugar
- 3/4 tsp. seasoned salt
- 1/4 tsp. pepper

Direction

- In a small saucepan, put in green beans and use water to cover the beans. Boil; cover up and cook till tender-crisp for 8 to 10 minutes. Drain off and wash under cold water.
- Mix onions, green pepper, zucchini, kidney beans and green beans in a big bowl. Mix pepper, seasoned salt, sugar, oil and vinegar in a small bowl. Put on top of bean mixture; coat by tossing. Keep it covered and chilled till serving.

Nutrition Information

- Calories: 127 calories
- Total Carbohydrate: 17 g
- Cholesterol: 0 mg
- Total Fat: 5 g
- Fiber: 5 g
- Protein: 6 g
- Sodium: 315 mg

131. Zucchini Coleslaw

"Every time I served this dish on every gathering, my guests would always compliment me on how amazing it is. This recipe is not just delicious, but it also looks elegant."
Serving: 8 servings. | Prep: 15m | Ready in: 15m

Ingredients

- 2 cups coarsely shredded zucchini
- 2 cups shredded cabbage
- 1 medium carrot, shredded
- 2 green onions, sliced
- 1/2 cup thinly sliced radishes
- 1/3 cup light mayonnaise
- 1/3 cup mild picante sauce
- 1/2 tsp. ground cumin

Direction

- Place the zucchini in between the layers of paper towels. Press the paper towel to drain the zucchini. In a large bowl, mix the drained zucchini, onions, radishes, carrot, and cabbage together. Combine all the remaining ingredients in a small bowl. Pour the mixture all over the vegetables and toss thoroughly. Once the vegetables are well-coated, cover the bowl and allow it to chill for at least 60 minutes.

Nutrition Information

- Calories: 55 calories
- Total Carbohydrate: 7 g
- Cholesterol: 2 mg
- Total Fat: 3 g
- Fiber: 0 g
- Protein: 1 g
- Sodium: 154 mg

132. Zucchini Harvest Salad

"Easy-to-prepare, stores well and colorful salad with pork and chicken and zucchini."
Serving: 8 servings. | Prep: 15m | Ready in: 15m

Ingredients

- 4 cups thinly sliced zucchini
- 1 cup sliced celery
- 1/2 cup sliced fresh mushrooms
- 1/2 cup sliced ripe olives
- 1/4 cup chopped green pepper
- 1/4 cup chopped sweet red pepper
- 1 cup mild or medium picante sauce or salsa
- 1/2 cup vinegar
- 3 tbsps. olive oil
- 3 tbsp. sugar
- 1/2 tsp. oregano
- 1 garlic clove, minced
- Lettuce leaves

Direction

- Mix the initial 6 ingredients together in a big bowl, toss to mix. Mix together all the leftover ingredients excluding lettuce in a jar or small bowl and shake/mix well. Put on top of the veggies. Keep it covered and chilled for a few hours or overnight. Serve in large lettuce-lined salad bowl or in individual "cups".

Nutrition Information

- Calories: 113 calories
- Total Carbohydrate: 13 g
- Cholesterol: 0 mg
- Total Fat: 7 g
- Fiber: 0 g
- Protein: 2 g
- Sodium: 37 mg

133. Zucchini Lettuce Salad

"This salad is a great way to use up an abundant crop of squash, you can this salad with cheese and bottled dressing."
Serving: 4 servings. | Prep: 10m | Ready in: 10m

Ingredients

- 2 cups shredded leaf lettuce
- 1/2 cup shredded zucchini
- 1/2 cup sliced ripe olives
- 1/4 cup chopped red onion
- 1/2 cup Italian salad dressing
- 1/4 cup shredded Parmesan cheese

Direction

- Mix onion, olives, zucchini and lettuce in a big serving bowl. Sprinkle dressing; coat by tossing. Use Parmesan cheese to drizzle. Serve right away.

Nutrition Information

- Calories: 160 calories
- Total Carbohydrate: 5 g
- Cholesterol: 4 mg

- Total Fat: 14 g
- Fiber: 2 g
- Protein: 3 g
- Sodium: 740 mg

134. Zucchini Orange Salad

"The ingredients in this recipe may surprise you, but not as much as the delightful flavor and refreshing crunch the blend produces!"
Serving: 16-20 servings. | Prep: 10m | Ready in: 15m

Ingredients

- 2 medium zucchini, thinly sliced
- 1 medium onion, thinly sliced
- 1 cup chopped celery
- 1 can (15 oz.) mandarin oranges, drained
- 1 can (14-1/2 oz.) cut green beans, drained, drained
- 1 can (14-1/2 oz.) cut wax beans, drained
- 1 can (8 oz.) sliced water chestnuts, drained
- 1-1/2 cups sugar
- 1 cup cider vinegar
- 1 tbsp. water
- 1 tsp. salt

Direction

- Mix together celery, onion and zucchini in a large bowl. Pour boiling water enough to cover and leave 1 hour.
- Drain well. Put in water chestnuts, beans and oranges. In a saucepan, add other ingredients and mix together. Bring it to a boil and let it boil in 1 minute. Drizzle onto the salad. Refrigerate with a cover 1 day before serving.

Nutrition Information

- Calories: 92 calories
- Total Carbohydrate: 23 g
- Cholesterol: 0 mg
- Total Fat: 0 g
- Fiber: 2 g
- Protein: 1 g

- Sodium: 256 mg

135. Zucchini Salad

"This easy-to-make zucchini salad is made all from our vegetable gardens."
Serving: 8 servings. | Prep: 15m | Ready in: 15m

Ingredients

- 4 medium zucchini, sliced (about 5 cups)
- 1 can (14 oz.) water-packed artichoke hearts, rinsed, drained and chopped
- 2 jars (4-1/2 oz. each) sliced mushrooms, drained
- 1 can (2-1/4 oz.) sliced ripe olives
- 1 can (8 oz.) sliced water chestnuts, drained
- 1 envelope ranch salad dressing mix
- 1 cup Italian salad dressing
- Leaf lettuce, optional

Direction

- Mix together water chestnuts, olives, mushrooms, artichokes and zucchini in a bowl. Mix Italian dressing and the ranch dressing mix together, drizzle onto the vegetable and toss so that it can be fully covered. Refrigerate overnight or for several hours with cover. Drain the mixture and use lettuce-lined bowl to serve (optional).

136. Zucchini Slaw

""A dish that works great on its own, but is also amazing topped over a burger!""
Serving: 4 | Prep: 10m | Ready in: 25m

Ingredients

- 1 tsp. olive oil
- 2 medium zucchini, finely chopped
- 1/2 medium onion, finely chopped
- 3 tbsps. Italian salad dressing
- 1 bunch chopped fresh parsley

Direction

- In a saucepan, pour in olive oil and heat it at a moderately low level of heat. Add onion and zucchini, cooking until they tenderize. Add parsley and Italian salad dressing. Proceed with stirring until thoroughly cooked. When it's warm enough, serve.

Nutrition Information

- Calories: 69 calories;
- Total Carbohydrate: 6.7 g
- Cholesterol: 0 mg
- Total Fat: 4.6 g
- Protein: 1.8 g
- Sodium: 201 mg

137. Zucchini Tomato Green Salad

"A party-pretty side dish of salad greens with diced tomato, zucchini, with fresh, flavorful dressing."
Serving: 2 servings. | Prep: 15m | Ready in: 15m

Ingredients

- 1/2 cup diced zucchini
- 1/2 cup seeded diced tomato, divided
- 2 tbsps. mayonnaise
- 1 tbsp. minced chives
- 1 tsp. prepared mustard
- 1/8 tsp. salt
- 1/8 tsp. pepper
- 1 cup ready-to-serve salad greens

Direction

- Mix pepper, salt, mustard, chives, mayonnaise, a quarter cup of tomato and zucchini in a small bowl. Chill in the refrigerator for 20 minutes. Serve over salad greens; drizzle with leftover tomato.

Nutrition Information

- Calories: 71 calories
- Total Carbohydrate: 5 g
- Cholesterol: 5 mg

- Total Fat: 5 g
- Fiber: 2 g
- Protein: 1 g
- Sodium: 307 mg

138. Zucchini Tomato Salad

"This is a warm-served side dish that is easy and quick to make with onion, green pepper, zucchini and fresh tomatoes straight from the garden."
Serving: 2 servings. | Prep: 5m | Ready in: 15m

Ingredients

- 1/4 cup chopped green pepper
- 1 medium zucchini, cut into 1/4-inch slices
- 1 small onion, thinly sliced and separated into rings
- 1 garlic clove, minced
- 1 tsp. olive oil
- 2 small plum tomatoes, peeled and cut into wedges
- 1/2 tsp. salt
- Dash pepper
- 1 tbsp. minced fresh parsley

Direction

- Sauté garlic, onion, and zucchini and green pepper in oil in a non-stick skillet for 3-4 minutes or until they turn crisp-tender. Stir in pepper, salt and tomatoes. Lower the heat, cook with cover until everything is hot enough. Top with a sprinkle of parsley.

Nutrition Information

- Calories: 59 calories
- Total Carbohydrate: 9 g
- Cholesterol: 0 mg
- Total Fat: 3 g
- Fiber: 3 g
- Protein: 2 g
- Sodium: 597 mg

139. Zucchini Tomato Toss

"A flavorful medley of tomatoes and zucchini shared from a co-worker."
Serving: 8 servings. | Prep: 10m | Ready in: 10m

Ingredients

- 4 cups thinly sliced zucchini
- 2 medium tomatoes, cut into wedges
- 1/4 cup thinly sliced green onions
- 3/4 cup red wine vinegar
- 2/3 cup vegetable oil
- 1 garlic clove, minced
- 2 tbsps. sugar
- 1 tsp. salt
- 1 tsp. dried basil
- Dash to 1/8 tsp. pepper

Direction

- Mix the onions, tomatoes and zucchini in a serving bowl. Mix the leftover ingredients in a tight-fitting lidded jar; shake the mixture well. Put on top of zucchini mixture and coat by lightly tossing. Keep it covered and let chilled in the fridge for at least 2 hours. Use a slotted spoon to serve.

Chapter 4: Zucchini Soup Recipes

***

140. "après-ski" Soup

"A great microwave soup recipe."
Serving: 6 servings (1-1/2 qt.). | Prep: 10m | Ready in: 30m

Ingredients

- 1 tbsp. butter
- 1-1/4 cups cubed acorn squash
- 1 carrot, thinly sliced
- 1 medium leek (white portion only), thinly sliced
- 3 cans (14-1/2 oz. each) reduced-sodium chicken broth
- 1 small zucchini, halved and sliced
- 1/2 cup uncooked elbow macaroni
- 1 bay leaf
- 1/2 tsp. dried basil
- 1/4 tsp. dried thyme
- 1/8 tsp. salt
- 1/8 tsp. pepper

Direction

- Microwave butter on high in 3-qt. microwave-safe bowl till melted for 15-20 minutes. Add leek, carrot and squash; mix to coat. Cook for 6 minutes on high, covered.
- Mix leftover ingredients in; cook on high for 12-14 minutes till macaroni and veggies are tender, covered, mixing twice. Discard bay leaf.

Nutrition Information

- Calories: 92 calories
- Total Carbohydrate: 15 g
- Cholesterol: 5 mg
- Total Fat: 2 g
- Fiber: 3 g
- Protein: 4 g
- Sodium: 594 mg

141. Alaskan Salmon Chowder

""My husband likes catching red salmon along with our son, and we use it in this soup to make its rich taste.""
Serving: 7 servings. | Prep: 10m | Ready in: 40m

Ingredients

- 1/2 cup chopped onion
- 1/2 cup chopped celery
- 1/4 cup chopped green pepper
- 1 garlic clove, minced
- 1 can (14-1/2 oz.) chicken broth, divided
- 2 cups diced peeled potatoes
- 1 cup sliced carrots
- 1 tsp. seasoned salt, optional
- 1/2 tsp. dill weed
- 1 small zucchini, thinly sliced
- 1 can (14-3/4 oz.) cream-style corn
- 1 can (12 oz.) evaporated milk
- 2 cups cooked salmon chunks or 2 cans (7-1/2 oz. each) salmon, drained and bones removed

Direction

- Cook the celery, onion, green pepper, and garlic in a big saucepan with 1/4 cup of broth until it softens.
- Mix in the carrots, potatoes, dill, seasoned salt, and the leftover broth.
- Let it simmer for 20 minutes while covered. The vegetables should cook to a soft texture. Mix in the zucchini, and let it simmer for 5 minutes. Pour in the milk along with corn and salmon. Let it heat thoroughly.

Nutrition Information

- Calories: 225 calories
- Total Carbohydrate: 29 g
- Cholesterol: 27 mg
- Total Fat: 4 g
- Fiber: 0 g
- Protein: 20 g
- Sodium: 147 mg

142. Baked Potatoes With Chili

"I experimented this recipe with handy ingredients and the result is awesome with perfect taste! You can double it to serve more people. You don't need a side dish because it is enough."
Serving: 4 servings. | Prep: 10m | Ready in: 30m

Ingredients

- 4 large baking potatoes
- 1/2 lb. ground beef
- 1 small zucchini, diced
- 1/2 cup chopped onion
- 1 can (16 oz.) chili
- Butter, optional
- 1 cup shredded cheddar cheese
- Sour cream
- Salsa

Direction

- Bake potatoes in a conventional oven or microwave. Cook ground beef till browned in a skillet, then drain. Put in zucchini and onion, then sauté till onion turns transparent. Heat chili in a saucepan and stir in vegetables and ground beef. Slice baked potatoes open and put in a pat of butter if wanted. Scoop chili in every potato, then put salsa, sour cream and cheese atop.

Nutrition Information

- Calories: 595 calories
- Total Carbohydrate: 84 g
- Cholesterol: 68 mg
- Total Fat: 15 g
- Fiber: 10 g
- Protein: 31 g
- Sodium: 732 mg

143. Barley Peasant Soup

"This grain with vegetables is so good-tasting."
Serving: 20 servings (5 quarts). | Prep: 10m | Ready in: 01h20m

Ingredients

- 1 lb. beef stew meat, cut into 3/4-inch cubes
- 1 tbsp. olive oil
- 2 cups chopped onions
- 1 cup sliced celery
- 2 garlic cloves, minced
- 5 cups water
- 5 cups beef broth
- 2 cups sliced carrots
- 1-1/2 cups medium pearl barley
- 1 can (15 oz.) garbanzo beans or chickpeas, rinsed and drained
- 1 can (15 oz.) kidney beans, rinsed and drained
- 4 cups sliced zucchini
- 3 cups diced plum tomatoes
- 2 cups chopped cabbage
- 1/4 cup minced fresh parsley
- 1 tsp. dried thyme
- 1-1/2 tsps. Italian seasoning
- Salt and pepper to taste
- Grated Parmesan cheese, optional

Direction

- In a stockpot, brown the meat in oil. Put in the celery and onions. Cook till beef is not pink anymore. Put in the garlic and cook 60 seconds more. Pour in broth and water; boil. Put in the barley and carrots. Lower the heat; keep covered and simmer till the barley softens, about 45 to 60 minutes.
- Put in the seasonings, parsley, cabbage, tomatoes, zucchini and beans; simmer till veggies soften, about 15 to 20 minutes. If you want, add parmesan cheese on top of each of the servings.

Nutrition Information

- Calories: 159 calories
- Total Carbohydrate: 24 g
- Cholesterol: 14 mg
- Total Fat: 3 g
- Fiber: 6 g
- Protein: 10 g
- Sodium: 292 mg

144. Bean Cabbage Soup

"You can adjust the amount of ingredients according to the number of people to serve."
Serving: 2 servings. | Prep: 15m | Ready in: 50m

Ingredients

- 2 tbsps. chopped celery
- 1 tbsp. chopped onion
- 1 tsp. olive or 1 tbsp. canola oil
- 1 garlic clove, minced
- 1/3 cup cubed zucchini
- 1/3 cup cubed peeled potato
- 1/3 cup sliced carrot
- 1 can (14-1/2 oz.) beef broth
- 1/2 cup canned cannellini beans or white kidney beans, rinsed and drained
- 2 tsps. minced fresh basil or 1/2 tsp. dried basil
- Dash pepper
- 1/2 cup coarsely chopped cabbage
- 1/4 cup cooked rice
- 1 tbsp. grated Parmesan cheese

Direction

- Sauté onion and celery in oil in a saucepan for 2-3 minutes. Add garlic, sauté for a minute. Add carrot, potato, and zucchini; sauté for 3 minutes. Stir in pepper, basil, beans, and beef broth. Boil. Then add in cabbage and stir.
- Turn down the heat; put a cover and let simmer until the potatoes become tender, for 20 minutes. Stir in cheese and rice just before serving.

Nutrition Information

- Calories: 162 calories

- Total Carbohydrate: 25 g
- Cholesterol: 6 mg
- Total Fat: 3 g
- Fiber: 5 g
- Protein: 7 g
- Sodium: 566 mg

145. Bean Vegetable Chili

"My family and friends request this hearty chili all the time."
Serving: 9 servings (2-1/4 quarts). | Prep: 25m | Ready in: 55m

Ingredients

- 1 medium zucchini, sliced 1/4 inch thick
- 1 medium green pepper, chopped
- 1 cup chopped onion
- 1 cup shredded carrots
- 1/2 cup finely chopped celery
- 2 garlic cloves, minced
- 1/4 cup olive oil
- 1 can (28 oz.) no-salt-added diced tomatoes, undrained
- 1 jar (8 oz.) picante sauce
- 1 tsp. reduced-sodium beef bouillon granules
- 1-1/2 tsps. ground cumin
- 1 can (16 oz.) chili beans, undrained
- 1 can (15 oz.) garbanzo beans or chickpeas, rinsed and drained
- 1 can (2-1/4 oz.) sliced ripe olives, drained

Direction

- In a Dutch oven, sauté garlic, celery, carrots, onion, green pepper, and zucchini in oil until vegetables are softened. Mix in cumin, bouillon, picante sauce, and tomatoes; bring to a boil.
- Lower heat; simmer without covering, stirring from time to time for 30 minutes. Add olives and beans; cook through.

Nutrition Information

- Calories: 211 calories
- Total Carbohydrate: 30 g
- Cholesterol: 0 mg
- Total Fat: 8 g
- Fiber: 7 g
- Protein: 7 g
- Sodium: 647 mg

146. Beef And Bean Chili

"This recipe is a fine version of hearty classic."
Serving: Makes 6 servings

Ingredients

- 1 tbsp. olive oil
- 2 large red onions, chopped
- 5 tbsps. chopped jalapeño chilies with seeds
- 8 garlic cloves, chopped
- 2 1/3 lbs. ground beef (15% fat)
- 1/4 cup chili powder
- 2 tbsps. ground cumin
- 1 tsp. sweet paprika
- 1 28-oz. can diced tomatoes in juice
- 2 15 1/4-oz. cans kidney beans, drained
- 1 14-oz. can beef broth
- Sour cream
- Grated cheddar cheese
- Chopped green onions
- Chopped fresh cilantro

Direction

- In a big heavy pot, heat oil over medium-high heat. Add onions, sauté for 6 minutes until turning brown. Add garlic and jalapeños, sauté for 1 minute. Add beef, sauté for 5 minutes until turning brown, crumble using the back of a fork. Add paprika, cumin, and chili powder, and then mix in broth, beans, and tomatoes with juices; boil it. Lower the heat and simmer for 45 minutes until the flavors combine and the chili thickens, whisking sometimes. Remove any fat from the surface of chili. (You can prepare 2 days in advance. Let cool slightly. Chill without a cover until cold, and then cover and keep chilled. Simmer before continuing, whisking sometimes).

- Spoon the chili into bowls. Enjoy, passing bowls of cilantro, green onions, grated cheese, and sour cream individually.

147. Beef And Pasta Vegetable Soup

"This rich soup is a wonderful dish to warm you up during chilly days. Remember to lightly dust with Parmesan cheese."
Serving: 10 servings (2-1/2 quarts). | Prep: 25m | Ready in: 50m

Ingredients

- 1-1/2 lbs. beef shanks or meaty beef soup bones
- 1 tbsp. canola oil
- 6 cups water
- 2 medium carrots, sliced
- 2 celery ribs, diced
- 1 medium red potato, cut into 1/2-inch cubes
- 1 small onion, chopped
- 1 garlic clove, minced
- 1 bay leaf
- 1 tsp. salt
- 1 tsp. dried basil
- 1 tsp. dried thyme
- 1/4 tsp. pepper
- 1 can (16 oz.) kidney beans, rinsed and drained
- 1 can (14-1/2 oz.) diced tomatoes, undrained
- 1 medium zucchini, diced
- 1/2 cup uncooked elbow macaroni

Direction

- Allow to brown both sides of the beef in oil in a pressure cooker on medium-high heat. Put in the seasonings, garlic, onion, potato, celery, carrots, and water. Place the cover on and seal securely; put the pressure regulator on the

vent pipe. Take the cooker to full pressure on high heat. Turn down the heat to medium-high; cook for 15 minutes. (Pressure regulator should remain in a slow and steady rocking motion; change the heat if necessary). Take away from the heat. Cool right away following the manufacturer's instructions to completely reduce the pressure. Discard the bay leaf. Use a slotted spoon to take the beef out; debone when the beef is cool enough to handle. Discard the bones and dice the meat.

- Bring the meat back to the pan. Put in the zucchini, tomatoes, and beans. Simmer the soup. Stir the macaroni in. Uncover and cook until zucchini and macaroni become tender, 8-10 minutes.

148. Beef Zucchini Soup

"A succulent garden-fresh soup loaded with tasty zucchini."
Serving: 6 servings. | Prep: 20m | Ready in: 40m

Ingredients

- 1/2 lb. lean ground beef (90% lean)
- 2 celery ribs, thinly sliced
- 1/3 cup chopped onion
- 1/2 cup chopped green pepper
- 1 can (28 oz.) diced tomatoes, undrained
- 3 medium zucchini, cubed
- 2 cups water
- 1-1/2 tsps. Italian seasoning
- 1 tsp. salt, optional
- 1 tsp. beef bouillon granules
- 1/2 tsp. sugar
- Pepper to taste
- Shredded Parmesan cheese, optional

Direction

- Cook the green pepper, onion, celery, and beef in a large saucepan on medium heat until the vegetables become tender and the meat is not pink anymore; then drain. Stir in pepper, sugar, bouillon, salt (if desired), Italian seasoning, water, zucchini, and tomatoes. Boil. Turn down the heat; put a cover and let simmer until the zucchini becomes tender, for 20-25 minutes. If desired, add Parmesan cheese to decorate.

Nutrition Information

- Calories: 106 calories
- Total Carbohydrate: 10 g
- Cholesterol: 14 mg
- Total Fat: 4 g
- Fiber: 2 g
- Protein: 10 g
- Sodium: 628 mg

149. Best Chicken Tortilla Soup

"This veggie-filled soup can be richer by grilling the vegetables and chicken first."
Serving: 3-1/2 cups. | Prep: 30m | Ready in: 55m

Ingredients

- 2 medium tomatoes
- 1 small onion, cut into wedges
- 1 garlic clove, peeled
- 4 tsps. canola oil, divided
- 1 boneless skinless chicken breast half (6 oz.)
- 1/4 tsp. lemon-pepper seasoning
- 1/8 tsp. salt
- 2 corn tortillas (6 inches)
- 1/2 cup diced zucchini
- 2 tbsps. chopped carrot
- 1 tbsp. minced fresh cilantro
- 3/4 tsp. ground cumin
- 1/2 tsp. chili powder
- 1 cup reduced-sodium chicken broth
- 1/2 cup Spicy Hot V8 juice
- 1/3 cup frozen corn
- 2 tbsps. tomato puree
- 1-1/2 tsps. chopped seeded jalapeno pepper
- 1 bay leaf
- 1/4 cup cubed or sliced avocado
- 1/4 cup shredded Mexican cheese blend

Direction

- Brush 1 tsp. of oil onto the garlic, onion, and tomatoes. Broil them 4 inches from the heat, turning once, for 6 - 8 minutes or until tender. Peel and throw away the charred skins from the tomatoes and place them in a blender. Add the garlic and onion, then process with a cover for 1 - 2 minutes or until smooth.
- Sprinkle chicken with salt and lemon pepper then broil on each side for 5 - 6 minutes, or until a thermometer reads out 170 degrees. Cut up one tortilla into 1/4 inch strips and chop the remaining tortilla coarsely.
- Heat the remaining oil in a large saucepan and fry the strips of tortilla until brown and crisp, then remove using a slotted spoon.
- In the same pan, cook the chopped tortilla, chili powder, cumin, cilantro, carrot, and zucchini on medium heat for 4 minutes. Stir in the bay leaf, jalapeno, tomato puree, corn, V8 juice, broth, and tomato mixture, then set to boil. Lower the heat and simmer while uncovered for 20 minutes.
- Cut up the chicken into strips and add them into the soup, heating it through. Throw away the bay leaf and garnish the soup with the tortilla strips, cheese, and avocado.

Nutrition Information

- Calories: 284 calories
- Total Carbohydrate: 24 g
- Cholesterol: 40 mg
- Total Fat: 14 g
- Fiber: 5 g
- Protein: 18 g
- Sodium: 617 mg

150. Black Bean Gazpacho

"A colorful cold soup made of fresh ingredients to make a big hit on any meal."
Serving: 10 servings. | Prep: 10m | Ready in: 10m

Ingredients

- 3 cans (11-1/2 oz. each) spicy hot V8 juice
- 4 medium tomatoes, seeded and chopped
- 1 can (15 oz.) black beans, rinsed and drained
- 1 cup cubed fully cooked ham
- 1/2 cup each chopped green, sweet yellow and red pepper
- 1/2 cup chopped cucumber
- 1/2 cup chopped zucchini
- 1/4 cup finely chopped green onions
- 2 tbsps. Italian salad dressing
- 3/4 tsp. salt
- 1/8 to 1/4 tsp. hot pepper sauce

Direction

- In a big bowl, mix entire ingredients together, then place a cover and chill for a minimum of 2 hours.

Nutrition Information

- Calories: 95 calories
- Total Carbohydrate: 13 g
- Cholesterol: 7 mg
- Total Fat: 3 g
- Fiber: 3 g
- Protein: 6 g
- Sodium: 591 mg

151. Black Bean Zucchini Gazpacho

"My friends enjoy this soup a lot. I created the recipe when trying to make use of our fresh garden zucchini."
Serving: 6 servings. | Prep: 10m | Ready in: 10m

Ingredients

- 3 cans (5-1/2 oz. each) spicy hot V8 juice
- 1 can (15 oz.) black beans, rinsed and drained
- 1 medium onion, chopped
- 2 large tomatoes, seeded and chopped
- 2 medium zucchini, chopped
- 2 tbsps. olive oil
- 2 tbsps. white wine vinegar
- 1 garlic clove, minced
- 1/4 tsp. salt
- 1/4 tsp. pepper
- 1/4 tsp. cayenne pepper

Direction

- Mix all ingredients together in a large bowl. Chill, covered for 8 hours or overnight.

Nutrition Information

- Calories: 149 calories
- Total Carbohydrate: 20 g
- Cholesterol: 0 mg
- Total Fat: 5 g
- Fiber: 6 g
- Protein: 6 g
- Sodium: 574 mg

152. Bow Tie Beef Soup

"The simplest yet delicious one-dish meal."
Serving: 8 servings (about 2 quarts). | Prep: 5m | Ready in: 30m

Ingredients

- 2 cups sliced zucchini
- 1 can (14-1/2 oz.) beef broth
- 1 cup uncooked bow tie pasta
- 3/4 cup water
- 1/2 tsp. dried oregano
- 1/4 to 1/2 tsp. dried thyme
- 1/4 to 1/2 tsp. crushed red pepper flakes
- 1-1/2 lbs. ground beef
- 1 cup chopped onion
- 2 tsps. minced garlic
- 4 plum tomatoes, cut into chunks
- 1/4 cup minced fresh basil
- 1/2 cup shredded Parmesan cheese

Direction

- Blend together the first 7 ingredients in a Dutch oven. Allow to boil. Use a spoon to press pasta into the broth mixture. Turn down the heat; cover, allow to simmer until the pasta becomes tender, about 15 minutes, stirring once.
- At the same time, cook the garlic, onion, and beef in a large skillet over medium heat until no pink remains in meat; allow to drain.
- Put the basil, tomatoes, and beef mixture into the broth mixture; heat through. Use the Parmesan cheese to decorate.

153. Butternut Goulash

"The taste of cayenne and chili powder will warm you up."
Serving: 8 servings (2-1/2 quarts). | Prep: 25m | Ready in: 01h10m

Ingredients

- 2 tbsps. butter
- 1 lb. lean ground beef (90% lean)
- 1 large red pepper, chopped
- 1 cup chopped onion
- 1 can (28 oz.) no-salt-added crushed tomatoes
- 1-1/2 cups peeled butternut squash, cut into 1/2-inch cubes
- 1 can (8 oz.) no-salt-added tomato sauce
- 1 cup reduced-sodium beef broth
- 1 tsp. salt
- 1/2 to 3/4 tsp. chili powder
- 1/8 to 1/4 tsp. cayenne pepper
- 1/8 tsp. dried oregano
- 2 cups chopped zucchini
- Shredded cheddar cheese, optional

Direction

- Cook the butter in a Dutch oven on medium-high heat. Add onion, red pepper, and beef; cook and crumble the beef for 6-8 minutes until the vegetables become tender and no pink remains in the meat; let drain.

- Add the following 8 ingredients. Allow to boil; turn down the heat to low. Cover and simmer for around 20 minutes; put in zucchini. Keep on simmering for 20-25 more minutes until the vegetables become tender. If desired, use cheese to dust over just before serving.

Nutrition Information

- Calories: 196 calories
- Total Carbohydrate: 17 g
- Cholesterol: 44 mg
- Total Fat: 8 g
- Fiber: 5 g
- Protein: 14 g
- Sodium: 450 mg

154. Cabbage Zucchini Borscht

"Healthy and hearty soup."
Serving: 12-14 servings (4 quarts). | Prep: 10m | Ready in: 03h40m

Ingredients

- 1 lb. meaty beef soup bones (beef shanks or short ribs)
- 8 cups water
- 4 cups shredded cabbage
- 2 cups cubed peeled potatoes
- 2 cups sliced carrots
- 2 cups diced peeled tomatoes
- 1 onion, chopped
- 1/2 cup chopped fresh parsley
- 2 tbsps. dill weed
- 1-1/2 tsps. salt
- 1/2 tsp. pepper
- 1 tbsp. aniseed
- 3 cups shredded zucchini
- 2 cups chopped cooked beets

Direction

- Boil water and soup bones in a stockpot. Lower heat; simmer for 40-45 minutes, uncovered.

- Skim fat off. Add pepper, salt, dill, parsley, onion, tomatoes, carrots, potatoes and cabbage. On a double thickness of cheesecloth, put aniseed; bring cloth corners up and tie with string to make a bag. Put into stockpot; simmer for 2 1/2-3 hours, uncovered.
- From soup bones, remove meat; discard bones. Put meat in soup; mix beets and zucchini in. Simmer till zucchini is tender, about 15-20 minutes more. Before serving, remove spice bag.

155. Calico Chili

"This food is delicious even the second day."
Serving: 8-10 servings (10 cups). | Prep: 15m | Ready in: 40m

Ingredients

- 1 lb. ground beef
- 1 medium green pepper, chopped
- 1 medium onion, chopped
- 1 celery rib, chopped
- 2 garlic cloves, minced
- 1 can (28 oz.) diced tomatoes, undrained
- 2 cans (16 oz. each) kidney beans, rinsed and drained
- 1 can (15-1/4 oz.) whole kernel corn, drained
- 1 cup cooked rice
- 1 cup diced zucchini, optional
- 1 cup water
- 2 tbsps. cider vinegar
- 1 tbsp. dried parsley flakes
- 1 tbsp. chili powder
- 1 tbsp. Worcestershire sauce
- 1/4 tsp. each dried oregano, thyme and rosemary, crushed
- Salt and pepper to taste

Direction

- Cook garlic, celery, onion, green pepper, and beef over medium heat in a Dutch oven, until beef is not pink anymore. Drain.

- Mix in the rest ingredients; heat to a boil. Decrease heat, simmer 20 minutes without cover until heated through and thickened, mixing from time to time.

Nutrition Information

- Calories: 229 calories
- Total Carbohydrate: 30 g
- Cholesterol: 22 mg
- Total Fat: 5 g
- Fiber: 7 g
- Protein: 16 g
- Sodium: 456 mg

156. Carrot Zucchini Soup

"This recipe is an easy way for kids to eat vegetables."
Serving: 2-4 servings. | Prep: 30m | Ready in: 60m

Ingredients

- 2 small onions
- 2 cups water
- 1/2 lb. carrots, cut into 1-inch pieces
- 1/8 tsp. celery salt
- 1/8 tsp. pepper
- 2 cups diced zucchini (3 to 4 medium)
- 1-1/2 tsps. olive oil
- 1-1/2 tsps. butter
- 1/2 cup chopped seeded tomatoes
- 2/3 cup evaporated milk
- 2 tbsps. minced fresh parsley

Direction

- Chop an onion and set it aside. In a 3 quart saucepan, place another onion, quartered. Add pepper, celery salt, carrots, and water, then allow to boil. Turn the heat down, and simmer while covered for 20 minutes or until the carrots become tender. Move the mixture into a blender, and process, covered, until they are pureed, then return it to the pan.
- Sauté chopped onion and zucchini in a large frying pan with butter and oil until they are

tender, then add into the carrot mixture. Stir in the tomatoes and simmer, covered, until the tomatoes are tender, or for 10 minutes. Stir in the parsley and milk, then heat through.

Nutrition Information

- Calories: 133 calories
- Total Carbohydrate: 16 g
- Cholesterol: 17 mg
- Total Fat: 6 g
- Fiber: 3 g
- Protein: 5 g
- Sodium: 127 mg

157. Celery Zucchini Soup

"Full of fresh flavors!"
Serving: 6 servings. | Prep: 10m | Ready in: 30m

Ingredients

- 3 green onions, thinly sliced
- 2 garlic cloves, minced
- 2 tbsps. butter
- 4 celery ribs, chopped
- 2 medium carrots, chopped
- 2 cups water
- 1 tbsp. reduced-sodium chicken bouillon granules or 1-1/2 vegetable bouillon cubes
- 3/4 tsp. salt
- 3/4 tsp. dried thyme
- 5 medium red potatoes, cut into small chunks (about 1 lb.)
- 3 cups fat-free milk
- 2 cups shredded zucchini
- 2 tbsps. cornstarch
- 1/4 cup cold water

Direction

- Sauté garlic and onions in butter till tender in a big saucepan. Add carrots and celery; mix and cook for 4 minutes. Mix thyme, salt, bouillon and water in then add potatoes; boil.

- Lower the heat; cover. Simmer till potatoes are tender for 15 minutes. Mix zucchini and milk in; boil. Mix cold water and cornstarch till smooth in a small bowl; whisk into the soup slowly. Boil; mix and cook till slightly thick for 2 minutes.

Nutrition Information

- Calories: 175 calories
- Total Carbohydrate: 28 g
- Cholesterol: 13 mg
- Total Fat: 4 g
- Fiber: 3 g
- Protein: 7 g
- Sodium: 651 mg

158. Chicken Minestrone

"This recipe is minestrone soup dressed up in croutons, portobello mushrooms, zucchini, and chicken. It's very easy to make but it tastes like a very complicated dish."
Serving: 5 servings. | Prep: 10m | Ready in: 30m

Ingredients

- 1 package (9.3 oz.) minestrone soup mix
- 1 medium zucchini, quartered lengthwise and sliced
- 1 cup chopped baby portobello mushrooms
- 1 lb. boneless skinless chicken breasts, cubed
- 1 tbsp. olive oil
- 1/4 cup butter, melted
- 1 tsp. dried parsley flakes
- 6 slices day-old French bread (1 inch thick), cubed
- 2 tbsps. grated Parmesan cheese

Direction

- Cook the soup mix following the package's instructions, add mushrooms and zucchini. In the meantime, cook chicken in oil in a big frying pan until the chicken is not pink anymore, or for about 10-12 minutes. Mix into the soup.

- To prepare the croutons, mix parsley and butter in a big bowl. Add bread cubes and coat by tossing. On a non-oiled baking sheet, put in 1 layer.
- Scatter with cheese. Bake at 400° until turning golden brown, mixing sometimes, or for about 7-8 minutes. Enjoy with soup.

Nutrition Information

- Calories: 588 calories
- Total Carbohydrate: 64 g
- Cholesterol: 95 mg
- Total Fat: 19 g
- Fiber: 6 g
- Protein: 36 g
- Sodium: 2164 mg

159. Chili Non Carne

"A zesty meatless chili full of flavors."
Serving: 10 servings. | Prep: 10m | Ready in: 50m

Ingredients

- 1 large onion, chopped
- 2 garlic cloves, minced
- 3 tbsps. olive oil
- 4 cups diced zucchini
- 1 cup coarsely chopped carrots
- 2 tbsps. chili powder
- 1/4 tsp. dried oregano
- 1/4 tsp. dried basil
- 1/4 tsp. ground cumin
- 2 cans (one 28 oz., one 14-1/2 oz.) stewed tomatoes
- 3 cans (16 oz. each) kidney beans, rinsed and drained

Direction

- Sauté garlic and onion in oil in a big saucepan. Mix in cumin, basil, oregano, chili powder, carrots, and zucchini; blend well. Add beans and tomatoes; boil. Lower heat and simmer, covered, until tender for 30-45 minutes.

Nutrition Information

- Calories: 266 calories
- Total Carbohydrate: 44 g
- Cholesterol: 0 mg
- Total Fat: 5 g
- Fiber: 15 g
- Protein: 12 g
- Sodium: 269 mg

160. Chunky Chicken Veggie Soup

"Try making this soup of veggies for a big group of Super Bowl fans or Christmas crowd."
Serving: 20 servings. (6-1/2 quarts). | Prep: 25m | Ready in: 50m

Ingredients

- 8 cups chicken broth
- 6 medium carrots, sliced
- 2 medium onions, chopped
- 2 small zucchini, chopped
- 4 garlic cloves, minced
- 6 cups cubed cooked chicken
- 2 cans (28 oz. each) crushed tomatoes
- 1 can (14-1/2 oz.) diced tomatoes, undrained
- 1 can (10 oz.) diced tomatoes with green chilies, undrained
- 1 can (8 oz.) tomato sauce
- 4 tsps. sugar
- 1 tsp. salt
- 1 tsp. celery salt
- 1 tsp. Creole seasoning
- 1/2 tsp. pepper

Direction

- Bring onions, carrots, and broth in a large stockpot to a boil. Lower heat; simmer without a cover for 5 minutes. Add garlic and zucchini; simmer until vegetables are crisp-tender, or for 5 more minutes. Mix in the remaining ingredients; cook until thoroughly heated.

Nutrition Information

- Calories: 130 calories
- Total Carbohydrate: 11 g
- Cholesterol: 37 mg
- Total Fat: 3 g
- Fiber: 2 g
- Protein: 15 g
- Sodium: 825 mg

Nutrition Information

- Calories: 188 calories
- Total Carbohydrate: 31 g
- Cholesterol: 10 mg
- Total Fat: 4 g
- Fiber: 4 g
- Protein: 9 g
- Sodium: 353 mg

---

161. Chunky Veggie Chowder

"A colorful chowder!"
Serving: 8 servings (2 quarts). | Prep: 15m | Ready in: 45m

Ingredients

- 2 medium onions, finely chopped
- 2 garlic cloves, minced
- 2 tbsps. butter
- 3 medium carrots, chopped
- 2 celery ribs, sliced
- 2 medium potatoes, cubed
- 1 small zucchini, cubed
- 2 cans (10-1/2 oz. each) condensed chicken broth, undiluted
- 1/4 cup minced fresh parsley
- 3/4 tsp. dried thyme
- 1 cup frozen peas
- 1 cup frozen corn
- 1/4 cup all-purpose flour
- 3 cups milk
- Salt and pepper to taste

Direction

- Sauté garlic and onions in butter till tender in a big saucepan/soup kettle. Add thyme, parsley, broth, zucchini, potatoes, celery and carrots; boil. Lower heat; cover. Simmer for 20 minutes till veggies are tender; mix corn and peas in.
- Mix pepper, salt (optional), milk and flour till smooth in a big bowl; add to soup slowly. Boil; mix and cook till thick, about 2 minutes.

---

162. Confetti Chowder

"This golden chowder is one of my grandmother's favorite recipes. It has zucchini, broccoli, and carrots and they add amazing flavors and beautiful colors to the dish."
Serving: 8 servings (2 quarts). | Prep: 15m | Ready in: 30m

Ingredients

- 3 tbsps. butter
- 1 cup chopped carrots
- 1 cup diced zucchini
- 1 cup broccoli florets
- 1/2 cup chopped onion
- 1/2 cup chopped celery
- 1/4 cup all-purpose flour
- 1/2 tsp. salt
- 1/2 tsp. pepper
- 1/4 tsp. sugar
- 3 cups whole milk
- 1 cup chicken broth
- 1 cup whole kernel corn
- 1 cup diced fully cooked ham
- 1/2 cup peas
- 1 jar (2 oz.) sliced pimiento, drained
- 1 cup shredded cheddar cheese

Direction

- In a saucepan, melt the butter. Then mix in the onion, broccoli, zucchini, celery, and carrots. Keep cooking and stirring for about 5 minutes or until they turn crisp-tender. Sprinkle some flour, sugar, pepper, and salt over the vegetables. Mix really well.

- Stir in the chicken broth and milk. Continue cooking and stirring until it turns bubbly and thick. Mix in the ham, peas, pimiento, and corn then cook until heated through. Remove the pot from the heat and stir in the cheese until melted.

Nutrition Information

- Calories: 237 calories
- Total Carbohydrate: 17 g
- Cholesterol: 48 mg
- Total Fat: 13 g
- Fiber: 2 g
- Protein: 12 g
- Sodium: 762 mg

163. Contest-winning Garden Harvest Chili

"You can be creative with the ingredients in this recipe. In my case, I use all kinds of veggies."
Serving: 6 servings (2-1/2 quarts). | Prep: 20m | Ready in: 30m

Ingredients

- 2 tbsps. vegetable oil
- 2 garlic cloves, minced
- 1 medium green pepper, chopped
- 1 medium sweet red pepper, chopped
- 1-1/2 cups sliced fresh mushrooms
- 1/2 cup chopped onion
- 1 can (28 oz.) diced tomatoes, undrained
- 1 can (15 oz.) tomato sauce
- 2 tbsps. chili powder
- 2 tsps. sugar
- 1 tsp. ground cumin
- 1 can (16 oz.) kidney beans, rinsed and drained
- 2 cups sliced zucchini
- 2 cups frozen sweet corn, thawed
- 1-1/2 cups shredded cheddar cheese, optional

Direction

- Heat oil in a skillet on medium-high heat. Sauté onion, mushrooms, peppers, and garlic until tender. Add cumin, sugar, chili powder, tomato sauce, and tomatoes with liquid; boil. Lower heat to low. Add corn, zucchini, and beans. Simmer for 10 minutes, uncovered, until zucchini becomes tender. Serve in bowls. Top with cheese if you want.

Nutrition Information

- Calories: 252 calories
- Total Carbohydrate: 44 g
- Cholesterol: 0 mg
- Total Fat: 7 g
- Fiber: 0 g
- Protein: 10 g
- Sodium: 675 mg

164. Contest-winning Vegetarian Chili

"This makes a big chili pot full of flavor and color. When you finish chopping, it's easy to make."
Serving: 16 servings. | Prep: 20m | Ready in: 60m

Ingredients

- 4 medium zucchini, chopped
- 2 medium onions, chopped
- 1 medium green pepper, chopped
- 1 medium sweet red pepper, chopped
- 1/4 cup olive oil
- 4 garlic cloves, minced
- 2 cans (28 oz. each) Italian stewed tomatoes, cut up
- 1 can (15 oz.) tomato sauce
- 1 can (15 oz.) pinto beans, rinsed and drained
- 1 can (15 oz.) black beans, rinsed and drained
- 1 jalapeno pepper, seeded and chopped
- 1/4 cup minced fresh cilantro
- 1/4 cup minced fresh parsley
- 2 tbsps. chili powder
- 1 tbsp. sugar

- 1 tsp. salt
- 1 tsp. ground cumin

Direction

- Sauté peppers, onions, and zucchini in oil in a Dutch oven until tender. Stir in garlic. Cook for a minute.
- Mix in all the other ingredients. Boil on medium heat. Lower heat and simmer, covered, until heated through for 30 minutes while occasionally stirring.

Nutrition Information

- Calories: 131 calories
- Total Carbohydrate: 18 g
- Cholesterol: 0 mg
- Total Fat: 4 g
- Fiber: 6 g
- Protein: 5 g
- Sodium: 622 mg

165. Country Italian Soup

"My mom shared this recipe to me a few years ago and my family loves it. It's very delicious."
Serving: 10 servings (2-1/2 quarts). | Prep: 20m | Ready in: 55m

Ingredients

- 1 lb. Johnsonville® Ground Mild Italian sausage
- 1 large onion, sliced
- 2 celery ribs, sliced
- 2 garlic cloves, minced
- 5 cups water
- 2 medium potatoes, peeled and chopped
- 1 can (14-1/2 oz.) diced tomatoes, undrained
- 2 medium carrots, sliced
- 2 tsps. salt
- 1 tsp. dried basil
- 1 tsp. dried thyme
- 1/2 tsp. dried oregano
- 1/2 tsp. pepper

- 1/4 tsp. cayenne pepper, optional
- 1 bay leaf
- 2 medium zucchini, sliced

Direction

- In a Dutch oven, cook celery, onion, and sausage over medium heat until the meat is not pink anymore; strain. Add garlic, cook for another 1 minute.
- Add seasonings, carrots, potatoes, tomatoes and water. Boil it. Lower the heat, put an on cover and simmer for 15 minutes. Mix in zucchini; simmer until the vegetables are soft, or for about another 8-10 minutes. Throw away the bay leaf.

Nutrition Information

- Calories: 211 calories
- Total Carbohydrate: 13 g
- Cholesterol: 34 mg
- Total Fat: 14 g
- Fiber: 2 g
- Protein: 8 g
- Sodium: 876 mg

166. Country Vegetable Soup

"This recipe is very reasonable in price."
Serving: 18-20 servings (5 quarts). | Prep: 20m | Ready in: 01h35m

Ingredients

- 2 quarts water
- 2 cans (10-1/2 oz. each) condensed French onion soup, undiluted
- 1 can (28 oz.) diced tomatoes, undrained
- 3 cups chopped zucchini
- 1 cup diced carrots
- 1 cup sliced celery
- 1 cup diced peeled potato
- 1/2 cup chopped fresh parsley
- 1 garlic clove, minced
- 1 tsp. beef bouillon granules

- 1 bay leaf
- 1/2 tsp. each dried basil, thyme and marjoram
- 1/4 tsp. pepper
- 8 bacon strips, cooked and crumbled
- 2 cups broken uncooked wide egg noodles
- 2 cans (15 oz. each) butter beans, rinsed and drained
- 1/4 cup grated Parmesan cheese
- 4 cups cubed cooked roast beef, optional

Direction

- In the soup kettle or Dutch oven, mix together the seasonings, bouillon, garlic, parsley, potato, celery, carrots, zucchini, tomatoes, soup and water; boil. Lower the heat; keep it covered and simmer for 60 minutes. Put in the noodles and bacon; let it simmer for 15 minutes, mixing often. If you want, mix in beef, parmesan cheese and beans; heat through. Take out the bay leaf prior to serving.

Nutrition Information

- Calories: 76 calories
- Total Carbohydrate: 12 g
- Cholesterol: 7 mg
- Total Fat: 2 g
- Fiber: 2 g
- Protein: 4 g
- Sodium: 350 mg

167. Cream Of Zucchini Soup

"I use vegan mimic cream to lessen calories, but you may use real cream."
Serving: 6 | Prep: 10m | Ready in: 45m

Ingredients

- 2 tbsps. olive oil
- 1 tbsp. vegan margarine
- 1 onion, chopped
- 2 lbs. zucchini, sliced
- 1 tsp. dried oregano
- salt and pepper to taste

- 2 1/2 tsps. vegetable bouillon powder
- 2 1/2 cups water
- 6 oz. crumbled Gorgonzola cheese
- 1 cup non-dairy creamer (such as MimicCreme®)

Direction

- Heat margarine and olive oil in a big pot; mix and cook onion in hot margarine and oil for 5-7 minutes till soft. Add zucchini; season with pepper, salt and oregano. Mix and cook for 10 minutes till zucchini is tender.
- Put water into the pot; mix bouillon powder in. Boil liquid; lower heat to medium-low. Simmer for 10 minutes longer. Add Gorgonzola cheese; let it melt into soup.
- No more than halfway full, fill pitcher of a blender with soup. Use a folded kitchen towel to secure the blender lid; start blender carefully, starting with a few quick pulses to move soup then leave on to puree. In batches, puree till smooth; put into a clean pot. Or, puree soup in the cooking pot with a stock blender. Before serving hot, mix creamer through the soup.

Nutrition Information

- Calories: 242 calories;
- Total Carbohydrate: 11.5 g
- Cholesterol: 30 mg
- Total Fat: 18.6 g
- Protein: 8.5 g
- Sodium: 353 mg

168. Creamy Sweet Potato And Veggie Soup

"This soup with sweet potatoes is so yummy."
Serving: 16 servings (4 quarts). | Prep: 10m | Ready in: 30m

Ingredients

- 1 large onion, chopped

- 1/4 cup butter
- 3 medium sweet potatoes, peeled and chopped
- 3 medium zucchini, chopped
- 1 bunch broccoli, chopped
- 2 cartons (32 oz. each) chicken broth
- 2 medium potatoes, peeled and shredded
- 1 tsp. celery seed
- 1 to 2 tsps. ground cumin
- 2 tsps. salt
- 1 tsp. pepper
- 2 cups half-and-half cream

Direction

- Sauté onion in butter in a stockpot till becoming transparent but not brown. Put in the broccoli, zucchini and sweet potatoes; sauté a bit till tender-crisp, about 5 minutes. Mix in broth; simmer for several minutes. Put in the seasonings and potatoes; cook till veggies become soft, about 10 minutes more. Mix in the cream and heat through.

Nutrition Information

- Calories: 137 calories
- Total Carbohydrate: 16 g
- Cholesterol: 25 mg
- Total Fat: 6 g
- Fiber: 3 g
- Protein: 4 g
- Sodium: 839 mg

169. Creamy Zucchini Soup

"A creamy soup is never a boring dish that you can change the flavor to fit your taste."
Serving: 6 | Prep: 15m | Ready in: 1h

Ingredients

- 1 tbsp. butter
- 2 tbsps. olive oil
- 1 onion, chopped
- 1 1/2 lbs. zucchini, sliced
- 1/2 (14 oz.) package firm tofu, cubed

- 2 tsps. red pepper flakes
- 1 tsp. dried oregano
- 3 cups vegetable stock
- 1/2 cup cottage cheese
- salt and pepper to taste

Direction

- In a large skillet, melt the butter and heat the oil over medium heat. Stir in the onion, and cook for 5 minutes. Blend in tofu and zucchini. Flavor with oregano and red pepper flakes. Keep cooking and stirring for 10 minutes, until zucchini is soft.
- In the skillet, pour the vegetable stock. Heat to a boil, lower the heat to low, and simmer for 35 minutes.
- In a blender, blend cottage cheese and soup until smooth. Flavor with salt and pepper.

Nutrition Information

- Calories: 159 calories;
- Total Carbohydrate: 8.8 g
- Cholesterol: 8 mg
- Total Fat: 10.9 g
- Protein: 9.5 g
- Sodium: 243 mg

170. Curried Zucchini Soup

"A soup that's super easy to make. Cook a tasty soup using simple ingredients."
Serving: 6 | Prep: 15m | Ready in: 45m

Ingredients

- 2 tbsps. extra virgin olive oil
- 1 large onion, halved and thinly sliced
- 1 tbsp. curry powder
- sea salt to taste
- 4 small zucchini, halved lengthwise and cut into 1 inch slices
- 1 quart chicken stock

Direction

- In a large pot, heat some oil. Sauté onions. Season with salt and curry powder. Stir and cook until the onion is soft. Add zucchini and cook until soft. Add the chicken stock and let it boil. Put the lid on and lower the heat to low. Let it simmer for 20 minutes.
- Remove from heat. Transfer to a blender or use a hand blender. Blend the soup in batches until almost smooth.

Nutrition Information

- Calories: 74 calories;
- Total Carbohydrate: 6.3 g
- Cholesterol: < 1 mg
- Total Fat: 5.2 g
- Protein: 1.8 g
- Sodium: 537 mg

171. Easy Minestrone

"Soup recipe serve topped with grated Parmesan cheese."
Serving: 8 | Prep: 20m | Ready in: 1h20m

Ingredients

- 3 tbsps. olive oil
- 3 cloves garlic, chopped, or more to taste
- 2 onions, chopped
- 5 carrots, sliced
- 4 cups chicken broth
- 2 (15 oz.) cans diced tomatoes with garlic and oregano
- 1/2 cup red wine (optional)
- 1 (16 oz.) package frozen green beans
- 1 (15 oz.) can pinto beans, rinsed and drained
- 1 (10 oz.) package frozen chopped spinach
- 2 tbsps. chopped fresh basil
- 1 tbsp. chopped fresh oregano
- salt and pepper to taste
- 1/2 cup seashell pasta, or more to taste
- 1/4 cup freshly grated Parmesan cheese, or to taste

Direction

- In a big pot, heat the olive oil over moderately-low heat. In hot oil, cook and mix the garlic for 2 to 3 minutes till aromatic. Put in the onion; cook and mix for 4 to 5 minutes till lightly softened. Mix in the carrots for 1 to 2 minutes till heated through.
- In the onion mixture, put the diced tomatoes and chicken broth; boil, mixing often. Put the red wine, lower the heat down to low, and mix black pepper, salt, oregano, basil, spinach, pinto beans and green beans into the broth mixture. Simmer, turn heat down to moderately-low, and allow to simmer for 40 minutes till vegetables are soft.
- Boil a big pot of slightly salted water. Cook the seashell pasta in boiling water for 8 minutes, mixing from time to time till cooked completely yet firm to the bite. Drain and mix the pasta into soup. Scoop the soup into the bowls, and put Parmesan cheese on top.

Nutrition Information

- Calories: 216 calories;
- Total Carbohydrate: 29.3 g
- Cholesterol: 2 mg
- Total Fat: 6.6 g
- Protein: 7.7 g
- Sodium: 388 mg

172. Favorite Italian Sausage Stew

"This chunky stew will surely warm your whole body during the winter season."
Serving: 4 servings. | Prep: 15m | Ready in: 45m

Ingredients

- 1/2 lb. Johnsonville® Ground Mild Italian sausage
- 2 garlic cloves, minced
- 1 can (14-1/2 oz.) Italian diced tomatoes, undrained
- 4 small red potatoes, quartered

- 1/4 cup sliced fresh carrots
- 1 tbsp. minced fresh basil
- 1/2 cup sliced zucchini
- 1 can (14-1/2 oz.) reduced-sodium beef broth
- 1 tbsp. cornstarch
- 1/4 cup shredded Parmesan cheese, optional

Direction

- Over medium heat, cook sausage in a big saucepan until it is not pink anymore. Put in garlic and cook for one more minute. Let it drain.
- Put carrots, potatoes, basil and tomatoes into the sausage mixture. Let it boil. Lower the heat and put in zucchini. Let it simmer with the cover on for 10 minutes.
- Mix together cornstarch and broth until it becomes smooth. Mix into the stew. Let it simmer for 5-10 minutes more until stew thickens and veggies become tender. Drizzle with cheese if you want.

Nutrition Information

- Calories: 187 calories
- Total Carbohydrate: 20 g
- Cholesterol: 25 mg
- Total Fat: 8 g
- Fiber: 2 g
- Protein: 9 g
- Sodium: 868 mg

173. Fire-roasted Tomato Minestrone

"This dish is for vegetarians, but it's so tasty and everyone wants to try it. You can also cook it on the stove on a low simmer for 2 hours."
Serving: 8 servings (about 3 quarts). | Prep: 20m | Ready in: 04h50m

Ingredients

- 1 medium sweet onion, chopped
- 1 cup cut fresh green beans

- 1 small zucchini, cubed
- 1 medium carrot, chopped
- 1 celery rib, chopped
- 2 garlic cloves, minced
- 2 tbsps. olive oil
- 1/4 tsp. salt
- 1/4 tsp. pepper
- 2 cans (14-1/2 oz. each) fire-roasted diced tomatoes
- 1 can (15 oz.) cannellini beans, rinsed and drained
- 1 carton (32 oz.) vegetable broth
- 1 cup uncooked small pasta shells
- 1 cup chopped fresh spinach

Direction

- Mix together the first 9 ingredients in a 5-quart slow cooker. Add beans and tomatoes; add broth. Put on a cover and cook over low heat for 4-6 hours until the vegetables are soft. Mix in pasta, put on a cover and cook for 30-40 minutes on low heat until the pasta is soft. Mix in spinach right before eating.

Nutrition Information

- Calories: 175 calories
- Total Carbohydrate: 29 g
- Cholesterol: 0 mg
- Total Fat: 4 g
- Fiber: 5 g
- Protein: 6 g
- Sodium: 767 mg

174. Flower Garden Soup

"Fresh vegetables give a flavor for this bountiful blend."
Serving: 8 servings (2 quarts). | Prep: 15m | Ready in: 45m

Ingredients

- 6 medium carrots
- 1 medium zucchini
- 4 celery ribs, chopped

- 1 medium onion, chopped
- 8 cans (14-1/2 oz. each) chicken broth
- 1 tsp. dried basil
- 1 tsp. dried oregano
- 4 cups cubed cooked chicken

Direction

- Slice a longways strip on each carrot with a paring knife or a zest stripper, forming a notch. Next, remake at equal spans around the carrot. Repeat the process with zucchini. Slice zucchini and carrots into 1/4-in. slices; put zucchini aside.
- Combine the carrots, oregano, basil, broth, onion, and celery in a Dutch oven or soup kettle. Next, boil, reduce the flame; cover and simmer until the greens are crisp-tender, about 20-30 minutes.
- Put in the reserved zucchini and chicken; simmer for 10 minutes, uncovered, or until the zucchini is softened.

Nutrition Information

- Calories: 171 calories
- Total Carbohydrate: 8 g
- Cholesterol: 62 mg
- Total Fat: 5 g
- Fiber: 3 g
- Protein: 22 g
- Sodium: 306 mg

175. Forgotten Minestrone

""*Prepare this simple recipe while doing your own work. I dust servings with Parmesan cheese and pair with garlic bread.*""
Serving: 8 servings (2 quarts). | Prep: 15m | Ready in: 08h45m

Ingredients

- 1 lb. beef stew meat, cut into 1/2-inch cubes
- 1 can (28 oz.) diced tomatoes, undrained
- 1 medium onion, chopped
- 2 tbsps. minced dried parsley

- 1 tsp. salt
- 1-1/2 tsps. ground thyme
- 1 beef bouillon cube
- 1/2 tsp. pepper
- 6 cups water
- 1 medium zucchini, halved and thinly sliced
- 2 cups chopped cabbage
- 1 can (15 oz.) garbanzo beans or chickpeas, rinsed and drained
- 1 cup uncooked elbow macaroni
- Grated Parmesan cheese, optional

Direction

- Mix the first 9 ingredients in a 5-qt. slow cooker. Cook on low for 8-10 hours, covered, or until meat is soft.
- Mix in the macaroni, beans, cabbage and zucchini; cook on high for 30-45 minutes, covered, or until vegetables and macaroni become tender. Dust servings with cheese if wished.

Nutrition Information

- Calories: 202 calories
- Total Carbohydrate: 24 g
- Cholesterol: 35 mg
- Total Fat: 5 g
- Fiber: 5 g
- Protein: 16 g
- Sodium: 661 mg

176. French Onion Tortellini Soup

"*This soup is so quick to make, beautiful and yummy.*"
Serving: 6-8 servings. | Prep: 5m | Ready in: 30m

Ingredients

- 1 lb. ground beef
- 3-1/2 cups water
- 1 can (28 oz.) diced tomatoes, undrained
- 1 can (10-1/2 oz.) condensed French onion soup, undiluted
- 1 package (9 oz.) frozen cut green beans

- 1 package (9 oz.) refrigerated cheese tortellini
- 1 medium zucchini, chopped
- 1 tsp. dried basil

Direction

- In the big saucepan, cook the beef on medium heat till meat is not pink anymore; drain off. Put in rest ingredients; boil. Cook, while uncovering, till the tortellini is softened or for 7 to 9 minutes.

Nutrition Information

- Calories: 241 calories
- Total Carbohydrate: 25 g
- Cholesterol: 43 mg
- Total Fat: 9 g
- Fiber: 4 g
- Protein: 16 g
- Sodium: 608 mg

177. Garden Chowder

""Use garden-fresh ingredients and this chowder will be a sure hit to your family gatherings and potlucks!""
Serving: 4-6 servings. | Prep: 15m | Ready in: 01h05m

Ingredients

- 1/4 cup chopped onion
- 1/2 cup chopped celery
- 1/4 cup butter, cubed
- 1/4 cup all-purpose flour
- 1/2 tsp. salt
- 1/4 tsp. pepper
- 2 cups chicken broth
- 1 medium tomato, peeled and diced
- 1 cup fresh broccoli florets
- 1 cup chopped carrots
- 1 cup frozen corn
- 1 cup thinly sliced zucchini
- 2 cups half-and-half cream
- 1/4 cup grated Parmesan cheese

Direction

- Sauté the celery and onion in butter in a large cooking pan for 5 minutes. Mix in the salt, flour, and pepper and stir the mixture until it forms a smooth paste. Pour in the broth slowly with constant stirring. Bring the soup to a boil and stir for 2 minutes or until it has thickened. Toss in the broccoli, tomato, corn, zucchini, and carrots then bring the soup back to a boil. Lower the heat, cover the pan and let it simmer until the vegetables are tender, or for 40 minutes. Pour in the cream and cheese and let it heat through.

Nutrition Information

- Calories: 261 calories
- Total Carbohydrate: 18 g
- Cholesterol: 63 mg
- Total Fat: 17 g
- Fiber: 3 g
- Protein: 7 g
- Sodium: 709 mg

178. Garden Harvest Chili

"If you want to use squash and zucchini, this is the best way to use it!"
Serving: 7 servings (1-3/4 quarts). | Prep: 20m | Ready in: 40m

Ingredients

- 1 medium sweet red pepper, chopped
- 1 medium onion, chopped
- 4 garlic cloves, minced
- 2 tbsps. canola oil
- 1 tbsp. chili powder
- 1 tsp. ground cumin
- 1 tsp. dried oregano
- 2 cups cubed peeled butternut squash
- 1 can (28 oz.) diced tomatoes, undrained
- 2 cups diced zucchini
- 1 can (15 oz.) black beans, rinsed and drained
- 1 can (8-3/4 oz.) whole kernel corn, drained

- 1/4 cup minced fresh parsley

Direction

- Sauté garlic, onion, and red pepper in oil in a big saucepan until tender. Mix in tomatoes, butternut squash, oregano, cumin, and chili powder and boil. Lower heat and simmer, covered, until squash is nearly tender for 10-15 minutes.
- Mix in the remaining ingredients and simmer, covered, until heated through for another 10 minutes.

Nutrition Information

- Calories: 193 calories
- Total Carbohydrate: 33 g
- Cholesterol: 0 mg
- Total Fat: 5 g
- Fiber: 0 g
- Protein: 8 g
- Sodium: 167 mg

179. Garden Minestrone Soup

"An invigorating and nutritious soup with freshly picked vegetables like garbanzo beans, zucchini, carrots."
Serving: 8 servings. | Prep: 10m | Ready in: 45m

Ingredients

- 4 medium carrots, chopped
- 1 medium zucchini, sliced
- 1/4 cup chopped onion
- 1 garlic clove, minced
- 1 tbsp. olive oil
- 2 cans (14-1/2 oz. each) vegetable broth
- 3 cups V8 juice
- 1 can (15 oz.) garbanzo beans or chickpeas, drained
- 1 can (14-1/2 oz.) diced tomatoes, undrained
- 1 cup frozen cut green beans
- 1/2 cup uncooked elbow macaroni
- 1 tsp. dried basil
- 1 tbsp. minced fresh parsley

Direction

- Add the garlic, onion, zucchini and carrots into a Dutch oven, cook in oil until onion gets tender, or for 7 minutes. Add the basil, macaroni, green beans, tomatoes, garbanzo beans, V8 juice and broth. Boil them up.
- Lower the heat, let it simmer while uncovering for 15 minutes. Mix in parsley. Cook for 5 more minutes or until macaroni gets tender.

Nutrition Information

- Calories: 166 calories
- Total Carbohydrate: 30 g
- Cholesterol: 0 mg
- Total Fat: 3 g
- Fiber: 5 g
- Protein: 6 g
- Sodium: 900 mg

180. Garden Vegetable Rice Soup

"This soup is fantastic despite not including meat."
Serving: 8 servings (2 quarts). | Prep: 25m | Ready in: 45m

Ingredients

- 1-1/2 tsps. minced garlic
- 2 tbsps. olive oil
- 1/4 cup uncooked long grain rice
- 2 cans (14-1/2 oz. each) chicken broth
- 1 cup chopped sweet red pepper
- 1 cup chopped green pepper
- 1/2 cup thinly sliced fresh carrots
- 1 tsp. salt
- 1/2 tsp. dried basil
- 1/4 tsp. dried rosemary, crushed
- Dash pepper
- 2 medium zucchini, sliced
- 6 plum tomatoes, chopped

Direction

- In a big saucepan, in oil, cook garlic for 1 minute. Mix in rice, stir and cook 1 minute.

Add seasonings, carrots, peppers, and broth; heat to a boil. Decrease heat, simmer with cover until rice is tender, 15-20 minutes.

- Mix in tomatoes and zucchini; cook 3 minutes then let cool down. Remove to freezer containers (it can be frozen for up to 3 months).
- To serve right away, cook soup until zucchini is tender, about 3-5 minutes more.
- To serve frozen soup: place soup in the fridge and thaw all night. Remove to a saucepan. Put on cover and cook until heated through on medium heat.

Nutrition Information

- Calories: 87 calories
- Total Carbohydrate: 11 g
- Cholesterol: 2 mg
- Total Fat: 4 g
- Fiber: 2 g
- Protein: 2 g
- Sodium: 753 mg

181. Golden Squash Soup

"Great for chilly nights."
Serving: 12-14 servings (3-1/2 quarts). | Prep: 35m | Ready in: 01h05m

Ingredients

- 3 leeks (white portion only), sliced
- 4 medium carrots, chopped
- 5 tbsps. butter
- 3 lbs. butternut squash, peeled and cubed
- 6 cups chicken broth
- 3 medium zucchini, peeled and sliced
- 2 tsps. salt
- 1/2 tsp. dried thyme
- 1/4 tsp. white pepper
- 1 cup half-and-half cream
- 1/2 cup 2% milk
- Grated Parmesan cheese and chives, optional

Direction

- Sauté carrots and leeks in butter in a Dutch oven, occasionally mixing, for 5 minutes. Add pepper, thyme, salt, zucchini, broth and squash; boil. Lower heat. Cover. Simmer till vegetables are tender for 30-35 minutes. Cool till lukewarm.
- In small batches, puree soup till smooth in a blender; put in pan. Mix milk and cream in; heat through and don't boil. Sprinkle chives and cheese if desired.

Nutrition Information

- Calories: 133 calories
- Total Carbohydrate: 17 g
- Cholesterol: 21 mg
- Total Fat: 7 g
- Fiber: 4 g
- Protein: 4 g
- Sodium: 804 mg

182. Ham 'n' Veggie Soup

"This multicolor dish of flavorful veggies broth with additional ham can be a complete meal."
Serving: 8-10 servings. | Prep: 5m | Ready in: 30m

Ingredients

- 1 medium onion, thinly sliced and separated into rings
- 1 medium zucchini, cubed
- 1 tbsp. olive oil
- 1 lb. sliced fresh mushrooms
- 3 cups fresh or frozen corn
- 3 cups cubed fully cooked ham
- 6 medium tomatoes, peeled, seeded and chopped
- 1/2 cup chicken broth
- 1-1/2 tsps. salt
- 1/2 tsp. garlic powder
- 1/2 tsp. pepper
- Shredded part-skim mozzarella cheese

Direction

- Sauté zucchini and onion in oil in a big saucepan for 5 minutes or until onion is soft. Add ham, corn and mushrooms; cook and stir for 5 minutes.
- Stir in pepper, garlic powder, salt, broth and tomatoes. Cook to a boil. Lower heat; simmer with the cover on for 5 minutes. Remove cover; continue simmering for additional 5-8 minutes. Top with mozzarella cheese.

Nutrition Information

- Calories: 160 calories
- Total Carbohydrate: 18 g
- Cholesterol: 22 mg
- Total Fat: 6 g
- Fiber: 3 g
- Protein: 12 g
- Sodium: 955 mg

183. Harvest Chicken Soup

"A healthy soup with delicious avocados and veggies would always keep you busy in the kitchen."
Serving: 8-10 servings (2-1/4 quarts). | Prep: 15m | Ready in: 02h55m

Ingredients

- 3 medium onions
- 3 bone-in chicken breast halves, skin removed
- 4 cups water
- 3 celery ribs, halved
- 1 tsp. salt
- 1/8 tsp. pepper
- 1 can (14-1/2 oz.) diced tomatoes, undrained
- 3 medium carrots, thinly sliced
- 4 tsps. chicken bouillon granules
- 1 small zucchini, halved and thinly sliced
- 1 cup frozen peas
- 1 avocado, peeled and sliced

Direction

- Chop an onion then put aside. Cut each of the other two into 4 parts; put into a Dutch oven along with pepper, salt, celery, water, and chicken. Allow to simmer, covered, until the vegetables and chicken become tender, 2 hours. Take the chicken out; put aside. Discard onion and celery.
- Put the chopped onion, bouillon, carrots, and tomatoes in the broth. Allow to simmer, covered, until the carrots become tender, 30 minutes.
- Separate the chicken meat from the bones and cube the meat; add the meat, peas and zucchini to the soup. Allow to simmer, covered, until zucchini becomes tender, 10 minutes. Fill the bowls and decorate with avocado.

Nutrition Information

- Calories: 133 calories
- Total Carbohydrate: 12 g
- Cholesterol: 27 mg
- Total Fat: 4 g
- Fiber: 4 g
- Protein: 12 g
- Sodium: 684 mg

184. Hearty Meatless Chili

"I switched the spices, lessened oil, and added veggies to this chili and it's amazing!"
Serving: 8 servings (2-1/2 quarts). | Prep: 20m | Ready in: 01h15m

Ingredients

- 1 small onion, chopped
- 1 tbsp. olive oil
- 3 garlic cloves, minced
- 2 medium zucchini, finely chopped
- 2 medium carrots, finely chopped
- 3 tbsps. cornmeal
- 2 tbsps. chili powder

- 2 tbsps. paprika
- 1 tbsp. sugar
- 1/2 tsp. ground cumin
- 1/4 to 1/2 tsp. cayenne pepper
- 2 cans (one 28 oz., one 14-1/2 oz.) diced tomatoes, undrained
- 2 cans (15 oz. each) pinto beans, rinsed and drained
- 1 can (16 oz.) kidney beans, rinsed and drained
- GARNISH:
- 8 tbsps. fat-free sour cream
- 8 tbsps. thinly sliced green onions
- 8 tsps. minced fresh cilantro

Direction

- Sauté onion in oil in a Dutch oven until tender. Add garlic and cook for a minute. Mix in carrots and zucchini. Add cayenne, cumin, sugar, paprika, chili powder, and cornmeal. Sauté for a minute.
- Mix in beans and tomatoes; boil. Lower the heat and simmer, covered, for 45 minutes. Top every serving with cilantro, green onions, and sour cream.

Nutrition Information

- Calories: 254 calories
- Total Carbohydrate: 47 g
- Cholesterol: 3 mg
- Total Fat: 3 g
- Fiber: 12 g
- Protein: 13 g
- Sodium: 466 mg

185. Hearty Minestrone

"A variation of Italian classic soup called Minestrone."
Serving: 4 | Ready in: 45m

Ingredients

- 2 tsps. extra-virgin olive oil
- 3 medium leeks, trimmed, washed (see Tip) and thinly sliced

- 4 cups reduced-sodium chicken broth, or vegetable broth
- 1 cup water
- 1 large red potato, diced
- 2 tsps. dried thyme
- ¼ tsp. salt
- ½ tsp. freshly ground pepper
- ½ cup whole-wheat orzo
- 1 15-oz. can white beans, rinsed
- 2 medium zucchini, quartered and thinly sliced
- 1 lb. fresh spinach, stems removed
- 2 tbsps. cider vinegar
- 2 tbsps. freshly grated Parmesan cheese, preferably Parmigiano-Reggiano

Direction

- In a big soup pot or Dutch oven, heat the oil over medium-high heat. Put leeks and allow to cook for 3 minutes, mixing from time to time, till tender. Put pepper, salt, thyme, potato, water and broth. Boil, turn heat to low and allow to simmer with cover for 5 minutes.
- Put orzo, partially cover and let cook for 5 minutes, mixing from time to time to keep form sticking. Put zucchini and beans, partly cover and keep cooking, till pasta and vegetables are soft for 8 minutes longer.
- Mix in the spinach and let cook for 2 minutes, mixing, till wilted. Put vinegar to season the soup. Scoop into the bowls and garnish with Parmesan.

Nutrition Information

- Calories: 299 calories;
- Total Carbohydrate: 54 g
- Cholesterol: 2 mg
- Total Fat: 5 g
- Fiber: 14 g
- Protein: 18 g
- Sodium: 1,080 mg
- Sugar: 7 g
- Saturated Fat: 1 g

186. Hearty Minestrone Soup

"If you're having a lot of homegrown zucchini, this recipe is the right one to make. You can use hot bulk Italian sausage if you want a little more spiciness."
Serving: 9 servings. | Prep: 25m | Ready in: 55m

Ingredients

- 1 lb. Johnsonville® Ground Mild Italian sausage
- 2 cups sliced celery
- 1 cup chopped onion
- 6 cups chopped zucchini
- 1 can (28 oz.) diced tomatoes, undrained
- 1-1/2 cups chopped green pepper
- 1-1/2 tsps. Italian seasoning
- 1-1/2 tsps. salt
- 1 tsp. dried oregano
- 1 tsp. sugar
- 1/2 tsp. dried basil
- 1/4 tsp. garlic powder

Direction

- Cook sausage in a big saucepan until it is not pink anymore. Transfer to a paper towel to strain using a slotted spoon, saving 1 tbsp. of drippings. In the drippings, sauté onion and celery for 5 minutes. Add the rest of the ingredients and sausage, boil it. Lower the heat, put on a cover and simmer until the vegetables are soft, or about 20-30 minutes.

Nutrition Information

- Calories: 224 calories
- Total Carbohydrate: 12 g
- Cholesterol: 38 mg
- Total Fat: 16 g
- Fiber: 4 g
- Protein: 10 g
- Sodium: 901 mg

187. Hearty Pasta Tomato Soup

"I modified the original recipe a bit so it can be cooked in a slow cooker. It's a really great option for staff luncheons at my workplace.""
Serving: 14 servings (about 3-1/2 quarts). | Prep: 15m | Ready in: 03h45m

Ingredients

- 1 lb. Johnsonville® Ground Mild Italian sausage
- 6 cups beef broth
- 1 can (28 oz.) stewed tomatoes
- 1 can (15 oz.) tomato sauce
- 2 cups sliced zucchini
- 1 large onion, chopped
- 1 cup sliced carrots
- 1 cup sliced fresh mushrooms
- 1 medium green pepper, chopped
- 1/4 cup minced fresh parsley
- 2 tsps. sugar
- 1 tsp. dried oregano
- 1 tsp. dried basil
- 1 garlic clove, minced
- 2 cups frozen cheese tortellini
- Grated Parmesan cheese, optional

Direction

- Cook sausage in a skillet over medium heat until it is no longer pink; drain well. Transfer cooked sausage to a 5-quart slow cooker; put in the next 13 ingredients. Cook, covered, on high setting until vegetables are softened, about 3 to 4 hours.
- Cook tortellini as directed on package; drain. Transfer into the slow cooker and stir to combine; cook, covered, for 30 more minutes. If desired, serve with Parmesan cheese.

Nutrition Information

- Calories: 149 calories
- Total Carbohydrate: 16 g
- Cholesterol: 16 mg
- Total Fat: 6 g
- Fiber: 2 g

- Protein: 8 g
- Sodium: 809 mg

188. Hearty Turkey Vegetable Soup

"This recipe is more nutritious than the one that I found on the Internet. You can double this recipe and share it with your friends or store inside the freezer for the next day."
Serving: 10 servings (3-3/4 quarts). | Prep: 20m | Ready in: 01h05m

Ingredients

- 1 lb. lean ground turkey
- 1 medium onion, chopped
- 2 small zucchini, quartered lengthwise and sliced
- 1 large carrot, cut into 1-inch julienne strips
- 3 cans (14 oz. each) reduced-sodium beef broth
- 1 jar (26 oz.) garden-style pasta sauce or meatless spaghetti sauce
- 1 can (16 oz.) kidney beans, rinsed and drained
- 1 can (15-1/2 oz.) great northern beans, rinsed and drained
- 1 can (14-1/2 oz.) Italian diced tomatoes, undrained
- 1 tbsp. dried parsley flakes
- 2 tsps. dried oregano
- 1 tsp. pepper
- 1 tsp. hot pepper sauce
- 1 cup uncooked small shell pasta

Direction

- Coat the Dutch oven with cooking spray. Stir in onion and turkey and cook them over medium heat until the meat is not anymore pinkish. Drain the mixture. Add the carrot and zucchini. Cook and stir the mixture for 1 minute. Mix in pasta sauce, parsley, pepper, hot pepper sauce, oregano, broth, beans, and tomatoes.
- Bring the mixture to a boil. Lower the heat and cover the pot. Simmer the mixture for 45 minutes. Follow the package directions to cook

the pasta; drain. Stir in pasta into the mixture and serve.

Nutrition Information

- Calories: 242 calories
- Total Carbohydrate: 34 g
- Cholesterol: 38 mg
- Total Fat: 4 g
- Fiber: 7 g
- Protein: 17 g
- Sodium: 888 mg

189. Hearty Vegetable Bean Soup

"This healthy soup made with beans and veggies will satisfy your appetite on chilly winter nights."
Serving: 6 servings. | Prep: 10m | Ready in: 50m

Ingredients

- 1 cup sliced carrots
- 1 cup thinly sliced zucchini
- 3/4 cup chopped onion
- 1/2 cup chopped sweet red pepper
- 1 tbsp. olive oil
- 2 cans (14-1/2 oz. each) vegetable broth
- 1 can (16 oz.) kidney beans, rinsed and drained
- 1 can (16 oz.) chili beans, undrained
- 1 can (15 oz.) garbanzo beans or chickpeas, rinsed and drained
- 1 can (14-1/2 oz.) stewed tomatoes, cut up
- 1 cup frozen white or frozen shoepeg corn
- 4 tsps. ground cumin
- 1/4 tsp. cayenne pepper
- 2 tbsps. minced fresh cilantro

Direction

- Sauté the red pepper, onion, zucchini, and carrots in oil in a Dutch oven or a large saucepan until tender-crisp. Put in cayenne, cumin, corn, tomatoes, beans, and broth; allow to boil.
- Turn down the heat; uncover, allow to simmer and occasionally stir until the vegetables

become tender for 30-35 minutes. Add in cilantro and stir.

Nutrition Information

- Calories: 285 calories
- Total Carbohydrate: 52 g
- Cholesterol: 0 mg
- Total Fat: 5 g
- Fiber: 11 g
- Protein: 13 g
- Sodium: 1356 mg

---

minutes or until the vegetables are soft. Add in the macaroni and heat through.

Nutrition Information

- Calories: 202 calories
- Total Carbohydrate: 23 g
- Cholesterol: 28 mg
- Total Fat: 6 g
- Fiber: 3 g
- Protein: 14 g
- Sodium: 869 mg

---

190. Hearty Vegetable Hamburger Soup

"You can substitute ground turkey instead of the beef in this veggie-filled soup. You can also double or triple this recipe easily to serve more."
Serving: 2 servings. | Prep: 15m | Ready in: 30m

Ingredients

- 1/4 lb. ground beef
- 1/4 cup chopped onion
- 1-1/2 cups water
- 1/4 cup thinly sliced carrot
- 1-1/2 tsps. beef bouillon granules
- 1 can (5-1/2 oz.) V8 juice
- 1/4 cup frozen corn
- 1/4 cup frozen peas
- 1/4 cup sliced fresh mushrooms
- 1/4 cup sliced zucchini
- 1/8 tsp. dried basil
- Dash pepper
- 1/2 cup cooked elbow macaroni

Direction

- Cook onion and beef in a small saucepan on medium heat until the beef is no longer pink, then drain. Add bouillon, carrot, and water, then set to boil. Decrease the heat and simmer without a cover for 5 minutes.
- Add pepper, basil, zucchini, mushrooms, peas, corn, and V8 juice. Simmer for another 6 - 8

---

191. Herbed Vegetable Soup

"The garden-fresh flavor is in every single spoon of this delicious soup."
Serving: 8 servings. | Prep: 5m | Ready in: 30m

Ingredients

- 3 cups finely shredded cabbage
- 1 package (16 oz.) frozen cut green beans
- 2 celery ribs, thinly sliced
- 2 medium carrots, thinly sliced
- 2 small zucchini, chopped
- 1 small onion, chopped
- 3 cups tomato juice
- 2 tsps. chicken bouillon granules
- 1 tsp. salt-free seasoning blend
- 1/2 tsp. dried basil
- 1/4 tsp. dried rosemary, crushed

Direction

- Combine tomato juice, onion, zucchini, carrots, celery, beans, and cabbage in a large saucepan; bring to a boil. Next, reduce the heat; cover and cook until the vegetables are tender, about 15 minutes. Add rosemary, basil, the seasoning blend, and bouillon; bring to a boil. Then reduce the flame; cover and simmer for another 10 minutes.

Nutrition Information

- Calories: 66 calories

- Total Carbohydrate: 13 g
- Cholesterol: 1 mg
- Total Fat: 1 g
- Fiber: 5 g
- Protein: 3 g
- Sodium: 493 mg

192. Italian Chicken Chili

"Every bite brings different flavor, in taste and texture."
Serving: 8 servings (2-3/4 quarts). | Prep: 20m | Ready in: 07h05m

Ingredients

- 1/2 lb. Johnsonville® Ground Mild Italian sausage
- 1 tsp. olive oil
- 1 lb. boneless skinless chicken breasts, cut into 1-inch cubes
- 1 can (28 oz.) crushed tomatoes
- 1 can (28 oz.) diced tomatoes, undrained
- 1 can (15 oz.) white kidney or cannellini beans, rinsed and drained
- 2 celery ribs, chopped
- 1 cup chopped onion
- 1 small sweet red pepper, chopped
- 1/2 cup dry red wine or chicken broth
- 2 tbsps. chili powder
- 2 tsps. dried oregano
- 2 tsps. minced garlic
- 1 tsp. dried thyme
- 1 medium zucchini, diced
- 1 cup sliced fresh mushrooms
- 1/4 cup minced fresh parsley
- Shredded Italian cheese blend, optional

Direction

- In oil, cook sausage in a large skillet over medium heat till not pink anymore; drain.
- Put to a 5-qt. slow cooker. Mix in the thyme, garlic, oregano, chili powder, broth or wine, red pepper, onion, celery, beans, tomatoes and chicken. Put cover and cook till chicken is not pink anymore for 6 hours and on low.

- Mix in the mushrooms and zucchini. Put cover and cook on high till vegetables are soft for 45 minutes. Top with parsley. If wished, serve with cheese.

Nutrition Information

- Calories: 243 calories
- Total Carbohydrate: 25 g
- Cholesterol: 43 mg
- Total Fat: 7 g
- Fiber: 8 g
- Protein: 20 g
- Sodium: 516 mg

193. Italian Chicken Sausage Soup

"This hearty soup is filled with tasty Italian flavors. Serve this meal with crusty rolls and you'll have a wonderful dinner."
Serving: 6 servings (2-1/2 quarts). | Prep: 15m | Ready in: 55m

Ingredients

- 1 package (12 oz.) fully cooked Italian chicken sausage links, halved lengthwise and sliced
- 1 medium onion, chopped
- 1 tbsp. olive oil
- 3 garlic cloves, minced
- 2 cans (15 oz. each) white kidney or cannellini beans, rinsed and drained
- 2 cans (14-1/2 oz. each) no-salt-added diced tomatoes
- 2 medium zucchini, quartered and sliced
- 1 can (14-1/2 oz.) reduced-sodium chicken broth
- 8 oz. whole fresh mushrooms, quartered
- 1 cup water
- 1/4 cup prepared pesto
- 1/4 cup dry red wine or additional reduced-sodium chicken broth
- 1 tbsp. balsamic vinegar
- 1 tsp. minced fresh oregano or 1/4 tsp. dried oregano
- 1/2 tsp. pepper

- Grated Parmesan cheese

Direction

- Cook sausage and onion in oil in a Dutch oven until it becomes brown in color. Put in garlic and cook for one more minute.
- Mix in the pepper, oregano, vinegar, wine, pesto, water, mushrooms, broth, zucchini, tomatoes and beans. Let it boil. Lower the heat and let it simmer without cover until veggies become tender, about 25-30 minutes. Drizzle with cheese.

Nutrition Information

- Calories: 337 calories
- Total Carbohydrate: 35 g
- Cholesterol: 47 mg
- Total Fat: 12 g
- Fiber: 10 g
- Protein: 22 g
- Sodium: 838 mg

194. Italian Chili

"This slow-simmered hearty dish is an Italian spin on traditional Southwestern-style chili with fresh veggies and Italian seasoning."
Serving: 6 servings. | Prep: 20m | Ready in: 06h50m

Ingredients

- 1 lb. ground beef
- 1/2 lb. Johnsonville® Ground Mild Italian sausage
- 1 can (28 oz.) diced tomatoes
- 1 can (8 oz.) tomato sauce
- 1 cup chopped onion
- 1 cup chopped sweet red pepper
- 1 cup water
- 1/2 cup chopped celery
- 1/4 cup beef broth
- 1 tbsp. chili powder
- 1 tbsp. Italian seasoning
- 1 tsp. sugar

- 1 tsp. minced garlic
- 1/2 tsp. salt
- 1 can (16 oz.) kidney beans, rinsed and drained
- 1 cup sliced fresh mushrooms
- 1 cup diced zucchini
- 3 tbsps. minced fresh parsley
- Shredded part-skim mozzarella cheese, optional

Direction

- Cook sausage and beef together in a big skillet on moderate heat until it is not pink anymore. At the same time, mix together salt, garlic, sugar, Italian seasoning, chili powder, broth, celery, water, red pepper, onion, tomato sauce and tomatoes in a 3-quart slow cooker.
- Drain the beef mixture and put into the slow cooker. Cover and cook on low setting until vegetables are softened, about 6 hours.
- Put in parsley, zucchini, mushrooms and beans. Cover and cook on high setting until vegetables are softened, about a half hour. Top with cheese, if wanted.

Nutrition Information

- Calories: 316 calories
- Total Carbohydrate: 28 g
- Cholesterol: 52 mg
- Total Fat: 12 g
- Fiber: 8 g
- Protein: 25 g
- Sodium: 947 mg

195. Italian Sausage Orzo Soup

"This delicious soup features Italian sausage with a lot of ingredients."
| Prep: 20m

Ingredients

- 1 lb. Italian Sausage, hot or sweet or a mix of both
- 2 cloves Garlic, minced
- 1 Small yellow onion, diced

- 3 cans Beef broth, 14 oz cans
- 1 can 14.5 oz. can Italian-style diced tomatoes
- 1 can 14.5 oz. can fire-roasted diced tomatoes
- 1 cups carrots, sliced 2 medium
- 3/4 cup Stalks of celery, sliced 2
- 2 cups Red potatoes 1-small
- 1 Green bell pepper
- 1 tsp. Italian seasoning
- 2 tsps. Dried oregano
- 1 tbsp. Dried basil
- 3/4 cup Orzo pasta, uncooked
- 2 cups Fresh spinach, packed
- 1/2 cup Fresh grated Parmesan cheese
- 1 Optional-fresh rosemary, fresh Italian flat leaf parsley, salt and pepper, 1/4 tsp. red pepper flakes

Direction

- Preparation
- Put diced yellow onion, minced garlic and Italian sausage in a Dutch oven or a big stockpot.
- Brown the sausage while crumbling.
- When the onion is tender and sausage is cooked through, mix in chopped bell pepper, diced red potatoes that are cut pretty small, sliced celery, sliced carrots, undrained cans of tomatoes, and broth.
- Season with basil, oregano, and Italian seasoning to taste. Put in pepper and salt for added taste. But you may not need more salt depending on the saltiness of the broth.
- Let it boil and lower the heat. Simmer with cover until all vegetables are tender crisp, about 20-25 minutes.
- Follow package instructions to cook the Orzo to al dente in a separate pan. Let it drain and wash in cold water.
- Take out the soup from the heat and mix in the orzo that you drained. Then gently stir in the spinach.
- Depending on your preference, you can taste and adjust the seasoning. If you have red pepper, add it in and some fresh herbs. Serve with crusty bread and Parmesan cheese.

196. Italian Sausage Tortellini Soup

"This recipe tops the list of the best soup because it is rich in vegetables. It also features tortellini and Italian sausage."
Serving: 6 | Prep: 15m | Ready in: 1h10m

Ingredients

- 1 (3.5 oz.) link sweet Italian sausage, casings removed
- 1 cup chopped onions
- 2 cloves garlic, minced
- 5 cups beef stock
- 1/3 cup water
- 1/2 cup red wine
- 4 tomatoes - peeled, seeded and chopped
- 1 cup chopped carrots
- 1/2 tsp. dried basil
- 1/2 tsp. dried oregano
- 1 cup tomato sauce
- 1 zucchini, chopped
- 8 oz. cheese tortellini
- 1 green bell pepper, chopped
- 1 tbsp. chopped fresh parsley
- 2 tbsps. grated Parmesan cheese for topping

Direction

- In a big pot, sauté sausage for 10 minutes over medium high heat until it is properly browned. Drain the grease but leave about 1 tbsp. and stir in garlic and onion. Sauté for about 5 minutes.
- Mix in tomato sauce, oregano, basil, carrots, tomatoes, wine, water, and beef stock. Let it boil and adjust heat to low. Let it simmer, while skimming any fat that may float, for 30 minutes.
- Mix in parsley, green bell pepper, tortellini and zucchini for added taste. Let it simmer until the tortellini is completely cooked, about 10 minutes. Put into individual bowls and top with cheese.

Nutrition Information

- Calories: 249 calories;
- Total Carbohydrate: 27.7 g
- Cholesterol: 22 mg
- Total Fat: 8.9 g
- Protein: 12.4 g
- Sodium: 542 mg

197. Italian Zucchini Soup

"A tasty vegetable soup that you can make prior time and store in freezer for cold days."
Serving: 10 | Prep: 20m | Ready in: 50m

Ingredients

- 8 cups sliced zucchini
- 8 cups chopped tomatoes
- 2 cups chopped green bell pepper
- 2 cups chopped celery
- 2 cups chopped onion
- 1 (10.75 oz.) can condensed tomato soup (such as Campbell's®) (optional)
- 5 tbsps. white sugar
- 4 tsps. salt
- 1 tsp. black pepper

Direction

- In a stock pot, combine the pepper, salt, sugar, tomato soup, onion, celery, bell pepper, tomatoes and zucchini; mix and boil them together. Lower to low heat and let it simmer for about half an hour until the zucchini gets tender.

Nutrition Information

- Calories: 108 calories;
- Total Carbohydrate: 24.2 g
- Cholesterol: 0 mg
- Total Fat: 1 g
- Protein: 3.7 g
- Sodium: 1137 mg

198. Kidney Bean Vegetable Soup

"A tasty veggie soup."
Serving: 8 servings (2 quarts). | Prep: 15m | Ready in: 30m

Ingredients

- 1 can (16 oz.) kidney beans, rinsed and drained
- 1 medium zucchini, cubed
- 1 medium carrot, diced
- 2 celery ribs, chopped
- 3 green onions, sliced
- 1/4 cup chopped fresh spinach
- 3 tbsps. quick-cooking barley
- 3 cans (14-1/2 oz. each) reduced-sodium chicken broth
- 1/4 cup minced fresh parsley
- 1 garlic clove, minced
- 1/2 tsp. garlic salt
- 1 can (14-1/2 oz.) Italian diced tomatoes, undrained

Direction

- Boil initial 11 ingredients in a big saucepan. Lower the heat; cover. Simmer till veggies and barley are tender for 10-12 minutes. Add tomatoes; heat through.

Nutrition Information

- Calories: 103 calories
- Total Carbohydrate: 19 g
- Cholesterol: 0 mg
- Total Fat: 0 g
- Fiber: 4 g
- Protein: 7 g
- Sodium: 939 mg

199. Kielbasa Bean Soup

"This nice vegetable soup with plenty of meat can be stored in freezer so that you don't have to worry about busy day meals or friends coming."
Serving: 12 servings (about 3 quarts). | Prep: 10m | Ready in: 01h25m

Ingredients

- 4-1/2 cups water
- 2 cans (14-1/2 oz. each) diced tomatoes, undrained
- 1 can (16 oz.) kidney beans, rinsed and drained
- 1 can (15-1/2 oz.) great northern beans, rinsed and drained
- 1 can (15 oz.) garbanzo beans or chickpeas, rinsed and drained
- 2 medium green peppers, chopped
- 2 medium onions, chopped
- 2 celery ribs, chopped
- 1 medium zucchini, sliced
- 2 tsps. chicken bouillon granules
- 2 garlic cloves, minced
- 2-1/2 tsps. chili powder
- 2 tsps. dried basil
- 1-1/2 tsps. salt
- 1/2 tsp. pepper
- 2 bay leaves
- 3/4 lb. Johnsonville® Fully Cooked Polish Kielbasa Sausage Rope, halved lengthwise and sliced

Direction

- Mix all ingredients, apart from sausage in a Dutch oven or a soup kettle. Boil them up. Lower the heat, let it simmer while covering for 60 minutes. Add sausage and cook through. Take out bay leaves and throw away.

Nutrition Information

- Calories: 212 calories
- Total Carbohydrate: 24 g
- Cholesterol: 19 mg
- Total Fat: 9 g
- Fiber: 7 g
- Protein: 10 g
- Sodium: 988 mg

200. Lasagna Soup

"Combine soup and lasagna into one delicious recipe."
Serving: 10 | Prep: 15m | Ready in: 1h19m

Ingredients

- 1 tsp. olive oil
- 1 lb. hot Italian sausage
- 1 lb. mild Italian sausage
- 2 sweet onions, chopped
- 5 cloves garlic, minced
- 2 tsps. dried oregano
- 1 tsp. red pepper flakes
- 1 (6 oz.) can tomato paste
- 1 (48 oz.) can beef broth
- 1 (14.5 oz.) can diced tomatoes with basil
- 1 (14.5 oz.) can crushed tomatoes with basil
- 1/2 cup sweet wine (optional)
- 2 sprigs fresh basil, or to taste
- salt and ground black pepper to taste
- 1 (8 oz.) container ricotta cheese, or more to taste
- 1/2 cup shredded mozzarella cheese
- 1/2 cup grated Parmesan cheese, or more to taste
- 1 (16 oz.) package farfalle (bow tie) pasta

Direction

- In a big pot over medium heat, heat olive oil. Let hot and mild sausage for 5 minutes cook till browned, mixing to break up into pieces. Put in onions; cook and mix for 5 minutes till translucent. Mix in red pepper flakes, oregano and garlic; cook for 2 minutes till aromatic.
- Mix tomato paste into the paste. With water, fill the tomato paste can and add in; combine thoroughly. Add in wine, crushed tomatoes, diced tomatoes and beef broth. Mix in basil pepper, salt and sprigs. Boil soup; lower heat and let simmer for minimum of half hour till flavors incorporate.

- In a bowl, combine together Parmesan cheese, mozzarella cheese and ricotta cheese; put salt and pepper to season.
- Boil a big pot of lightly salted water. Allow bow-tie pasta to cook at a boil for 12 minutes, mixing from time to time, till tender yet firm to the bite. Drain.
- Distribute pasta between serving bowls; spoon the ricotta cheese mixture over. Ladle soup atop cheese mixture.

Nutrition Information

- Calories: 511 calories;
- Total Carbohydrate: 49.6 g
- Cholesterol: 53 mg
- Total Fat: 21.7 g
- Protein: 26.1 g
- Sodium: 1529 mg

201. Macaroni Vegetable Soup

""This vivid veggie soup with a hint of cayenne was first made in Hebron, Indiana. A great break from heavy cream soups, this hearty yet nutritious combo can be presented as a light meal or as a side dish.""
Serving: 8 servings (2 quarts). | Prep: 10m | Ready in: 30m

Ingredients

- 1 medium zucchini, julienned
- 1/2 cup finely chopped onion
- 1 medium carrot, halved and thinly sliced
- 1 tbsp. butter
- 2 cans (14-1/2 oz. each) chicken broth
- 1 cup tomato or vegetable juice
- 1/2 cup uncooked elbow macaroni
- 1/8 to 1/4 tsp. cayenne pepper
- 1 can (15 oz.) white kidney or cannellini beans, rinsed and drained
- 1/2 cup frozen corn

Direction

- Put butter in a large saucepan and fry carrot, onion and zucchini until softened. Stir in the

tomato juice and broth. Allow to boil; mix in cayenne and macaroni. And cook for 10 minutes or until macaroni is soft. Mix in corn and beans; and heat through.

Nutrition Information

- Calories: 96 calories
- Total Carbohydrate: 18 g
- Cholesterol: 3 mg
- Total Fat: 1 g
- Fiber: 3 g
- Protein: 5 g
- Sodium: 325 mg

202. Make-ahead Squash Soup

"A lovely summer treat."
Serving: 3 cups per batch. | Prep: 25m | Ready in: 45m

Ingredients

- SOUP BASE:
- 3 lbs. zucchini, sliced
- 2 cups water
- 1 can (14-1/2 oz.) beef broth
- 1 cup chopped onion
- 1-1/2 tsps. salt
- 1/8 tsp. garlic powder
- ADDITIONAL INGREDIENTS (for each batch):
- 1 cup half-and-half cream
- Grated Parmesan cheese and crumbled cooked bacon, optional

Direction

- Boil the soup base ingredients in a 6-qt. stockpot. Lower the heat; simmer till zucchini is tender for 18-20 minutes; slightly cool.
- In batches, puree in a food processor/blender; cool. In each of the 4 freezer containers, put 2 cups; makes 4 batches.
- Prepare 1 soup batch: In the fridge, thaw the soup base. Put into a saucepan then add cream; mix and cook on medium heat to heat

through. Sprinkle with bacon and cheese if desired.

Nutrition Information

- Calories: 51 calories
- Total Carbohydrate: 5 g
- Cholesterol: 10 mg
- Total Fat: 2 g
- Fiber: 2 g
- Protein: 2 g
- Sodium: 428 mg

203. Meaty Vegetable Chili

"This chili is great to enjoy with spaghetti."
Serving: 12 servings (3 quarts). | Prep: 10m | Ready in: 45m

Ingredients

- 1 lb. ground beef
- 2 medium onions, chopped
- 4 cups chopped zucchini
- 2 cans (16 oz. each) kidney beans, rinsed and drained
- 1 jar (24 oz.) spaghetti sauce with mushrooms
- 1 can (14-1/2 oz.) diced tomatoes, undrained
- 1 cup water
- 2 tbsps. chili powder
- 1 tsp. ground cumin

Direction

- Cook onions and beef over medium heat in a big saucepan, until the beef is not pink anymore; drain. Put in the rest ingredients, heat to a boil. Lower heat, cover and let simmer until vegetables are tender, or for 20 minutes.

Nutrition Information

- Calories: 151 calories
- Total Carbohydrate: 19 g
- Cholesterol: 19 mg
- Total Fat: 4 g

- Fiber: 5 g
- Protein: 11 g
- Sodium: 478 mg

204. Mexi-stroni Soup

"This Mexican-flavored soup with spices, veggies and pasta is amazing."
Serving: 10 servings (3-3/4 quarts). | Prep: 25m | Ready in: 07h55m

Ingredients

- 1-1/2 lbs. beef stew meat (1-inch pieces)
- 1-1/2 cups shredded carrots
- 1/2 cup chopped onion
- 1 jalapeno pepper, seeded and minced, optional
- 1 tsp. ground cumin
- 1 tsp. chili powder
- 3/4 tsp. seasoned salt
- 1/2 tsp. Italian seasoning
- 2 cans (10 oz. each) diced tomatoes and green chilies, undrained
- 2 cups spicy hot V8 juice
- 1 carton (32 oz.) reduced-sodium beef broth
- 1 medium zucchini, halved and thinly sliced
- 2 cups finely shredded cabbage
- 2 celery ribs, thinly sliced
- 1 can (16 oz.) kidney beans, rinsed and drained
- 1 can (15 oz.) black beans, rinsed and drained
- 1 cup small pasta shells
- 1/4 cup chopped fresh cilantro

Direction

- Add the initial 11 ingredients in a 6-7-quart slow cooker. Cook, while covered, on low heat setting for 7 to 9 hours or till the meat softens.
- Mix in the rest of ingredients. Cook, while covered, on high heat setting for 30 to 45 minutes or till the veggies soften, mixing once in a while.

Nutrition Information

- Calories: 249 calories
- Total Carbohydrate: 29 g
- Cholesterol: 44 mg
- Total Fat: 5 g
- Fiber: 6 g
- Protein: 21 g
- Sodium: 816 mg

205. Microwave Minestrone

"This tasty soup is loaded with pasta and vegetables."
Serving: 5 servings. | Prep: 30m | Ready in: 30m

Ingredients

- 1 cup each sliced carrots, celery and zucchini
- 1/2 cup diced sweet yellow pepper
- 1 small onion, chopped
- 1 tbsp. olive oil
- 1 can (15 oz.) cannellini or white kidney beans, rinsed and drained
- 1 can (14-1/2 oz.) beef broth
- 1 can (14-1/2 oz.) diced tomatoes, undrained
- 1 cup medium pasta shells, cooked and drained
- 1/2 to 1 tsp. dried basil
- 1/2 tsp. salt
- 1/4 tsp. pepper

Direction

- Mix together onion, yellow pepper, zucchini, celery, and carrots in a 2-quart microwave-safe bowl. Drizzle oil over, stir to coat.
- Put on a cover and microwave on high, about 3 minutes. Mix in the rest of the ingredients. Put on a cover and cook on high, about 9-11 minutes.

Nutrition Information

- Calories: 220 calories
- Total Carbohydrate: 39 g
- Cholesterol: 0 mg
- Total Fat: 4 g

- Fiber: 7 g
- Protein: 9 g
- Sodium: 765 mg

206. Minestrone

Serving: Makes about 10 cups, serving 6 to 8

Ingredients

- 1/2 lb. (about 1 1/4 cups) dried white beans such as Great Northern, picked over and rinsed
- 1/2 tsp. salt
- 1/4 lb. pancetta (Italian cured pork belly, available at Italian markets and specialty foods shops) or sliced lean bacon, chopped
- 1/3 cup olive oil
- 1 onion, chopped
- 1 large carrot, cut into 1/2-inch dice
- 1 rib of celery, cut into 1/2-inch dice
- 3 garlic cloves, chopped fine
- 2 zucchini, scrubbed and cut into 1/2-inch dice
- 1/4 lb. green beans, trimmed and cut into 1/2-inch pieces
- 1/2 lb. boiling potatoes
- 4 cups shredded green cabbage (preferably Savoy)
- 1/2 lb. kale, rinsed, drained, stems discarded, and the leaves chopped (about 6 cups)
- a 28-oz. can tomatoes, chopped coarse and drained well
- 4 1/2 cups chicken broth (preferably low-salt)
- freshly grated Parmesan, garlic bruschetta , and dry-cured sausages as accompaniments

Direction

- Preparation:
- In a big bowl, allow white beans to steep in enough water to cover them by 2 in. overnight or quick-steep them. Drain white beans, in a saucepan, mix the white beans with enough water to cover them by 2 in., and simmer them, while uncovered, pouring in extra water if needed to keep the white beans barely

covered, for 45-60 minutes, or till they soften. Put in salt and simmer white beans for 5 minutes longer. Take pan out of heat and allow white beans to rest while uncovered.

- In a heavy kettle, cook pancetta in oil over moderate heat, mixing, till it becomes crisp and pale golden, put in onion, and cook mixture, mixing, till onion becomes tender. Put in garlic, celery and carrots and cook mixture, mixing, for 4 minutes. Put in green beans and zucchini with potatoes, peeled and chopped into the three-quarter-in. dice, and cook mixture, mixing, for 4 minutes. Put in kale and cabbage and cook mixture, mixing, till cabbage wilts. Put in broth and tomatoes and simmer soup, while covered, for 60 minutes.

- Drain white beans, saving liquid, in the food process or the blender, purée 1/2 of them along with 1 cup reserved liquid, and mix the purée and rest of white beans into soup. Simmer soup, while uncovered, for 15 minutes, if you want, use some of leftover reserved liquid to make the soup thinner, and use pepper and salt to season. Soup can be cooked 3 days ahead, covered and chilled. Reheat soup; make it thinner with water as you wish. Serve soup along with sausages, bruschetta and Parmesan.

Nutrition Information

- Calories: 498
- Total Carbohydrate: 52 g
- Cholesterol: 19 mg
- Total Fat: 25 g
- Fiber: 13 g
- Protein: 20 g
- Sodium: 653 mg
- Saturated Fat: 6 g

207. Minestrone In Minutes

"It may take long for this dish to simmer and get cooked, but it will worth your time."
Serving: 2 quarts. | Prep: 10m | Ready in: 01h15m

Ingredients

- 3 sweet or Johnsonville® Hot Italian Sausage Links,, sliced
- 1 cup chopped onion
- 1 can (14-1/2 oz.) diced tomatoes, undrained
- 2 small zucchini, cubed
- 3 tsps. beef bouillon granules
- 3 cups water
- 2 cups finely chopped cabbage
- 1 can (15-1/2 oz.) great northern beans, rinsed and drained
- 1 tsp. dried basil
- 2 tbsps. minced fresh parsley
- Grated Parmesan cheese

Direction

- Add onion and sausage in a soup kettle or a Dutch oven, cook over medium heat until sausage is not pink anymore; drain. Mix in the rest of ingredients but cheese. Boil them up. Cover and let it simmer for 60 minutes. Scatter cheese over.

Nutrition Information

- Calories: 117 calories
- Total Carbohydrate: 15 g
- Cholesterol: 7 mg
- Total Fat: 4 g
- Fiber: 4 g
- Protein: 6 g
- Sodium: 645 mg

208. Minestrone Soup With Hamburger

"This rich broth loaded with macaroni, ground beef, healthy vegetables, and Italian seasoning will warm you up."
Serving: 9 servings (about 3 quarts). | Prep: 10m | Ready in: 30m

Ingredients

- 1 lb. lean ground beef (90% lean)
- 1/2 cup chopped onion
- 1 garlic clove, minced
- 6 cups water
- 1 can (16 oz.) kidney beans, rinsed and drained
- 1 can (28 oz.) diced tomatoes, undrained
- 1-1/2 cups frozen whole kernel corn
- 1-1/2 cups sliced zucchini
- 1 cup shredded cabbage
- 1 celery rib, chopped
- 2 tsps. beef bouillon granules
- 2 tsps. Italian seasoning
- 1/4 tsp. salt
- 1/2 cup uncooked elbow macaroni

Direction

- Cook garlic, onion, and beef in a Dutch oven on medium heat until no pink remains in the beef, 6-8 minutes, shredding the beef into crumbles; let drain. Put in the seasonings, vegetables, beans, and water; allow to boil. Stir the macaroni in. Turn down the heat; put a cover on, allow to simmer and constantly stir for 10-15 minutes until the macaroni becomes tender.

Nutrition Information

- Calories: 186 calories
- Total Carbohydrate: 22 g
- Cholesterol: 31 mg
- Total Fat: 5 g
- Fiber: 5 g
- Protein: 15 g
- Sodium: 496 mg

209. Minestrone With Italian Sausage

"This recipe makes a big batch of soup. You can freeze it and will taste the same when reheated."
Serving: 11 servings (about 3 quarts). | Prep: 25m | Ready in: 01h25m

Ingredients

- 1 lb. Johnsonville® Ground Mild Italian sausage
- 1 large onion, chopped
- 2 large carrots, chopped
- 2 celery ribs, chopped
- 1 medium leek (white portion only), chopped
- 1 medium zucchini, cut into 1/2-inch pieces
- 1/4 lb. fresh green beans, trimmed and cut into 1/2-inch pieces
- 3 garlic cloves, minced
- 6 cups beef broth
- 2 cans (14-1/2 oz. each) diced tomatoes with basil, oregano and garlic
- 3 cups shredded cabbage
- 1 tsp. dried basil
- 1 tsp. dried oregano
- 1/4 tsp. pepper
- 1/2 cup uncooked small pasta shells
- 1 can (15 oz.) garbanzo beans or chickpeas, rinsed and drained
- 3 tbsps. minced fresh parsley
- 1/3 cup grated Parmesan cheese

Direction

- Over medium heat, cook onion and sausage in a Dutch oven until sausage is not pink anymore. Let it drain. Mix in the leek, celery and carrots and cook for 3 minutes. Put in the garlic, green beans and zucchini and cook for one more minute.
- Mix in pepper, oregano, basil, cabbage, tomatoes and broth. Let it boil. Lower the heat and simmer with cover for 45 minutes.

- Bring to a boil again and mix in parsley, pasta, and garbanzo beans. Cook until pasta becomes tender, about 6-9 minutes. Serve with cheese.

Nutrition Information

- Calories: 253 calories
- Total Carbohydrate: 18 g
- Cholesterol: 33 mg
- Total Fat: 15 g
- Fiber: 4 g
- Protein: 12 g
- Sodium: 910 mg

210. Mock Minestrone

"This soup is the favorite and so simple to make."
Serving: 20-22 servings (5-1/2 quarts). | Prep: 30m | Ready in: 30m

Ingredients

- 2 lbs. Johnsonville® Ground Mild Italian sausage
- 1 large onion, chopped
- 1 garlic clove, minced
- 6 cups water
- 1 jar (24 oz.) chunky pasta sauce
- 2 cans (10-3/4 oz. each) condensed beef broth, undiluted
- 1 can (15 oz.) garbanzo beans or 15 oz. garbanzo beans, rinsed and drained
- 1 package (10 oz.) frozen chopped spinach, thawed and squeezed dry
- 1 cup diced zucchini
- 1 cup thinly sliced carrots
- 1-1/2 tsps. dried basil
- 1/2 tsp. pepper
- 4 cups cooked pasta
- Grated Parmesan cheese, optional

Direction

- In the soup kettle or the Dutch oven, cook the garlic, onion and sausage till onion is softened and sausage turns brown; drain. Mix in all of the rest ingredients except cheese and pasta. Let it simmer for 20 minutes. Put in the pasta and heat through. If you want, use cheese to decorate on top.

211. Moroccan Chickpea Stew

"A great recipe featuring kale."
Serving: 4 | Prep: 15m | Ready in: 40m

Ingredients

- 1 tbsp. olive oil
- 1 small onion, chopped
- 2 cloves garlic, minced
- 2 tsps. ground cumin
- 2 tsps. ground coriander
- 1/2 tsp. cayenne pepper, or to taste
- 1 tsp. garam masala
- 1/2 tsp. curry powder
- 1 pinch salt
- 3 potatoes, cut into 1/2-inch cubes
- 1 (14.5 oz.) can diced tomatoes, undrained
- 1 cup tomato sauce
- 1 cup golden raisins
- water, or enough to cover
- 1 (14.5 oz.) can chickpeas, drained and rinsed
- 1 bunch kale, ribs removed, chopped
- 1/2 cup chopped fresh cilantro

Direction

- Heat olive oil in a big pot on medium heat; cook garlic and onion in hot oil for 5-7 minutes till onions are translucent. Mix salt, curry powder, garam masala, cayenne pepper, coriander and cumin into the garlic and onion; cook together for 1 minute till fragrant. Add raisins, tomato sauce, diced tomatoes and potatoes into the pot. Put enough water on mixture to cover; simmer. Cook for 10-15 minutes till potatoes are soft.
- Put kale and chickpeas into the pot; simmer for 3 minutes till kale wilts. Sprinkle cilantro on the stew; take pot off the heat immediately.

Nutrition Information

- Calories: 476 calories;
- Total Carbohydrate: 96.1 g
- Cholesterol: 0 mg
- Total Fat: 6.5 g
- Protein: 15.7 g
- Sodium: 1263 mg

---

212. Nutmeg Zucchini Bisque

"A great soup to use zucchini."
Serving: 6 servings. | Prep: 10m | Ready in: 30m

Ingredients

- 4 medium zucchini, shredded
- 1 medium onion, chopped
- 1/2 cup butter, cubed
- 2-1/2 cups chicken broth
- 1 cup heavy whipping cream
- 3/4 tsp. salt
- 1/2 tsp. minced fresh basil
- 1/2 tsp. pepper
- 1/4 tsp. ground nutmeg
- Sour cream and additional nutmeg, optional

Direction

- Sauté onion and zucchini in butter till tender in big saucepan for 5-6 minutes. Mix broth in; boil. Lower heat; simmer for 12-15 minutes, covered. Slightly cool.
- Put in food processor; process till smooth on low, covered. Put in pan; mix nutmeg, pepper, basil, salt and cream in. Boil. Simmer for 1-2 minutes till heated through, uncovered. Garnish with extra nutmeg (optional) and sour cream.

Nutrition Information

- Calories: 306 calories
- Total Carbohydrate: 8 g
- Cholesterol: 95 mg
- Total Fat: 30 g
- Fiber: 2 g

- Protein: 4 g
- Sodium: 857 mg

---

213. Oven Cheese Chowder

"This richly flavored dish is made up of a wonderful combination of ingredients. Zucchini and tomatoes add to its hearty flavor!"
Serving: 10-12 servings (3 quarts). | Prep: 20m | Ready in: 01h30m

Ingredients

- 1/2 lb. zucchini, cut into 1-inch chunks
- 2 medium onions, chopped
- 1 can (15 oz.) garbanzo beans or chickpeas, rinsed and drained
- 1 can (14-1/2 oz.) diced tomatoes, undrained
- 1 can (11 oz.) Mexicorn, drained
- 1 can (14-1/2 oz.) chicken broth
- 2 tsps. salt
- 1/4 tsp. pepper
- 1 garlic clove, minced
- 1 tsp. dried basil
- 1 bay leaf
- 1 cup shredded Monterey Jack cheese
- 1 cup grated Romano cheese
- 1-1/2 cups half-and-half cream
- Additional Monterey Jack cheese, optional

Direction

- Mix the first 11 ingredients in a 3-quart baking dish that's ungreased. Cover the dish and bake for 1 hour at 400°, stirring it once.
- Add the cream and the cheeses, stirring them in. Bake again for 10 more minutes, uncovered. Take out the bay leaf and discard. You can also add Monterey Jack as toppings if preferred.

Nutrition Information

- Calories: 190 calories
- Total Carbohydrate: 16 g
- Cholesterol: 33 mg

- Total Fat: 10 g
- Fiber: 3 g
- Protein: 10 g
- Sodium: 968 mg

214. Pesto Minestrone

"I make this vegetable soup with store-bought pesto with zucchini, but you can use whatever kinds of vegetables you like."
Serving: 4 servings. | Prep: 5m | Ready in: 30m

Ingredients

- 1/2 cup chopped onion
- 2 tsps. olive oil
- 1 tsp. minced garlic
- 2-1/4 cups water
- 2 cups frozen mixed vegetables
- 1 can (14-1/2 oz.) vegetable broth
- 3/4 tsp. dried oregano
- 1/2 tsp. salt
- 1/2 tsp. pepper
- 1 package (9 oz.) refrigerated cheese tortellini
- 2 cups diced zucchini
- 2 tbsps. prepared pesto

Direction

- Sauté onion in oil in a big saucepan until tender. Add garlic and cook for 60 more seconds. Add the pepper, salt, oregano, broth, mixed vegetables and water and stir to combine. Boil them up. Lower the heat, let it simmer while covering for 3 minutes.
- Add the pesto, zucchini and tortellini. Let it simmer while uncovering until vegetables and pasta get tender, or for another 7 to 9 minutes.

Nutrition Information

- Calories: 337 calories
- Total Carbohydrate: 47 g
- Cholesterol: 30 mg
- Total Fat: 12 g
- Fiber: 7 g

- Protein: 15 g
- Sodium: 1063 mg

215. Quick Cream Of Zucchini Soup

"This soup is very easy to make. Using more zucchini will make the soup taste better."
Serving: 4 servings. | Prep: 15m | Ready in: 45m

Ingredients

- 2 cups sliced zucchini
- 1/2 cup chopped onion
- 1/2 cup chopped carrot
- 1 tbsp. butter
- 2 cups chicken broth
- 3/4 tsp. dried tarragon
- 1/2 tsp. salt
- 1/4 tsp. pepper
- 1/4 to 1/2 tsp. garlic powder
- 2 cups milk
- Paprika and additional zucchini, optional

Direction

- Sauté carrot, onion, and zucchini with butter in a big saucepan until crunchy and soft. Add garlic powder, pepper, salt, tarragon, and broth. Boil it. Lower the heat, put a cover on and simmer until the vegetables are soft, about 15-20 minutes. Cool briefly.
- Move to a blender. Put the lid on and blend until pureed, put back into the pan. Pour in milk, thoroughly heat. Use zucchini and paprika to garnish if you want.

Nutrition Information

- Calories: 132 calories
- Total Carbohydrate: 12 g
- Cholesterol: 24 mg
- Total Fat: 7 g
- Fiber: 2 g
- Protein: 6 g
- Sodium: 857 mg

216. Ranchero Soup

"This soup is not only tasty but also colorful."
Serving: 8 servings (2-1/2 quarts). | Prep: 40m | Ready in: 55m

Ingredients

- 1 large onion, quartered
- 3 celery ribs
- 1 medium zucchini, halved lengthwise
- 1 large sweet red pepper, quartered and seeded
- 1 poblano pepper, quartered and seeded
- 1 tbsp. olive oil
- 2 cans (14-1/2 oz. each) diced tomatoes, undrained
- 2 cans (14-1/2 oz. each) vegetable broth
- 1 cup frozen sliced carrots
- 1 cup cooked rice
- 1/2 tsp. lemon-pepper seasoning

Direction

- Brush oil on peppers, zucchini, celery, and onion. Use cooking oil to moisten a paper towel; slightly coat the grill rack with long-handed tongs. Grill vegetables over medium heat without cover or broil 4 inches from heat until tender, or about 7-8 minutes per side (pepper skins will char).
- Transfer peppers to a bowl right away; cover and let sit for 15-20 minutes. Peel off and get rid of charred skin. Coarsely cut grilled vegetables.
- Combine carrots, broth, and tomatoes in a big saucepan; heat to a boil. Decrease heat; mix in lemon-pepper, rice, and grilled vegetables; heat through.

Nutrition Information

- Calories: 99 calories
- Total Carbohydrate: 18 g
- Cholesterol: 0 mg
- Total Fat: 2 g
- Fiber: 4 g
- Protein: 3 g
- Sodium: 623 mg

217. Rich Meaty Vegetable Chili

"This chili is amazingly tasty with variety of meats and vegetables."
Serving: 16 servings (4 quarts). | Prep: 20m | Ready in: 01h40m

Ingredients

- 1 lb. beef stew meat, cut into 1/2-inch cubes
- 1/2 lb. boneless skinless chicken breasts, cut into 1/2-inch cubes
- 1 to 2 tbsps. vegetable oil
- 3-1/2 cups water
- 3 medium carrots, cubed
- 2 zucchini, cubed
- 2 tomatoes, cubed
- 1 medium onion, chopped
- 1 medium turnip, cubed
- 1 green or sweet red pepper, chopped
- 2 cans (30 oz. each) dark red kidney beans, rinsed and drained
- 1 bottle (12 oz.) chili sauce

Direction

- In oil over medium-high heat, brown chicken and beef in a big Dutch oven; drain.
- Put in the green or red pepper, turnip, onion, tomatoes, zucchini, carrots and water; boil. Lower heat; put cover and allow to simmer till beef is tender, about an hour. Put chili sauce and beans in; simmer 15 minutes more.

Nutrition Information

- Calories: 158 calories
- Total Carbohydrate: 18 g
- Cholesterol: 27 mg
- Total Fat: 4 g
- Fiber: 4 g
- Protein: 13 g

- Sodium: 406 mg

---

218. Roasted Vegetable Chili

"This soup goes very well with a small salad, a small salad, cheese, and corn chips. You can use diced vegetables from a store to shorten the cooking time."
Serving: 13 servings (5 quarts). | Prep: 35m | Ready in: 01h05m

Ingredients

- 1 medium butternut squash, peeled and cut into 1-inch pieces
- 3 large carrots, sliced
- 2 medium zucchini, cut into 1-inch pieces
- 2 tbsps. olive oil, divided
- 1-1/2 tsps. ground cumin
- 2 medium green peppers, diced
- 1 large onion, chopped
- 3 cans (14-1/2 oz. each) reduced-sodium chicken broth
- 3 cans (14-1/2 oz. each) diced tomatoes, undrained
- 2 cans (15 oz. each) cannellini or white kidney beans, rinsed and drained
- 1 cup water
- 1 cup salsa
- 3 tsps. chili powder
- 6 garlic cloves, minced

Direction

- In a 15x10x1-inch baking pan, put zucchini, carrots, and squash. Stir together cumin and 1 tbsp. of oil, sprinkle over the vegetables and stir to coat. Bake without a cover at 450° until soft, or about 25-30 minutes, tossing 1 time.
- In the meantime, sauté onion and green peppers in a stockpot with the leftover oil until soft, or about 3-4 minutes. Mix in garlic, chili powder, salsa, water, beans, tomatoes, and broth. Boil it. Lower the heat, simmer without a cover for 10 minutes.

- Mix in the roasted vegetables. Boil again. Lower the heat; simmer without a cover until thoroughly heated, or about 5-10 minutes.

Nutrition Information

- Calories: 156 calories
- Total Carbohydrate: 28 g
- Cholesterol: 0 mg
- Total Fat: 3 g
- Fiber: 9 g
- Protein: 6 g
- Sodium: 559 mg

---

219. Roasted Vegetable Soup

"This is an extremely tasty soup made with veggies and beans."
Serving: 16 servings (about 4 quarts). | Prep: 25m | Ready in: 50m

Ingredients

- 1 medium eggplant, cut into 3/4-inch pieces
- 2 medium zucchini, cut into 3/4-inch pieces
- 2 large sweet red peppers, cut into 3/4-inch pieces
- 1/2 lb. fresh mushrooms, quartered
- 1 large sweet potato, peeled and cut into 3/4-inch pieces
- 1 large potato, peeled and cut into 3/4-inch pieces
- 1 medium leek (white part only), sliced
- 6 garlic cloves, minced
- 4 cans (14-1/2 oz. each) vegetable or chicken broth
- 1 can (16 oz.) kidney beans, rinsed and drained
- 1 can (15 oz.) garbanzo beans or chickpeas, rinsed and drained
- 1 can (15-1/2 oz.) black-eyed peas, rinsed and drained
- 2 to 3 tsps. red wine vinegar
- 1 tsp. dried rosemary, crushed
- 1 tsp. dried marjoram
- 1/2 tsp. rubbed sage
- 1/2 tsp. dried thyme

- Salt and pepper to taste

Direction

- Prepare two 15x10x1-inch baking pans lined with foil. Grease the foil with cooking spray. Place leek, potatoes, mushrooms, peppers, zucchini, and eggplant on the pans; liberally spray with cooking spray. Uncover and bake for 25 to 30 minutes at 425° or until tender.
- Coat a Dutch oven with cooking spray, and sauté garlic for 2 minutes. Add roasted vegetables, seasonings, vinegar, peas, beans, and broth. Bring the mixture to a boil. Lower heat; simmer, covered until heated through, or for 10 to 12 minutes.

Nutrition Information

- Calories: false

220. Roasted Veggie Chili

"This is a chili recipe that you will love."
Serving: 24 servings (6 quarts). | Prep: 30m | Ready in: 01h10m

Ingredients

- 2 cups fresh or frozen corn
- 2 cups each cubed zucchini, yellow summer squash and eggplant
- 2 each medium green peppers and sweet red peppers, cut into 1-inch pieces
- 2 large onions, chopped
- 1/2 cup garlic cloves, peeled
- 1/4 cup olive oil
- 4 quarts chicken broth
- 2 cans (14-1/2 oz. each) stewed tomatoes
- 2 cans (14-1/2 oz. each) tomato puree
- 1/4 cup lime juice
- 4 tsp. chili powder
- 1-1/4 tsp. cayenne pepper
- 1 tsp. ground cumin
- 1/2 cup butter
- 1/2 cup all-purpose flour

- 3 cans (15 oz. each) white kidney or cannellini beans, rinsed and drained
- 1/2 cup minced fresh cilantro
- Sour cream and chopped green onions, optional

Direction

- Combine garlic and vegetables in a roasting pan. Add oil; and stir until evenly coated. Bake, covered for 20 to 30 minutes at 400° or until vegetables are softened; allow to cool a bit. Remove and chop garlic cloves.
- Combine cumin, cayenne, chili powder, lime juice, tomato puree, tomatoes, and broth in a soup kettle or Dutch oven. Bring to a boil. Lower heat; simmer without a cover until the mixture is reduced by 1/4, or for 25 to 35 minutes.
- Melt butter in a Dutch oven or large saucepan; add flour into melted butter and stir until no lumps remain. Cook, stirring until flour mixture is bubbly and begins to brown. Gradually stir into tomato mixture. Add cilantro, beans, garlic, and roasted vegetables; mix to combine. Uncover and simmer until chili reaches your desired thickness. Top with green onions and sour cream if desired.

Nutrition Information

- Calories: 168 calories
- Total Carbohydrate: 22 g
- Cholesterol: 10 mg
- Total Fat: 7 g
- Fiber: 4 g
- Protein: 6 g
- Sodium: 802 mg

221. Salmon Zucchini Chowder

"This dish is light yet flavorful and creamy and gives out all sorts of wonderful flavors that are perfect on cold winter nights."
Serving: 6 servings. | Prep: 20m | Ready in: 45m

Ingredients

- 1 small onion, chopped
- 1 garlic clove, minced
- 1/4 tsp. dried thyme
- 1/4 tsp. dried basil
- 1 tbsp. butter
- 2 cups 1% milk
- 1 can (10-1/2 oz.) condensed chicken broth, undiluted
- 1/2 cup frozen corn
- 1/2 cup chopped carrot
- 1 medium red potato, cut into 1/2-inch cubes
- 3 tbsps. all-purpose flour
- 1/4 cup cold water
- 1/2 lb. salmon fillet, cut into 1-inch pieces
- 1/2 cup chopped zucchini
- 1/2 tsp. salt
- 1/4 tsp. pepper
- 1/2 cup shredded reduced-fat cheddar cheese

Direction

- Combine and cook the onion, thyme, basil, and garlic in butter in a big cooking pan on medium heat, stirring until the onion is tender. Pour in the milk, corn, broth, potato, and carrot, stirring them in then boil. Lower the heat, cover the pan, and let it simmer until the vegetables are tender, about 6 to 8 minutes.
- Mix the water and flour until it's smooth and pour this into the onion mixture. Bring the soup to a boil, cook and stir until it has thickened, about 2 minutes. Lower the heat then mix in the zucchini and salmon. Let it simmer uncovered until the fish is flaky, about 3 to 5 minutes. Season with salt and pepper while still stirring. Drizzle with cheese then serve.

Nutrition Information

- Calories: 214 calories
- Total Carbohydrate: 16 g
- Cholesterol: 38 mg
- Total Fat: 10 g
- Fiber: 2 g
- Protein: 16 g
- Sodium: 656 mg

222. Simple Italian Vegetable Soup

"So flavorful and hearty!"
Serving: 6-8 servings. | Prep: 10m | Ready in: 60m

Ingredients

- 2 medium carrots, diced
- 1 small onion, chopped
- 1 tbsp. olive oil
- 2 garlic cloves, minced
- 2 cans (14-1/2 oz. each) beef broth
- 1 can (14-1/2 oz.) diced tomatoes, undrained
- 2 cups water
- 1 small zucchini, diced
- 1 tsp. dried basil
- 1 tsp. salt
- 1/2 tsp. dried oregano
- 1/4 tsp. pepper
- 2 to 3 drops hot pepper sauce
- 1 can (16 oz.) kidney beans, rinsed and drained
- 1 cup chopped fresh spinach
- 3/4 cup uncooked elbow macaroni
- 2 tbsps. minced fresh parsley
- 1/2 cup shredded Parmesan cheese

Direction

- Sauté onion and carrots in oil till tender in a Dutch oven. Add garlic and cook for another 1 minute; mix in hot pepper sauce, pepper, oregano, salt, basil, zucchini, water, tomatoes and broth; boil. Lower the heat and cover; simmer for 15 minutes.
- Mix in parsley, macaroni, spinach and kidney beans; cover and cook till macaroni is tender

or for another 15 minutes; using cheese to garnish.

223. Simple Minestrone

"This dish is loaded with vegetables and has a smoky flavor that surely will warm up your cold winter days."
Serving: 2 servings. | Prep: 20m | Ready in: 45m

Ingredients

- 1 bacon strip, diced
- 1/3 cup smoked turkey kielbasa, quartered
- 1 small onion, chopped
- 1 garlic clove, minced
- 1/4 cup chopped carrot
- 2 tbsps. chopped celery
- 1 cup reduced-sodium chicken broth
- 1 cup canned diced tomatoes, undrained
- 1 can (5-1/2 oz.) reduced-sodium tomato juice
- 1/4 cup chopped zucchini
- 1/2 tsp. dried basil
- 1/4 tsp. dried oregano
- 1/8 tsp. pepper
- 1/3 cup canned pinto beans, rinsed and drained
- 1/4 cup cooked elbow macaroni
- 1 tbsp. grated Parmesan cheese

Direction

- Cook bacon in a big saucepan over medium heat until crisp. Transfer the bacon to a paper towel using a slotted spoon. Sauté garlic, onion, and sausage in the drippings, about 3 minutes. Mix in celery and carrot. Stir and cook until the sausage turns light brown, or about another 2 minutes; strain.
- Mix in seasonings, zucchini, tomato juice, tomatoes, and broth. Boil it. Lower the heat, put on a cover and simmer until the vegetables are soft, or about 10 minutes. Mix in macaroni and beans; thoroughly heat. Sprinkle bacon and Parmesan cheese over.

Nutrition Information

- Calories: 267 calories
- Total Carbohydrate: 28 g
- Cholesterol: 45 mg
- Total Fat: 9 g
- Fiber: 6 g
- Protein: 18 g
- Sodium: 1256 mg

224. Simple Sausage Minestrone

"This chunky soup is filled with veggies."
Serving: 2 servings. | Prep: 20m | Ready in: 45m

Ingredients

- 1 bacon strip, diced
- 2/3 cup Johnsonville® Fully Cooked Polish Kielbasa Sausage Rope, quartered
- 1 small onion, chopped
- 1 garlic clove, minced
- 1/4 cup chopped carrot
- 2 tbsps. chopped celery
- 1 cup chicken broth
- 1 cup canned diced tomatoes, undrained
- 1 can (5-1/2 oz.) tomato juice
- 1/4 cup chopped zucchini
- 1/2 tsp. dried basil
- 1/4 tsp. dried oregano
- 1/4 tsp. salt, optional
- 1/8 tsp. pepper
- 1/3 cup canned pinto beans, rinsed and drained
- 1/4 cup cooked elbow macaroni
- 1 tbsp. grated Parmesan cheese

Direction

- Cook bacon in a big saucepan on medium heat until they are crispy. Use a slotted spoon to transfer them onto paper towel. Sauté garlic, onion, and sausage in the drippings for 3 minutes. Stir in celery and carrot, then cook while stirring for another 2 minutes or until the sausage lightly browns, then drain.

- Stir in the seasonings, zucchini, tomato juice, tomatoes, and broth, then boil. Turn down the heat and simmer while covered until the vegetables are soft, or for about 10 minutes. Stir in the macaroni and beans, heating them through. Sprinkle with bacon and Parmesan cheese.

Nutrition Information

- Calories: 277 calories
- Total Carbohydrate: 33 g
- Cholesterol: 30 mg
- Total Fat: 9 g
- Fiber: 6 g
- Protein: 16 g
- Sodium: 1194 mg

225. Slow Cooker Vegetable Bean Soup

"This soup is so heart-warming and quick to prepare."
Serving: 7 servings. | Prep: 30m | Ready in: 06h30m

Ingredients

- 2 cans (14-1/2 oz. each) petite diced tomatoes
- 1 can (16 oz.) kidney beans, rinsed and drained
- 1 can (15-1/4 oz.) whole kernel corn, drained
- 1 can (15 oz.) garbanzo beans or chickpeas, rinsed and drained
- 1 can (15 oz.) black beans, rinsed and drained
- 1 can (10 oz.) diced tomatoes and green chilies
- 1 can (8 oz.) tomato sauce
- 1 cup chopped green pepper
- 1 cup chopped zucchini
- 3/4 cup water
- 1/2 cup chopped onion
- 1/2 cup chopped celery
- 2 tbsps. chili powder
- 4 tsps. dried oregano
- 2 garlic cloves, minced
- 1 tsp. ground cumin
- 1 tsp. pepper
- 1/2 tsp. salt

- 2 bay leaves

Direction

- In the 5-quart slow cooker, mix together all of the ingredients. Keep it covered and cook over low heat till the veggies are softened or for 6 to 8 hours. Throw away the bay leaves prior to serving.

Nutrition Information

- Calories: 268 calories
- Total Carbohydrate: 49 g
- Cholesterol: 0 mg
- Total Fat: 2 g
- Fiber: 14 g
- Protein: 13 g
- Sodium: 1296 mg

226. Spicy Kielbasa Soup

"This hearty soup has a little zip that comes from red pepper flakes. If you have any leftover of this soup, you can reheat it and wait some time for the flavors come together."
Serving: 5 servings. | Prep: 15m | Ready in: 08h15m

Ingredients

- 1/2 lb. reduced-fat smoked turkey kielbasa, sliced
- 1 medium onion, chopped
- 1 medium green pepper, chopped
- 1 celery rib with leaves, thinly sliced
- 4 garlic cloves, minced
- 2 cans (14-1/2 oz. each) reduced-sodium chicken broth
- 1 can (15-1/2 oz.) great northern beans, rinsed and drained
- 1 can (14-1/2 oz.) stewed tomatoes, cut up
- 1 small zucchini, sliced
- 1 medium carrot, shredded
- 1 tbsp. dried parsley flakes
- 1/4 tsp. crushed red pepper flakes
- 1/4 tsp. pepper

Direction

- Cook kielbasa in a nonstick frying pan over medium heat until brown lightly. Add celery, green pepper, and onion, stir and cook for 3 minutes. Add garlic, cook for another 1 minute.
- Move to a 5-qt. slow cooker. Mix in the rest of the ingredients. Put a cover on and cook on low until the vegetables are soft, about 8-9 hours.

Nutrition Information

- Calories: 194 calories
- Total Carbohydrate: 32 g
- Cholesterol: 16 mg
- Total Fat: 2 g
- Fiber: 7 g
- Protein: 14 g
- Sodium: 1187 mg

227. Spicy Zucchini Soup

"This recipe is amazing in the summer."
Serving: 14-16 servings (4 quarts). | Prep: 20m | Ready in: 01h50m

Ingredients

- 1 lb. Johnsonville® Ground Mild Italian sausage
- 3 cans (28 oz. each) diced tomatoes, undrained
- 3 cans (14-1/2 oz. each) beef broth
- 2 lbs. zucchini, diced
- 2 medium green peppers, diced
- 2 cups thinly sliced celery
- 1 cup chopped onion
- 2 tsps. Italian seasoning
- 1 tsp. dried basil
- 1 tsp. dried oregano
- 1 tsp. salt
- 1/2 tsp. sugar
- 1/4 tsp. pepper
- 1/4 tsp. garlic powder
- 3 cups cooked macaroni

Direction

- In the soup kettle or a Dutch oven, brown and crumble the sausage; drain off. Put in the seasonings, onion, celery, green peppers, zucchini, broth and tomatoes; boil. Lower the heat; keep it covered and let it simmer till the veggies are softened or for 1.25 – 1.5 hours. Put in the macaroni; thoroughly heat.

Nutrition Information

- Calories: 109 calories
- Total Carbohydrate: 13 g
- Cholesterol: 11 mg
- Total Fat: 4 g
- Fiber: 3 g
- Protein: 6 g
- Sodium: 449 mg

228. Summer Garden Soup

"This soup is even better when served chilled."
Serving: 8 servings (2 quarts). | Prep: 15m | Ready in: 30m

Ingredients

- 1 cup chopped onion
- 2 tbsps. olive oil
- 4 to 6 garlic cloves, minced
- 3 cups chopped fresh tomatoes
- 1 cup fresh or frozen cut green beans
- 1 tbsp. minced fresh basil or 1 tsp. dried basil
- 1 tsp. minced fresh tarragon or 1/4 tsp. dried tarragon
- 1/2 tsp. minced fresh dill or pinch dill weed
- 1/4 tsp. salt, optional
- 1/4 tsp. pepper
- 3-1/2 cups chicken broth
- 1 cup fresh or frozen peas
- 1 cup sliced zucchini or yellow summer squash

Direction

- Sauté onion in oil until tender in a large saucepan. Add garlic; cook for 1 more minute. Put the tomatoes, pepper, dill, tarragon, basil, and beans. You may add salt if desired.
- Boil, reduce the heat; stew for 10 minutes, uncovered. Pour the broth, zucchini, and peas; continue to simmer until vegetables are crisp-tender for 5-10 minutes.

Nutrition Information

- Calories: 86 calories
- Total Carbohydrate: 10 g
- Cholesterol: 2 mg
- Total Fat: 5 g
- Fiber: 0 g
- Protein: 4 g
- Sodium: 77 mg

229. Summer Vegetable Soup

"It's a simple garden vegetable soup that needs no cooking and is served chilled."
Serving: 4 | Prep: 30m | Ready in: 30m

Ingredients

- 1 cup chopped celery hearts
- 1 cup chopped cucumber
- 1/2 cup chopped red bell pepper
- 1/2 cup chopped avocado
- 1/4 cup lemon juice
- 1/4 cup chopped tomato
- 1 cup spinach
- 1/4 cup water
- 1/2 tsp. salt
- 1/4 tsp. cayenne pepper
- 1 tsp. paprika

Direction

- In a high-speed blender, blend together tomato, lemon juice, avocado, red bell pepper, cucumber and celery for half a minute, until smooth. Put in cayenne pepper, salt, water and spinach, then keep on blending until smooth. Scoop into soup bowls and decorate with paprika.

Nutrition Information

- Calories: 56 calories;
- Total Carbohydrate: 7.4 g
- Cholesterol: 0 mg
- Total Fat: 3 g
- Protein: 1.5 g
- Sodium: 325 mg

230. Summer's Bounty Soup

"This chunky is loaded with vegetables. You can add or leave out any vegetables you want."
Serving: 14 servings (about 3-1/2 quarts). | Prep: 5m | Ready in: 07h05m

Ingredients

- 4 medium tomatoes, chopped
- 2 medium potatoes, peeled and cubed
- 2 cups halved fresh green beans
- 2 small zucchini, cubed
- 1 medium yellow summer squash, cubed
- 4 small carrots, thinly sliced
- 2 celery ribs, thinly sliced
- 1 cup cubed peeled eggplant
- 1 cup sliced fresh mushrooms
- 1 small onion, chopped
- 1 tbsp. minced fresh parsley
- 1 tbsp. salt-free garlic and herb seasoning
- 4 cups reduced-sodium V8 juice

Direction

- In a 5-qt. slow cooker, mix all of the ingredients together. Put a cover on and cook on Low until the vegetables are soft, or for about 7-8 hours.

Nutrition Information

- Calories: 67 calories
- Total Carbohydrate: 15 g

- Cholesterol: 0 mg
- Total Fat: 0 g
- Fiber: 3 g
- Protein: 2 g
- Sodium: 62 mg

231. Swiss Chard Bean Soup

"This soup with nutritious Swiss chard is so hearty and flavorful."
Serving: 10 servings (2-1/2 quarts). | Prep: 25m | Ready in: 55m

Ingredients

- 1 medium carrot, coarsely chopped
- 1 small zucchini, coarsely chopped
- 1 small yellow summer squash, coarsely chopped
- 1 small red onion, chopped
- 2 tbsps. olive oil
- 2 garlic cloves, minced
- 3 cans (14-1/2 oz. each) reduced-sodium chicken broth
- 4 cups chopped Swiss chard
- 1 can (15-1/2 oz.) great northern beans, rinsed and drained
- 1 can (14-1/2 oz.) diced tomatoes, undrained
- 1 tsp. dried thyme
- 1/2 tsp. salt
- 1/2 tsp. dried oregano
- 1/4 tsp. pepper
- 1/4 cup grated Parmesan cheese

Direction

- In the Dutch oven, sauté onion, yellow squash, zucchini and carrot in oil till becoming softened. Put in the garlic; sauté 60 seconds more. Put in pepper, oregano, salt, thyme, tomatoes, beans, Swiss chard and broth.
- Boil. Lower the heat; let it simmer, uncovered, till the chard is softened or for 15 minutes. Just prior to serving, drizzle with cheese.

Nutrition Information

- Calories: 94 calories
- Total Carbohydrate: 12 g
- Cholesterol: 2 mg
- Total Fat: 4 g
- Fiber: 4 g
- Protein: 5 g
- Sodium: 452 mg

232. Tasty-italian Vegetable Soup

"Only 25 minutes to prepare, this warm and tasty soup would satisfy your appetite."
Serving: 6-8 servings (2 quarts). | Prep: 10m | Ready in: 25m

Ingredients

- 1 lb. Johnsonville® Ground Mild Italian sausage
- 1 medium onion, sliced
- 1-1/2 cups water
- 1 can (15 oz.) chickpeas, rinsed and drained
- 1 can (14-1/2 oz.) diced tomatoes, undrained
- 1 can (14-1/2 oz.) beef broth
- 2 medium zucchini, cut into 1/4-inch slices
- 1/2 tsp. dried basil
- Grated Parmesan cheese

Direction

- Cook onion and sausage in a large saucepan over medium heat until no pink remains in the meat; let drain. Stir in the basil, zucchini, broth, tomatoes, beans, and water.
- Allow to boil. Turn down the heat and allow to simmer until the zucchini becomes tender, about 5 minutes. Decorate with cheese.

Nutrition Information

- Calories: 173 calories
- Total Carbohydrate: 14 g
- Cholesterol: 23 mg
- Total Fat: 9 g
- Fiber: 3 g

- Protein: 10 g
- Sodium: 620 mg

233. Tex-mex Chicken Soup

"A simple and quick recipe for fast meal."
Serving: 12 servings (3 quarts). | Prep: 10m | Ready in: 55m

Ingredients

- 1/2 cup chopped onion
- 1 tbsp. canola oil
- 2 garlic cloves, minced
- 4 cups chicken broth
- 3 cups cubed cooked chicken
- 3 medium zucchini, sliced
- 1 can (14-1/2 oz.) diced tomatoes, undrained
- 1 can (11 oz.) whole kernel corn, drained
- 1 can (8 oz.) tomato sauce
- 1/2 cup salsa
- 2 tsps. ground cumin
- 1 tsp. salt, optional
- 3/4 tsp. pepper
- 1/2 tsp. dried oregano
- Shredded cheddar cheese, optional
- Tortilla chips, optional

Direction

- Sauté onion in oil in a big stockpot until tender. Put in garlic, cook for 1 more minute. Add in the following 11 ingredients; heat to a boil. Lower the heat. Allow to simmer 30 minutes with cover. Serve with tortilla chips and cheese.

Nutrition Information

- Calories: 110 calories
- Total Carbohydrate: 6 g
- Cholesterol: 31 mg
- Total Fat: 4 g
- Fiber: 2 g
- Protein: 12 g
- Sodium: 296 mg

234. Tomato Zucchini Soup

"A tomato soup that is easy and versatile."
Serving: 4 | Prep: 5m | Ready in: 15m

Ingredients

- 1 (26 oz.) can tomato soup
- 26 fluid oz. milk
- 1 (14.5 oz.) can zucchini in Italian-style tomato sauce
- 1 1/2 tsps. dried basil
- 1 tsp. minced garlic
- 4 slices Swiss cheese

Direction

- In a big pot, mix milk and tomato soup together on medium-low heat; put in garlic, basil, and zucchini. Simmer for 5 minutes until warm. Mix Swiss cheese slices into mixture, cook for 5 minutes longer until cheese is melted.

Nutrition Information

- Calories: 323 calories;
- Total Carbohydrate: 32 g
- Cholesterol: 45 mg
- Total Fat: 14 g
- Protein: 17.5 g
- Sodium: 1020 mg

235. Tortellini Minestrone

"This is a smart way to use zucchini."
Serving: 9 servings. | Prep: 20m | Ready in: 01h10m

Ingredients

- 1-1/4 lbs. Italian turkey sausage links, casings removed
- 1 large onion, chopped
- 2 garlic cloves, minced
- 6-1/2 cups reduced-sodium beef broth

- 1 can (14-1/2 oz.) diced tomatoes, undrained
- 2 cups thinly sliced carrots
- 1 cup thinly sliced celery
- 1 cup ketchup
- 1 tsp. Italian seasoning
- 2 cups sliced zucchini
- 1 medium green pepper, chopped
- 2 cups frozen cheese tortellini
- 1/4 cup minced fresh parsley
- 2 tbsps. grated Parmesan cheese

Direction

- Cook onion and sausage over medium heat in a large saucepan or a Dutch oven until the meat is no more pink. Add garlic and cook for 1 minute longer. Allow to drain. Add the Italian seasoning, ketchup, celery, carrots, tomatoes, and broth. Bring to a boil, and reduce the flame; simmer for 20-25 minutes, uncovered, or until the greens are softened.
- Next, add green pepper and zucchini; cook until the green pepper is tender, about 5-7 minutes more. Stir in parsley and tortellini. Bring to a boil, reduce the heat to medium; cook until the tortellini is tender, uncovered, about 5 minutes. Before serving, dust with cheese.

Nutrition Information

- Calories: 247 calories
- Total Carbohydrate: 27 g
- Cholesterol: 43 mg
- Total Fat: 8 g
- Fiber: 3 g
- Protein: 17 g
- Sodium: 1179 mg

236. Turkey Meatball And Vegetable Soup

"This main dish is not only hearty but also affordable to make."
Serving: 6 servings. | Prep: 30m | Ready in: 50m

Ingredients

- 1/2 cup dry bread crumbs
- 3 tbsps. milk
- 1 egg, lightly beaten
- 1/2 tsp. salt
- 1-1/4 lbs. ground turkey
- 2-1/2 cups water
- 1 can (14-1/2 oz.) stewed tomatoes
- 2 medium zucchini, halved and sliced
- 2 small carrots, thinly sliced
- 2/3 cup frozen corn
- 1/2 cup cut fresh green beans or frozen cut green beans
- 2 tsps. chicken bouillon granules
- 1 tsp. dried basil
- 1/4 tsp. pepper

Direction

- Combine salt, egg, milk, and breadcrumbs in a big bowl. Crumble the turkey over the mixture and blend well, then shape into 1/2 inch balls. In a nonstick pan, brown the meatballs in batches on medium heat, then drain if needed.
- Combine all of the remaining ingredients in a large saucepan, then boil. Slowly add in the meatballs and decrease the heat. Simmer, covered, until the vegetables become tender, 20 - 25 minutes.

237. Turkey Minestrone

""Italian turkey sausage provides the correct spice to the broth. I like serving this to my guests, especially for lunch. I became a better cook because of this recipe. Enjoy!""
Serving: 16 servings (4 quarts). | Prep: 30m | Ready in: 30m

Ingredients

- 2/3 cup chopped onion
- 2 tbsps. canola oil
- 1/2 lb. lean ground turkey
- 1/2 lb. hot Italian turkey sausage links, casings removed
- 1/2 cup minced fresh parsley
- 2 garlic cloves, minced
- 1 tsp. dried oregano
- 1 tsp. dried basil
- 2 cans (14-1/2 oz. each) Italian stewed tomatoes
- 6 cups chicken broth
- 1 medium zucchini, sliced
- 1 package (10 oz.) frozen mixed vegetables
- 1 can (16 oz.) kidney beans, rinsed and drained
- 1-1/2 cups cooked elbow macaroni
- 2 tbsps. cider vinegar
- 1/2 tsp. salt, optional
- Pinch pepper

Direction

- Sauté onion in oil in a stockpot that is set over medium heat for 4 minutes until tender. Add the next six ingredients. Cook the mixture until the meat is no longer pink.
- Add the broth, mixed vegetables, zucchini, and tomatoes. Cover the pot and cook the mixture on low heat for 5 minutes. Mix on vinegar, beans, macaroni, and salt and pepper if desired. Simmer the mixture for 3-4 minutes until heated through.

Nutrition Information

- Calories: 132 calories
- Total Carbohydrate: 15 g
- Cholesterol: 20 mg
- Total Fat: 4 g
- Fiber: 3 g
- Protein: 9 g
- Sodium: 538 mg

238. Vegetable Bean Barley Soup

"This appealing soup contains loads of carrots, tomatoes, barley, and zucchini."
Serving: 6 servings. | Prep: 20m | Ready in: 01h20m

Ingredients

- 1 medium onion, chopped
- 1/2 tsp. dried basil
- 1/2 tsp. dill weed
- 2 tbsps. canola oil
- 1 garlic clove, minced
- 2 cans (14-1/2 oz. each) reduced-sodium chicken broth
- 1-3/4 cups water
- 1 cup chopped carrots
- 1/2 cup medium pearl barley
- 1 can (15-3/4 oz.) pork and beans
- 2 small zucchini, sliced
- 1/2 tsp. salt
- 1/4 tsp. pepper
- 1 can (14-1/2 oz.) diced tomatoes, undrained
- 1 tsp. cider vinegar

Direction

- Sauté dill, basil, and onion, in oil in a large saucepan until onion is softened. Add garlic; cook for another minute. Mix in barley, carrots, water, and broth. Bring to a boil. Lower heat; simmer, covered for half an hour.
- Stir zucchini, beans, and pork into the mixture; season with pepper and salt. Simmer, covered until barley and vegetables are tender, or for 10 to 15 more minutes. Mix in vinegar and tomatoes just before serving; cook until thoroughly heated.

Nutrition Information

- Calories: 218 calories
- Total Carbohydrate: 36 g
- Cholesterol: 5 mg
- Total Fat: 6 g
- Fiber: 9 g
- Protein: 9 g
- Sodium: 1003 mg

Nutrition Information

- Calories: 250 calories
- Total Carbohydrate: 33 g
- Cholesterol: 4 mg
- Total Fat: 10 g
- Fiber: 0 g
- Protein: 11 g
- Sodium: 863 mg

239. Vegetable Bean Chili

"This is so hearty that no one even wants meat in this recipe!"
Serving: 9 servings (2-1/4 quarts). | Prep: 25m | Ready in: 55m

Ingredients

- 1 medium zucchini, sliced 1/4 inch thick
- 1 medium green pepper, chopped
- 1 cup chopped onion
- 1 cup shredded carrots
- 1/2 cup finely chopped celery
- 2 garlic cloves, minced
- 1/4 cup olive oil
- 1 can (28 oz.) diced tomatoes, undrained
- 1 jar (8 oz.) picante sauce
- 1 tsp. beef bouillon granules
- 1-1/2 tsps. ground cumin
- 1 can (16 oz.) chili beans, undrained
- 1 can (15 oz.) garbanzo beans or chickpeas, rinsed and drained
- 1 can (2-1/4 oz.) sliced ripe olives, drained
- 1 cup shredded cheddar cheese

Direction

- In a Dutch oven or 4-qt. kettle, sauté garlic, celery, carrots, onion, green pepper, and zucchini in oil until soft. Mix in cumin, bouillon, picante sauce, and tomatoes; boil. Lower heat and simmer for 30 minutes, uncovered, while stirring occasionally.
- Add olive and beans. Heat it through. Top with cheese.

240. Vegetable Chili

"Put some sour cream and grated cheddar cheese on top. Serves better with rice."
Serving: Serves 6

Ingredients

- 3 tbsps. olive oil
- 1 large onion, coarsely chopped
- 6 large garlic cloves, chopped
- 3 14 1/2-oz. cans diced tomatoes in juice
- 1 4-oz. can diced mild green chilies
- 3 tbsps. chili powder
- 1 tbsp. ground cumin
- 1 tbsp. dried oregano
- 2 15- to 16-oz. cans kidney beans, drained
- 2 green bell peppers, cut into 1/2-inch pieces
- 1 10-oz. package frozen corn kernels

Direction

- Heat oil in a heavy big pot over medium-high heat. Sauté onion and garlic for 5 minutes. Mix in green chilies, tomatoes with juices, cumin, oregano, and chili powder; cook for 10 minutes to incorporate the flavors. Add bell peppers, corn, and beans. Put the heat to medium-low and simmer until the chili is thickened; often stir it about 35 minutes. Season with salt and pepper to taste.

Nutrition Information

- Calories: 328
- Total Carbohydrate: 51 g
- Total Fat: 10 g

- Fiber: 15 g
- Protein: 13 g
- Sodium: 577 mg
- Saturated Fat: 1 g

241. Vegetable Minestrone

"A soup recipe to try out for an evening meal of busy people. You may replace beef with vegetable broth to create a vegetarian soup."
Serving: 8 servings (2-1/2 quarts). | Prep: 15m | Ready in: 06h45m

Ingredients

- 2 cans (14-1/2 oz. each) beef broth
- 1 can (16 oz.) kidney beans, rinsed and drained
- 1 can (15 oz.) great northern beans, rinsed and drained
- 1 can (14-1/2 oz.) Italian-style stewed tomatoes
- 1 large onion, chopped
- 1 medium zucchini, thinly sliced
- 1 medium carrot, shredded
- 3/4 cup tomato juice
- 1 tsp. dried basil
- 3/4 tsp. dried oregano
- 1/4 tsp. garlic powder
- 1 cup frozen cut green beans, thawed
- 1/2 cup frozen chopped spinach, thawed
- 1/2 cup small shell pasta
- 1/2 cup shredded Parmesan cheese

Direction

- Blend the first eleven ingredients in a 4- or 5-quart slow cooker. Put a cover on and cook on low heat until the vegetables become tender, 6-7 hours.
- Stir in the pasta, spinach, and green beans. Put a cover on and heat until cooked thoroughly, about 30 minutes. Use cheese to sprinkle.

Nutrition Information

- Calories: 181 calories

- Total Carbohydrate: 30 g
- Cholesterol: 4 mg
- Total Fat: 2 g
- Fiber: 8 g
- Protein: 12 g
- Sodium: 1027 mg

242. Vegetarian White Bean Soup

"Stew up this crisp tasting meatless soup. Generous with two sorts of beans, it makes a fantastic course. Round out the feast with Walnut Zucchini Muffins or warm supper rolls."
Serving: 7 servings. | Prep: 10m | Ready in: 30m

Ingredients

- 2 small zucchini, quartered lengthwise and sliced
- 1 cup each chopped onion, celery and carrot
- 2 tbsps. canola oil
- 3 cans (14-1/2 oz. each) vegetable broth
- 1 can (15-1/2 oz.) great northern beans, rinsed and drained
- 1 can (15 oz.) white kidney or cannellini beans, rinsed and drained
- 1 can (14-1/2 oz.) diced tomatoes, undrained
- 1/2 tsp. dried thyme
- 1/2 tsp. dried oregano
- 1/4 tsp. pepper

Direction

- Sauté the carrot, celery, onion and zucchini in oil in a big saucepan for 5-7 minutes until crisp-tender. Put in the rest of the ingredients. Take it to a boil. Lower the heat; cover then simmer until vegetables are soft, 15 minutes.

Nutrition Information

- Calories: 171 calories
- Total Carbohydrate: 25 g
- Cholesterol: 0 mg
- Total Fat: 5 g
- Fiber: 7 g

- Protein: 8 g
- Sodium: 1047 mg

243. Veggie Beef Chili

"A beautiful and nutritious food that makes use of vegetables."
Serving: 8 servings (2 quarts). | Prep: 10m | Ready in: 40m

Ingredients

- 1 lb. lean ground beef (90% lean)
- 1 large onion, chopped
- 1 medium zucchini, diced
- 1 medium yellow summer squash, diced
- 1 medium sweet red pepper, chopped
- 1 can (15-1/2 oz.) hominy, drained
- 1 can (15 oz.) black beans, rinsed and drained
- 1 can (14-1/2 oz.) diced tomatoes with green peppers and onions, undrained
- 1 cup light beer or beef broth
- 1 can (4 oz.) chopped green chilies
- 1 tbsp. minced fresh parsley
- 2 garlic cloves, minced
- 2 tsps. ground cumin
- 2 tsps. dried coriander
- 1 tsp. minced fresh cilantro
- 1 tsp. chili powder
- 1/4 tsp. cayenne pepper

Direction

- Cook onion and beef over medium heat in a big saucepan, until meat is not pink anymore; drain. Add red pepper, yellow squash, and zucchini; stir and cook until crisp-tender. Mix in the rest ingredients; boil. Lower heat, simmer with cover until vegetables are tender, about 20 minutes.

Nutrition Information

- Calories: 223 calories
- Total Carbohydrate: 23 g
- Cholesterol: 21 mg

- Total Fat: 6 g
- Fiber: 7 g
- Protein: 17 g
- Sodium: 439 mg

244. Veggie Soup With Meatballs

"This is the recipe you will make again and again."
Serving: 6 servings (2-1/2 quarts). | Prep: 20m | Ready in: 05h50m

Ingredients

- 1 package (12 oz.) frozen fully cooked Italian meatballs
- 1 can (28 oz.) diced tomatoes, undrained
- 3 cups beef broth
- 2 cups shredded cabbage
- 1 can (16 oz.) kidney beans, rinsed and drained
- 1 medium zucchini, sliced
- 1 cup fresh green beans, cut into 1-inch pieces
- 1 cup water
- 2 medium carrots, sliced
- 1 tsp. dried basil
- 1/2 tsp. minced garlic
- 1/4 tsp. salt
- 1/8 tsp. dried oregano
- 1/8 tsp. pepper
- 1 cup uncooked elbow macaroni
- 1/4 cup minced fresh parsley
- Grated Parmesan cheese, optional

Direction

- Combine the first 14 ingredients in a 5-qt. slow cooker. Cover and stew on low heat for 5-6 hours, or until the vegetables are almost soft.
- Stir in parsley and macaroni; continue to cook until the macaroni is tender, about 30 minutes more. Enjoy with cheese if desired.

Nutrition Information

- Calories: 335 calories
- Total Carbohydrate: 37 g
- Cholesterol: 27 mg

- Total Fat: 14 g
- Fiber: 9 g
- Protein: 19 g
- Sodium: 1295 mg

245. Very Veggie Soup

""I came up with the recipe of this soup when trying to make a healthier diet for my family. It contains lots of vegetables and is super tasty."
Serving: 6 servings (2 quarts). | Prep: 20m | Ready in: 55m

Ingredients

- 1 medium zucchini, chopped
- 1-1/3 cups chopped fresh mushrooms
- 1 small onion, chopped
- 1 tsp. canola oil
- 4 garlic cloves, minced
- 1 carton (32 oz.) reduced-sodium chicken broth
- 2 cans (14-1/2 oz. each) diced tomatoes with basil, oregano and garlic, undrained
- 1 package (16 oz.) frozen chopped broccoli, thawed
- 2 medium carrots, shredded
- 1 cup meatless spaghetti sauce
- 1 tsp. Italian seasoning
- 1 tsp. adobo seasoning
- 1 package (10 oz.) frozen chopped spinach, thawed and squeezed dry
- Parmesan cheese

Direction

- Sauté onion, mushrooms, and zucchini in oil in a Dutch oven until softened. Add garlic; cook for 1 minute longer. Add seasonings, spaghetti sauce, carrots, broccoli, tomatoes, and broth. Bring to a boil. Lower heat; simmer, covered until vegetables are tender, or for 10 to 15 minutes. Mix in spinach; cook through, top each portion with cheese.

Nutrition Information

- Calories: 134 calories
- Total Carbohydrate: 24 g
- Cholesterol: 0 mg
- Total Fat: 2 g
- Fiber: 7 g
- Protein: 10 g
- Sodium: 1527 mg

246. Zesty Chicken Soup

"A healthy soup from lots of vegetables and chicken."
Serving: 10 servings (3-3/4 quarts). | Prep: 25m | Ready in: 01h05m

Ingredients

- 1-1/4 lbs. boneless skinless chicken breasts
- 4 cups water
- 1 tbsp. canola oil
- 1 medium onion, chopped
- 2 celery ribs, chopped
- 4 garlic cloves, minced
- 1 can (14-1/2 oz.) Mexican diced tomatoes
- 1 can (14-1/2 oz.) diced tomatoes
- 1 can (8 oz.) tomato sauce
- 1 cup medium salsa
- 3 medium zucchini, halved and sliced
- 2 medium carrots, sliced
- 1 cup frozen white corn
- 1 can (4 oz.) chopped green chilies
- 3 tsps. ground cumin
- 2 tsps. chili powder
- 1 tsp. dried basil
- Shredded cheddar cheese and tortilla chips, optional

Direction

- In a Dutch oven, put chicken and pour in water. Heat to a boil then lower heat. Allow to simmer 10-15 minutes with cover, or until chicken juices run clear. Take chicken out, chop into 1/2-inch cubes; put aside.

- Heat oil in a big skillet over medium-high heat. Put in garlic, celery, and onion; stir and cook until tender.
- Put into cooking juices in the Dutch oven. Mix in basil, chili powder, cumin, chilies, corn, carrots, zucchini, salsa, tomato sauce, and tomatoes; heat to a boil. Lower the heat, simmer with cover until vegetables are tender, or about 20-25 minutes. Add in chicken and heat through.
- Serve with tortilla chips and cheese if wished. Frozen soup can be kept for up to 3 months in the fridge.

Nutrition Information

- Calories: 152 calories
- Total Carbohydrate: 16 g
- Cholesterol: 31 mg
- Total Fat: 3 g
- Fiber: 5 g
- Protein: 14 g
- Sodium: 518 mg

247. Zesty Turkey Tomato Soup

"You can leave off the jalapeno pepper in this chunky soup if you don't want too much heat. You can also make it vegetarian by adding in a small can of garbanzos near the end of cooking instead of using turkey."
Serving: 3 cups. | Prep: 15m | Ready in: 30m

Ingredients

- 1/4 lb. lean ground turkey
- 1 small zucchini, diced
- 1 small onion, chopped
- 1 can (14-1/2 oz.) reduced-sodium chicken broth
- 1 cup canned Mexican diced tomatoes
- 1/3 cup uncooked whole wheat spiral pasta
- 1/2 tsp. minced fresh basil
- 1/4 tsp. ground cumin
- 1/8 tsp. pepper
- 1 tbsp. chopped jalapeno pepper, optional
- Shredded fat-free cheddar cheese, optional

Direction

- Cook onion, zucchini, and turkey in a big saucepan on medium heat until the turkey is no longer pink, then drain.
- Stir in jalapeno (if desired), pepper, cumin, basil, pasta, tomatoes, and broth, then allow to boil. Lower the heat and simmer while uncovered for 13 - 15 minutes or until the pasta becomes tender. You can garnish the soup with cheese if you want.

Nutrition Information

- Calories: 143 calories
- Total Carbohydrate: 17 g
- Cholesterol: 30 mg
- Total Fat: 4 g
- Fiber: 3 g
- Protein: 11 g
- Sodium: 719 mg

248. Zippy Vegetarian Chili

"I like serving this with flour tortillas or cornbread. An affordable and tasty dish."
Serving: 12 servings (about 3 quarts). | Prep: 10m | Ready in: 40m

Ingredients

- 2 cans (15 oz. each) pinto beans, rinsed and drained
- 1 can (28 oz.) crushed tomatoes
- 1 can (16 oz.) kidney beans, rinsed and drained
- 1 can (15-1/2 oz.) hominy, rinsed and drained
- 1 can (15 oz.) garbanzo beans or chickpeas, rinsed and drained
- 1 can (6 oz.) tomato paste
- 1 can (4 oz.) chopped green chilies, undrained
- 2 small zucchini, halved and thinly sliced
- 1 medium onion, chopped
- 1-1/2 to 2 cups water
- 1 to 2 tbsps. chili powder
- 1 tsp. ground cumin
- 1 tsp. salt, optional

- 1/2 tsp. garlic powder
- 1/2 tsp. sugar
- 1/2 cup shredded Monterey Jack cheese

Direction

- Mix the first 15 ingredients in a Dutch oven; boil. Lower heat and simmer, covered, until veggies are tender for 30-35 minutes. Top with cheese.

Nutrition Information

- Calories: 210 calories
- Total Carbohydrate: 37 g
- Cholesterol: 4 mg
- Total Fat: 3 g
- Fiber: 9 g
- Protein: 11 g
- Sodium: 524 mg

249. Zucchini Beef Soup

"This soup and the broth is delicious."
Serving: 8 servings (2 quarts). | Prep: 20m | Ready in: 02h35m

Ingredients

- 1 lb. beef stew meat, cut into 1-inch cubes
- 1 tbsp. canola oil
- 6 cups water
- 1 can (8 oz.) tomato sauce
- 1 medium onion, chopped
- 1-1/2 tsps. salt
- 3/4 tsp. dried oregano
- 1/4 tsp. pepper
- 2 cups thinly sliced zucchini
- 1 cup broken uncooked spaghetti

Direction

- Brown beef in oil in a Dutch oven; let drain. Next, add pepper, oregano, salt, onion, tomato sauce, and water. Bring to a boil, then reduce the heat; cover and simmer for 2 hours. Add spaghetti and zucchini; bring back to a boil.

Put a lid on and cook until the zucchini and spaghetti are softened, about 15-18 minutes more.

Nutrition Information

- Calories: 155 calories
- Total Carbohydrate: 12 g
- Cholesterol: 35 mg
- Total Fat: 6 g
- Fiber: 1 g
- Protein: 13 g
- Sodium: 598 mg

250. Zucchini Bisque

"A light and nice soup."
Serving: 4-5 servings (5 cups). | Prep: 5m | Ready in: 30m

Ingredients

- 1 medium onion, diced
- 1/2 cup butter, cubed
- 2-1/2 cups shredded zucchini
- 2-1/2 cups chicken broth
- 1/2 tsp. dried basil
- 1/2 tsp. salt
- 1/2 tsp. pepper
- 1/4 tsp. ground nutmeg
- 1 cup half-and-half cream

Direction

- Sauté onion in butter in a big saucepan. Add chicken broth and zucchini; simmer for 15 minutes, covered. Add seasonings.
- In a blender, puree on low. Put in pan; mix cream in. Heat through.

Nutrition Information

- Calories: 318 calories
- Total Carbohydrate: 9 g
- Cholesterol: 91 mg
- Total Fat: 29 g
- Fiber: 2 g

- Protein: 5 g
- Sodium: 1141 mg

251. Zucchini Garden Chowder

"Zucchini is the special ingredients in this soup."
Serving: 8-10 servings (about 2-1/2 quarts). | Prep: 10m |
Ready in: 30m

Ingredients

- 2 medium zucchini, chopped
- 1 medium onion, chopped
- 2 tbsps. minced fresh parsley
- 1 tsp. dried basil
- 1/3 cup butter, cubed
- 1/3 cup all-purpose flour
- 1 tsp. salt
- 1/4 tsp. pepper
- 3 cups water
- 3 tsps. chicken bouillon granules
- 1 tsp. lemon juice
- 1 can (14-1/2 oz.) diced tomatoes, undrained
- 1 can (12 oz.) evaporated milk
- 1 package (10 oz.) frozen corn
- 1/4 cup grated Parmesan cheese
- 2 cups shredded cheddar cheese
- Pinch sugar, optional
- Additional minced fresh parsley, optional

Direction

- In a Dutch oven, in butter, sauté basil, parsley, onion, and zucchini till vegetables are tender. Mix in pepper, salt, and flour. Slowly blend in water. Put in lemon juice and bouillon; heat to a boil. Stir and cook until thick, about 2 minutes.
- Add in corn, milk, and tomatoes; heat to a boil. Lower the heat, simmer with cover until corn is tender, about 5 minutes.
- Add cheeses just before serving; mix until cheeses melt. Mix in sugar. If wished, sprinkle parsley over top.

Nutrition Information

- Calories: 258 calories
- Total Carbohydrate: 18 g
- Cholesterol: 55 mg
- Total Fat: 16 g
- Fiber: 2 g
- Protein: 11 g
- Sodium: 905 mg

252. Zucchini Sausage Soup

"This warm soup will satisfy you during winter season. You can enjoy leftovers because this recipe makes a lot."
Serving: 11 servings (2-3/4 quarts). | Prep: 15m | Ready in: 30m

Ingredients

- 1 lb. Johnsonville® Ground Mild Italian sausage
- 2/3 cup chopped onion
- 5 cups water
- 2 medium zucchini, sliced
- 1 can (14-1/2 oz.) diced tomatoes, undrained
- 1 jar (14 oz.) pizza sauce
- 3/4 cup uncooked orzo pasta
- 1 envelope au jus gravy mix
- 1 tbsp. dried basil
- 2 tsps. dried oregano

Direction

- Over medium heat, cook onion and sausage in a Dutch oven until sausage is not pink anymore. Let it drain. Mix in the rest of the ingredients and boil. Lower the heat. Put cover and let it simmer until pasta becomes tender, about 10-15 minutes.

Nutrition Information

- Calories: 233 calories
- Total Carbohydrate: 18 g
- Cholesterol: 31 mg
- Total Fat: 14 g
- Fiber: 2 g

- Protein: 9 g
- Sodium: 675 mg

253. Zucchini Soup

"A gluten-free, dairy-free and nightshade free zucchini soup."
Serving: 4 | Prep: 10m | Ready in: 40m

Ingredients

- 21 oz. zucchini, sliced
- 2 onions, chopped
- 2 cloves garlic, crushed
- 3 cups water, divided
- salt to taste
- 1 bunch chives, chopped

Direction

- In a nonstick skillet, mix together the 2 tbsp. water, garlic, onions and zucchini over medium heat. Let it cook for 5-10 minutes, until the zucchini becomes soft, then add leftover water and boil. Lower the heat and let it simmer for 5 minutes. Take it out of the heat and allow it to cool.
- Pour the zucchini mixture into a food processor not more than halfway full. Put cover and pulse several times prior to leaving on to blend. Puree in batches until it has a smooth consistency. Sprinkle salt on soup to season and put chives on top to garnish.

Nutrition Information

- Calories: 56 calories;
- Total Carbohydrate: 11.8 g
- Cholesterol: 0 mg
- Total Fat: 0.5 g
- Protein: 3.4 g
- Sodium: 62 mg

254. Zucchini Tomato Soup

"A simple with fresh taste. It is low in calories so I love to have it for lunch, with a roll and fruit."
Serving: 2 servings. | Prep: 10m | Ready in: 20m

Ingredients

- 2 small zucchini, coarsely chopped
- 1/4 cup chopped red onion
- 1-1/2 tsps. olive oil
- 1/8 tsp. salt
- 1 cup spicy hot V8 juice
- 1 small tomato, cut into thin wedges
- Dash each pepper and dried basil
- 2 tbsps. shredded cheddar cheese, optional
- 1 to 2 tbsps. crumbled cooked bacon, optional

Direction

- Add onion and zucchini into a big skillet, sauté in oil until crisp tender. Scatter salt over, Add the basil, pepper, tomato and V8 juice; cook until heated through. Scatter bacon and cheese if preferred.

Nutrition Information

- Calories: 89 calories
- Total Carbohydrate: 12 g
- Cholesterol: 0 mg
- Total Fat: 4 g
- Fiber: 3 g
- Protein: 3 g
- Sodium: 545 mg

255. Zucchini/potato Soup

"This zucchini soup with potato and eggs is so amazing."
Serving: about 2 quarts. | Prep: 15m | Ready in: 30m

Ingredients

- 5 cups chicken broth
- 4 small zucchini (about 1 lb.), thinly sliced
- 1 large potato, peeled, halved and thinly sliced
- 1 large onion, thinly sliced

- 3 large eggs
- 2 tbsps. lemon juice
- 2 tsps. dill weed
- Salt and pepper to taste

Direction

- Boil the broth in the saucepan. Mix in onion, potato and zucchini. Lower the heat. Keep it covered and let simmer till veggies become soft, about 15 minutes.
- Whip the eggs in the small-sized bowl; blend in half cup of hot broth and lemon juice. Bring back to saucepan. Heat over medium heat for 60 seconds, mixing continuously, but don't boil. Mix in pepper, salt and dill.

Nutrition Information

- Calories: 91 calories
- Total Carbohydrate: 13 g
- Cholesterol: 80 mg
- Total Fat: 2 g
- Fiber: 2 g
- Protein: 6 g
- Sodium: 611 mg

Chapter 5: Zucchini Bread Recipes

***

256. A-to-z Bread

"Whatever you have on hand, this recipe will be fantastic in the bread."
Serving: 2 loaves. | Prep: 15m | Ready in: 01h15m

Ingredients

- 1-1/2 cups sugar
- 1 cup canola oil
- 3 eggs, lightly beaten
- 2 cups A to Z ingredients (choose from list below)
- 1 tbsp. vanilla extract
- 3 cups all-purpose flour
- 2 tsps. ground cinnamon
- 2 tsps. baking powder
- 1 tsp. baking soda
- 1 tsp. salt
- 1 cup chopped walnuts
- A to Z INGREDIENTS:
- Apples, peeled and shredded
- Applesauce
- Apricots (dried), chopped
- Bananas (ripe), mashed
- Carrots, shredded
- Sweetened shredded coconut
- Dates, pitted and chopped
- Figs (dried), chopped
- Grapes (seedless), chopped
- Oranges, peeled and chopped
- Peaches, peeled and chopped
- Pears, peeled and chopped
- Pineapple (canned), crushed and drained
- Dried plums, pitted and chopped
- Pumpkin, canned
- Raisins
- Raspberries, unsweetened fresh or frozen
- Rhubarb, chopped fresh or frozen
- Strawberries, fresh or frozen
- Sweet potatoes, cooked and mashed
- Zucchini, peeled and grated

Direction

- Mix eggs, oil and sugar together in a bowl. Mix in ingredients of your choice from A to Z and vanilla. Mix together baking soda, salt, cinnamon, baking powder and flour. Mix into the liquid ingredients until it becomes moist then put the nuts in. Put the final mixture into 2 loaf pans that are 8x4 inches in size.
- Bake at 350 degrees until the toothpick comes out clean when inserted in the middle, about 50 to 55 minutes. Before transferring it from

pans to the wire racks, let it cool for 10 minutes.

257. Apple Zucchini Bread

"Apples and zucchini are used together in this recipe."
Serving: 3 loaves (16 slices each). | Prep: 15m | Ready in: 01h05m

Ingredients

- 4 cups all-purpose flour
- 1 tbsp. baking soda
- 1-1/2 tsps. ground cinnamon
- 1/2 tsp. ground nutmeg
- 1/4 tsp. salt
- 5 large eggs
- 1-1/2 cups vegetable oil
- 2 cups sugar
- 1 cup packed brown sugar
- 1 tbsp. vanilla extract
- 2 cups shredded unpeeled zucchini
- 1 cup shredded peeled apples
- 1-1/2 cups chopped pecans

Direction

- Mix salt, nutmeg, cinnamon, baking soda and flour in a big bowl. Beat eggs in a separate bowl. Put in vanilla, sugars and oil then pour the mixture on the dry ingredients. Combine well. Mix in pecans, apples and zucchini (the batter would be stiff) then spoon into 3 loaf pans that are 8x4 inches in size with grease. Bake it at 350 degrees until done, about 50 to 55 minutes. Let it cool for 10 minutes in the pans before letting it completely cool by transferring it to a wire rack.

Nutrition Information

- Calories: 185 calories
- Total Carbohydrate: 22 g
- Cholesterol: 22 mg
- Total Fat: 10 g
- Fiber: 1 g
- Protein: 2 g

- Sodium: 100 mg

258. Apple Zucchini Loaf

"This recipe is best if you want to make bread for dinner or to have with coffee."
Serving: 1 loaf (12 slices). | Prep: 15m | Ready in: 01h05m

Ingredients

- 1-1/2 cups all-purpose flour
- 1 cup sugar
- 1 tsp. ground cinnamon
- 1/2 tsp. baking soda
- 1/4 tsp. baking powder
- 1/4 tsp. salt
- 1 jar (4-1/2 oz.) diced apple baby food
- 1 large egg
- 1 tbsp. canola oil
- 1 cup finely shredded zucchini
- TOPPING:
- 1/4 cup quick-cooking oats
- 1/4 cup sweetened shredded coconut
- 1/4 cup packed brown sugar
- 2 tbsps. butter, melted
- Dash ground cinnamon

Direction

- Mix the salt, baking powder, sugar, baking soda, cinnamon and flour in a big bowl. Drain the apples and save the juice. Whisk the reserved juice, oil and egg in a separate bowl. Mix into the dry ingredients until combined. Fold in apples and zucchini until they become moist.
- In a loaf pan coated with cooking spray that is 8x4 inches in size, pour the mixture. Mix topping ingredients and sprinkle on top. Bake at 350 degrees until toothpick comes out clean when inserted in the middle, about 50 to 55 minutes. Allow to cool for 10 mins before transferring from the pan to a wire rack.

Nutrition Information

- Calories: 193 calories
- Total Carbohydrate: 37 g
- Cholesterol: 23 mg
- Total Fat: 4 g
- Fiber: 1 g
- Protein: 3 g
- Sodium: 139 mg

Nutrition Information

- Calories: 115 calories
- Total Carbohydrate: 11 g
- Cholesterol: 18 mg
- Total Fat: 7 g
- Fiber: 0 g
- Protein: 3 g
- Sodium: 162 mg

259. Baby Basil-zucchini Muffins

"Make the most of the basil and zucchini with these delicious treats."
Serving: about 4-1/2 dozen. | Prep: 20m | Ready in: 35m

Ingredients

- 2-1/2 cups all-purpose flour
- 1/4 cup sugar
- 3 tbsps. minced fresh basil or 1 tbsp. dried basil
- 1 tsp. baking powder
- 1 tsp. salt
- 1/2 tsp. baking soda
- 2 eggs
- 3/4 cup milk
- 2/3 cup vegetable oil
- 2 cups finely shredded peeled zucchini, squeezed dry
- 1/2 cup grated Parmesan cheese

Direction

- Mix baking powder, basil, baking soda, sugar, salt and flour in a big bowl. Beat the oil, milk and eggs then mix into the dry ingredients until it becomes moist. Fold the zucchini in.
- In paper-lined miniature or greased muffin cups, fill 2/3 full. Use cheese to sprinkle, then bake at 400 degrees until the toothpick comes out clean when inserted in the middle, about 12 to 15 minutes. Allow to cool for 5 minutes. Move from the pans to wire racks. Serve while warm.

260. Baked Zucchini Squares

"This zucchini bake loaded with cheese and veggies, is a perfect side dish with any meal."
Serving: 16 | Prep: 15m | Ready in: 55m

Ingredients

- 1 cup biscuit baking mix
- 1/2 cup grated Parmesan cheese
- 1/2 cup shredded mozzarella cheese
- 1 tbsp. minced fresh parsley
- 1 1/2 tsps. dried oregano
- 1 1/2 tsps. dried basil
- 1/2 tsp. salt
- 4 eggs
- 1/2 cup vegetable oil
- 1 small onion, chopped
- 3 zucchini, grated
- 1/2 cup chopped pepperoni

Direction

- Preheat the oven to 175°C or 350°F. Grease a 9x13-inch baking dish lightly.
- In a bowl, mix salt, basil, oregano, parsley, mozzarella cheese, Parmesan cheese and biscuit mix. In a bowl, combine onion, oil and eggs. Mix biscuit mixture into egg mixture till just incorporated; fold in pepperoni and zucchini. Put onto baking dish.
- In prepped oven, bake for 30 to 35 minutes till set and golden brown. Allow to slightly cool and slice into squares.

Nutrition Information

- Calories: 172 calories;
- Total Carbohydrate: 6.7 g
- Cholesterol: 58 mg
- Total Fat: 13.7 g
- Protein: 6.1 g
- Sodium: 366 mg

261. Banana-zucchini Bread

"You'll get a hint of the flavors of this combination in each bite."
Serving: 20 | Prep: 15m | Ready in: 1h5m

Ingredients

- 3 eggs
- 3/4 cup vegetable oil
- 2/3 cup packed brown sugar
- 1 cup white sugar
- 1 cup grated zucchini
- 2 bananas, mashed
- 2 tsps. vanilla extract
- 3 1/2 cups all-purpose flour
- 1 tbsp. ground cinnamon
- 1 1/2 tsps. baking powder
- 1 tsp. baking soda
- 1 tsp. salt
- 1/2 cup dried cranberries
- 1/2 cup chopped walnuts

Direction

- Preheat oven to 165 °C or 325 °F. Grease and flour 2 bread loaf pans that are 8x4 inches in size.
- Beat eggs until frothy and lightly yellow in a big bowl. Put in vanilla, bananas, grated zucchini, white sugar, brown sugar and oil. Mix together until blended well. Mix in baking soda, salt, cinnamon, baking powder and flour. Put in the nuts and cranberries. Evenly distribute the batter between the 2 loaf pans that were prepared.

- Bake in the prepared oven for about 50 minutes, or until the toothpick comes out clean when inserted in the middle. Before removing and serving, let it cool in the loaf pans on wire rack.

Nutrition Information

- Calories: 272 calories;
- Total Carbohydrate: 40.2 g
- Cholesterol: 28 mg
- Total Fat: 11.1 g
- Protein: 3.9 g
- Sodium: 230 mg

262. Carrot Zucchini Bread

"A moist bread, excellent for brunch."
Serving: 24 | Prep: 30m | Ready in: 2h30m

Ingredients

- 3 1/2 cups all-purpose flour
- 1 tbsp. baking powder
- 1 tsp. baking soda
- 1/2 tsp. salt
- 1 tsp. ground cinnamon
- 2 eggs, lightly beaten
- 1 1/2 cups buttermilk
- 2 tbsps. butter, melted
- 1/2 cup packed brown sugar
- 1 cup shredded zucchini
- 1 cup shredded carrot
- orange, zested
- lemon, zested
- 1/2 cup chopped walnuts

Direction

- Preheat the oven to 175°C or 350°F. Grease 2 loaf pans 9x5-inch in size. Sift together the cinnamon, salt, baking soda, baking powder and flour; reserve.
- In a mixing bowl, mix the melted butter, buttermilk and eggs. Mix in brown sugar. Put

in orange and lemon zests, carrots and zucchini.

- Mix dry ingredients into wet ingredients and mix softly till just incorporated. Fold in walnuts.
- Into prepped loaf pans, put the batter. Bake at 175°C or 350°F for 60 to 75 minutes till a toothpick pricked into the middle of the loaf comes out clean. Allow the loaf to cool in the pan for 10 minutes prior to taking out to a wire rack to cool fully.

Nutrition Information

- Calories: 125 calories;
- Total Carbohydrate: 20.6 g
- Cholesterol: 19 mg
- Total Fat: 3.3 g
- Protein: 3.4 g
- Sodium: 197 mg

263. Carrot Zucchini Fritters

"An entertaining dish even with or without dipping sauces."
Serving: 1-1/2 dozen fritters, 2/3 cup basil sauce and 1-1/2 cups horseradish sauce. | Prep: 20m | Ready in: 25m

Ingredients

- 2/3 cup plus 1/2 cup sour cream, divided
- 2/3 cup lightly packed fresh basil leaves
- 1 tsp. lemon juice
- Salt and pepper to taste
- 1/2 cup mayonnaise
- 1/2 cup horseradish sauce
- FRITTERS:
- 2 tbsps. finely chopped onion
- 1 tbsp. butter
- 1 egg, lightly beaten
- 2 medium zucchini, shredded and squeezed dry (about 1-1/2 cups)
- 1 large carrot, shredded
- 1/3 cup all-purpose flour
- 1/3 cup grated Parmesan cheese
- 1 tbsp. cornmeal

- 1/2 tsp. salt
- 1/8 tsp. pepper
- Oil for frying

Direction

- Put pepper, salt, lemon juice, basil, and 2/3 cup of sour cream in a blender; put a cover and pulse until combined. Place into a small bowl. Mix the rest of sour cream, horseradish sauce, and mayonnaise in a different bowl. Put a cover and store both sauces in the fridge.
- In a microwave-safe dish, put butter and onion. Put a cover and microwave on high until the onion becomes tender. Add carrot, zucchini, and egg. Mix pepper, salt, cornmeal, cheese, and flour in small bowl; add in the vegetable mixture until just blended.
- Heat 2 inches of oil in an electric skillet to 375 degrees. Drop rounded tablespoonfuls of batter into the hot oil, several each time. Fry for 1 1/2 minutes per side until golden brown. Place onto paper towels to drain.

264. Carrot Zucchini Muffins

"Luscious moist muffins loaded with raisins, nuts, and zucchini to serve as amazing snacks as well as dessert with cream cheese frosting."
Serving: about 16 muffins. | Prep: 10m | Ready in: 35m

Ingredients

- 1 package carrot cake mix (regular size)
- 1/2 cup applesauce
- 1/4 cup vegetable oil
- 1 egg
- 1-1/2 cups shredded zucchini
- 1/2 cup raisins
- 1/2 cup chopped pecans

Direction

- Mix egg, oil, applesauce, and cake mix in a large bowl for half a minute; whisk for half a minute at low speed. Whisk for 2 minutes at medium speed. Stir in pecans, raisins, and zucchini.

- Add into paper-lined or greased muffin cups to 3/4 full. Bake at 350 degrees until a toothpick comes out clean, for 25-30 minutes. Let cool for 10 minutes, then transfer from the pan onto a wire rack to cool entirely.

Nutrition Information

- Calories: 214 calories
- Total Carbohydrate: 31 g
- Cholesterol: 13 mg
- Total Fat: 9 g
- Fiber: 1 g
- Protein: 3 g
- Sodium: 208 mg

265. Cheddar Zucchini Wedges

"An appealing and savory round bread with a mixture of toasted almonds, cheddar cheese, tender zucchini, and biscuit mix."
Serving: 6-8 servings. | Prep: 20m | Ready in: 45m

Ingredients

- 1 medium onion, chopped
- 1/4 cup butter, cubed
- 2-1/2 cups biscuit/baking mix
- 1 tbsp. minced fresh parsley
- 1/2 tsp. dried basil
- 1/2 tsp. dried thyme
- 3 large eggs, lightly beaten
- 1/4 cup 2% milk
- 1-1/2 cups shredded zucchini
- 1 cup shredded cheddar cheese
- 3/4 cup chopped almonds, toasted

Direction

- Sauté onion in butter in a large skillet until it is tender. Mix the onion mixture, thyme, basil, parsley, and biscuit mix in a large bowl. Stir in milk and eggs until just mixed. Fold in almonds, cheese, and zucchini.

- Place into a 9-inch greased round baking pan. Bake at 400 degrees until a toothpick comes out clean when inserted into the center, for 25-30 minutes. Before slicing into wedges, let cool for a minute. Transfer onto a wire rack and cool.

Nutrition Information

- Calories: 368 calories
- Total Carbohydrate: 29 g
- Cholesterol: 111 mg
- Total Fat: 24 g
- Fiber: 3 g
- Protein: 11 g
- Sodium: 644 mg

266. Chocolate Chip Zucchini Bread

"You will love this recipe too."
Serving: 16 | Prep: 20m | Ready in: 1h50m

Ingredients

- 3 eggs
- 1 cup vegetable oil
- 2 cups white sugar
- 1 tbsp. vanilla extract
- 3 cups grated zucchini
- 3 cups all-purpose flour
- 3 tbsps. unsweetened cocoa powder
- 1 tsp. salt
- 1 tsp. baking soda
- 1/4 tsp. baking powder
- 1/2 cup chopped walnuts
- 1/2 cup chocolate chips

Direction

- Preheat oven at 165 °C or 325 °F.
- Grease and flour 2 loaf pans that are 4x8 inches in size.
- In a big bowl, beat eggs until foamy and light. Combine zucchini, vanilla extract, sugar and vegetable oil until blended thoroughly.

- In another bowl, whisk the baking powder, cocoa powder, baking soda, salt and flour together.
- Mix the flour mixture into the zucchini mixture.
- Mix in chocolate chips and chopped walnuts.
- In the prepared loaf pans, pour the batter.
- In the preheated oven, bake for about an hour until toothpick comes out clean when inserted in the middle.
- Let it cool for 10 mins in pans. Move to wire racks to complete cooking.

Nutrition Information

- Calories: 374 calories;
- Total Carbohydrate: 48.2 g
- Cholesterol: 35 mg
- Total Fat: 19.1 g
- Protein: 4.9 g
- Sodium: 248 mg

267. Chocolate Zucchini Bread

"There is a new take on your favorite veggie dessert with this dairy-free, chocolatey and rich zucchini bread."
Serving: 16 | Ready in: 1h45m

Ingredients

- ½ cup chopped walnuts, (1¾ oz.)
- 1 cup all-purpose flour
- 1 cup whole-wheat flour
- ¼ cup unsweetened cocoa, preferably Dutch-process
- ½ tsp. baking powder
- ½ tsp. baking soda
- ½ tsp. salt
- 3 large eggs, lightly beaten
- 1½ cups sugar
- ¾ cup unsweetened applesauce
- ¼ cup canola oil
- 1 tsp. vanilla extract
- 1 oz. unsweetened chocolate, melted
- 2 cups grated zucchini, (1 medium)

Direction

- Preheat oven at 325 °F. Use cooking spray to coat 2 loaf pans that are 8 1/2x4 1/2 inches in size.
- In a pie pan, spread walnuts then bake for 5 till 7 minutes until fragrant. To cool, set it aside.
- In a big bowl, whisk baking soda, cocoa, baking powder, whole wheat flour, salt and all-purpose flour.
- In a separate big bowl, whisk melted chocolate, vanilla, oil, applesauce, sugar and eggs until combined. Put mixture in the dry ingredients then mix until combined using a rubber spatula. Fold in the reserved walnuts and zucchini. Spoon the batter into the prepared pans and smooth the tops.
- Bake the loaves until skewer comes out clean when inserted in the middle and the tops are golden, about 55 to 60 mins. Allow to cool for 10 mins in pans on a wire rack. Cool completely by inverting onto rack.

Nutrition Information

- Calories: 249 calories;
- Total Carbohydrate: 43 g
- Cholesterol: 35 mg
- Total Fat: 8 g
- Fiber: 2 g
- Protein: 5 g
- Sodium: 142 mg
- Sugar: 24 g
- Saturated Fat: 1 g

268. Chocolate Zucchini Loaf

"Add in grated zucchini into this no-fuss loaf."
Serving: 1 loaf (12 slices). | Prep: 15m | Ready in: 01h15m

Ingredients

- 1/2 cup butter, softened
- 1 cup sugar

- 2 large eggs
- 1 tsp. vanilla extract
- 1-1/2 cups all-purpose flour
- 3 tbsps. baking cocoa
- 1/2 tsp. salt
- 1/2 tsp. baking soda
- 1/2 tsp. ground cinnamon
- 1 cup grated unpeeled zucchini
- 1/2 cup semisweet chocolate chips

Direction

- Cream the sugar and butter in a big bowl till fluffy and light. Whisk in vanilla and eggs. Mix the cinnamon, baking soda, salt, cocoa and flour; slowly put into creamed mixture just till moistened. Fold in the chocolate chips and zucchini.
- Scoop into a greased 8x4-inch loaf pan. Let bake at 350° for 60 to 70 minutes till a toothpick pricked in the middle comes out clean. Allow to cool for 10 minutes prior to taking out from pan to a wire rack.

Nutrition Information

- Calories: 180 calories
- Total Carbohydrate: 26 g
- Cholesterol: 42 mg
- Total Fat: 8 g
- Fiber: 1 g
- Protein: 3 g
- Sodium: 180 mg

269. Chocolaty Zucchini Bread

"The secret ingredient to this bread is zucchini."
Serving: 3 loaves (16 slices each). | Prep: 15m | Ready in: 01h10m

Ingredients

- 3 cups all-purpose flour
- 3 cups sugar
- 1/2 cup baking cocoa
- 1-1/2 tsps. baking powder

- 1-1/2 tsps. baking soda
- 1 tsp. salt
- 1/4 tsp. ground cinnamon
- 4 eggs
- 1-1/2 cups canola oil
- 2 tbsps. butter, melted
- 1-1/2 tsps. vanilla extract
- 1-1/2 tsps. almond extract
- 3 cups grated zucchini
- 1 cup chopped pecans
- 1/2 cup raisins

Direction

- Mix the first 7 ingredients in a big bowl. Whisk the extracts, butter, oil and eggs. Mix into the dry ingredients until it becomes moist. Fold in raisins, pecans and zucchini then put it into 3 loaf pans that are 8x4 inches in size with grease and flour.
- Bake at 350 degrees until the toothpick comes out clean when inserted in the middle, about 55 to 60 minutes. Let it cool for 10 minutes and transfer from the pans to wire racks.

Nutrition Information

- Calories: 174 calories
- Total Carbohydrate: 21 g
- Cholesterol: 19 mg
- Total Fat: 10 g
- Fiber: 1 g
- Protein: 2 g
- Sodium: 112 mg

270. Cinnamon Zucchini Bread

"This recipe of zucchini bread was lightened."
Serving: 1 loaf (12 slices). | Prep: 25m | Ready in: 01h15m

Ingredients

- 3/4 cup sugar
- 1/4 cup unsweetened applesauce
- 1/4 cup canola oil

- 2 egg whites
- 1 tsp. vanilla extract
- 1-1/2 cups all-purpose flour
- 1-1/2 tsps. ground cinnamon
- 1 tsp. baking powder
- 1/2 tsp. salt
- 1/2 tsp. ground nutmeg
- 1/4 tsp. baking soda
- 1-1/4 cups shredded peeled zucchini
- 1/2 cup raisins

Direction

- Beat vanilla, egg whites, oil, applesauce and sugar until mixed well in a small bowl. Combine baking soda, nutmeg, salt, baking powder, cinnamon and flour then beat gradually into the sugar mixture. Fold in raisins and zucchini.
- Put into an 8x4-inch loaf pan that is coated with cooking spray. At 350 degrees, bake it until a toothpick comes out clean when inserted in the middle or for 50 to 60mins. Allow to cool for 10mins. Move to wire rack from the pan to completely cool.

Nutrition Information

- Calories: 174 calories
- Total Carbohydrate: 31 g
- Cholesterol: 0 mg
- Total Fat: 5 g
- Fiber: 1 g
- Protein: 3 g
- Sodium: 170 mg

271. Cranberry Zucchini Bread

"Nutmeg and cinnamon and green zucchini and red cranberries add spice and give each slice a festive look."
Serving: 2 loaves. | Prep: 15m | Ready in: 01h15m

Ingredients

- 3 cups all-purpose flour
- 2 cups sugar

- 2-1/2 tsps. ground cinnamon
- 1-1/4 tsps. salt
- 1 tsp. baking soda
- 1/2 tsp. baking powder
- 1/4 tsp. ground nutmeg
- 3 eggs
- 1-1/2 cups shredded zucchini
- 1 cup vegetable oil
- 1 tbsp. vanilla extract
- 1 cup chopped fresh or frozen cranberries
- 1/2 cup chopped walnuts

Direction

- Mix together the first 7 ingredients in a big bowl. Beat eggs in a separate bowl; put in vanilla, oil and zucchini. Mix into dry ingredients just till combined. Fold in the walnuts and cranberries. Put into 2 greased and floured 8x4-inch loaf pans. Bake at 350° for 60 to 65 minutes till a toothpick pricked in the middle comes out clean. Allow to cool for 10 minutes prior to taking out from pans to wire racks.

Nutrition Information

- Calories: 174 calories
- Total Carbohydrate: 23 g
- Cholesterol: 20 mg
- Total Fat: 9 g
- Fiber: 1 g
- Protein: 2 g
- Sodium: 144 mg

272. Daughter's A-to-z Bread

"The version of this bread has a lower sugar and fat."
Serving: 2 loaves (12 slices each). | Prep: 20m | Ready in: 01h10m

Ingredients

- 1 cup sugar
- 1/2 cup canola oil
- 1/2 cup unsweetened applesauce

- 3 eggs
- 2 cups A to Z ingredients (choose from list below)
- 1 tbsp. vanilla extract
- 2 cups all-purpose flour
- 1 cup whole wheat flour
- 2 tsps. ground cinnamon
- 1 tsp. baking powder
- 1 tsp. baking soda
- 1 tsp. salt
- 1 cup chopped walnuts or pecans
- A TO Z INGREDIENTS:
- Peaches, peeled and chopped
- Pears, peeled and chopped
- Pineapple (canned), crushed and drained
- Dried plums, pitted and chopped
- Pumpkin, canned
- Raspberries, fresh or frozen
- Raisins
- Rhubarb, chopped fresh or frozen
- Strawberries, chopped fresh or frozen
- Sweet potatoes, cooked and mashed
- Zucchini, shredded

Direction

- In a big bowl, whisk the eggs, applesauce, oil and sugar. Mix in A to Z ingredients of your choice and vanilla. Mix salt, baking soda, baking powder, cinnamon, all-purpose flour, and whole wheat flour. Mix into liquid ingredients until just moistened. Mix the nuts in. In 2 greased loaf pans that are 8x4 inches in size, put the mixture.
- At 325 degrees, bake until toothpick comes out clean when inserted in the middle or for 50 to 55 minutes. Allow to cool for 10mins. Move to wire racks from pans.

273. Fruited Zucchini Bread

"Green zucchini and red cherries make this moist bread a must for Christmas season."
Serving: 2 loaves. | Prep: 30m | Ready in: 01h25m

Ingredients

- 3 cups all-purpose flour
- 2 cups sugar
- 2 tsps. ground cinnamon
- 1 tsp. salt
- 1 tsp. baking soda
- 1/2 tsp. baking powder
- 3 eggs
- 3/4 cup vegetable oil
- 2 tsps. vanilla extract
- 2 cups shredded zucchini
- 1 can (8 oz.) crushed pineapple, drained
- 1 cup chopped pecans
- 1/2 cup raisins
- 1/2 cup chopped dates
- 1/2 cup chopped maraschino cherries, patted dry

Direction

- Mix the baking powder, baking soda, salt, cinnamon, sugar and flour in a big bowl. Beat the vanilla, oil and eggs in a separate bowl. Mix into dry ingredients till just moistened. Fold in cherries, dates, raisins, pecans, pineapple and zucchini.
- Put into 2 greased loaf pans 9x5-inch in size. Allow to bake at 350° for 55 to 60 minutes till bread pulls away from the sides of pans and a toothpick pricked in the middle comes out with some moist crumbs. Allow to cool for 10 minutes prior to taking off from pans to wire racks to fully cool.

Nutrition Information

- Calories: 196 calories
- Total Carbohydrate: 29 g
- Cholesterol: 20 mg
- Total Fat: 8 g

- Fiber: 1 g
- Protein: 2 g
- Sodium: 128 mg

274. Garden Focaccia

"Delicious flat Italian bread with herb flavor in frozen bread dough base for a tasty appetizer at a summer get-together."
Serving: 20 slices. | Prep: 15m | Ready in: 45m

Ingredients

- 1 loaf (1 lb.) frozen bread dough, thawed
- 1 tbsp. olive oil
- 1 tbsp. minced fresh rosemary or 1 tsp. dried rosemary, crushed
- 1 tbsp. minced fresh thyme or 1 tsp. dried thyme
- 1 package (8 oz.) cream cheese, softened
- 1/4 cup finely chopped onion
- 1 garlic clove, minced
- 4 large fresh mushrooms, sliced
- 3 medium tomatoes, sliced
- 1 small zucchini, thinly sliced
- 1/4 cup grated Parmesan cheese

Direction

- Roll the dough on a lightly floured surface into a 15x10-inch rectangle. Then arrange in a 15x10x1-inch greased baking pan. Put a cover and allow to rise for half an hour.
- Make indentations in the dough with fingertips. Brush oil over; dust with thyme and rosemary. Bake at 400 degrees until golden brown, for 12-15 minutes. Let slightly cool.
- Mix garlic, onion, and cream cheese in a large bowl. Spread on the crust. Place zucchini, tomatoes, and mushrooms on top; dust with Parmesan cheese.
- Bake until brown lightly, for 12-15 minutes. Before slicing, let cool for 5 minutes.

Nutrition Information

- Calories: 109 calories

- Total Carbohydrate: 14 g
- Cholesterol: 7 mg
- Total Fat: 4 g
- Fiber: 1 g
- Protein: 5 g
- Sodium: 185 mg

275. Garden Vegetable Bread

"This moist loaf has a nice flavor and attractive color from green onions, zucchini, and red pepper."
Serving: 1 loaf (16 slices). | Prep: 10m | Ready in: 03h10m

Ingredients

- 1/2 cup warm buttermilk (70° to 80°)
- 3 tbsps. water (70° to 80°)
- 1 tbsp. canola oil
- 2/3 cup shredded zucchini
- 1/4 cup chopped red sweet pepper
- 2 tbsps. chopped green onions
- 2 tbsps. grated Romano or Parmesan cheese
- 2 tbsps. sugar
- 1 tsp. salt
- 1/2 tsp. lemon-pepper seasoning
- 1/2 cup old-fashioned oats
- 2-1/2 cups bread flour
- 1-1/2 tsps. active dry yeast

Direction

- Put all the ingredients into the pan of the bread machine in the order recommended by the manufacturer. Use the basic bread setting. If available select the crust color and loaf size.
- Bake as directed on the bread machine (after five minutes of mixing elapse, check the dough and feel free to add one to two tbsps. of flour or water if necessary).

Nutrition Information

- Calories: 94 calories
- Total Carbohydrate: 18 g
- Cholesterol: 1 mg

- Total Fat: 1 g
- Fiber: 1 g
- Protein: 4 g
- Sodium: 165 mg

276. Grilled Vegetable Cheese Bread

""Enjoy Fourth of July tomatoes with this bread recipe any time of the year.""
Serving: 8 servings. | Prep: 20m | Ready in: 35m

Ingredients

- 1 loaf (1 lb.) French bread, sliced lengthwise
- 1/4 cup olive oil
- 3 large tomatoes, thinly sliced
- 2 cups thinly sliced zucchini
- 1 cup shredded cheddar cheese
- 1 jar (4 oz.) sliced pimientos, drained
- 1 can (4-1/4 oz.) chopped ripe olives, drained
- 2 tsps. Creole seasoning
- 1/4 cup grated Parmesan cheese

Direction

- Cut the side of the bread and brush with oil. Place tomatoes and zucchini in layer then drizzle cheddar cheese, olives, pimientos and Creole seasoning.
- Prepare the grill over indirect heat, place bread on grill rack and grill it covered, over indirect medium heat for about 10 to 12 minutes or until the zucchini is crisp-tender. Add Parmesan cheese on top and cook for another 2 to 4 minutes more or until melted.

Nutrition Information

- Calories: 312 calories
- Total Carbohydrate: 35 g
- Cholesterol: 18 mg
- Total Fat: 15 g
- Fiber: 3 g
- Protein: 10 g
- Sodium: 729 mg

277. Jumbo Zucchini Chip Muffins

"There is a cinnamon flavor in this recipe."
Serving: 1 dozen. | Prep: 30m | Ready in: 60m

Ingredients

- 3 cups all-purpose flour
- 1-1/2 cups sugar
- 3 tsps. ground cinnamon
- 2 tsps. baking powder
- 1 tsp. salt
- 1/2 tsp. baking soda
- 3 large eggs, beaten
- 2/3 cup canola oil
- 3 tsps. vanilla extract
- 2 cups shredded zucchini
- 1 package (11-1/2 oz.) milk chocolate chips
- 1 cup chopped walnuts
- MASCARPONE FROSTING:
- 1/2 cup butter, softened
- 3 oz. cream cheese, softened
- 1/3 cup Mascarpone cheese
- 1/4 cup confectioners' sugar
- 1/2 tsp. vanilla extract
- 1/4 cup finely chopped walnuts

Direction

- Combine the first 6 ingredients in a big bowl. Mix vanilla, oil and eggs in a separate bowl then mix into dry ingredients just until it becomes moist. Fold the walnuts, chips and zucchini in.
- Put 3/4 full into paper-lined jumbo muffin cups. Bake at 350 degrees until toothpick comes out clean when inserted in the middle or for 30 to 35 minutes. Allow to cool for 5mins in the pan. Move from pans to wire racks to completely cool.
- Beat the Mascarpone cheese, cream cheese and butter until fluffy in a big bowl. Put in vanilla and confectioners' sugar then whip until smooth. On each muffin, pipe a dollop of frosting then sprinkle walnuts over.

Nutrition Information

- Calories: 726 calories
- Total Carbohydrate: 71 g
- Cholesterol: 103 mg
- Total Fat: 46 g
- Fiber: 3 g
- Protein: 11 g
- Sodium: 439 mg

278. Lemony Zucchini Bread

"Flecks of zucchini to the popular lemon and poppy seed combination."
Serving: 2 loaves (16 slices each). | Prep: 25m | Ready in: 01h15m

Ingredients

- 4 cups all-purpose flour
- 1-1/2 cups sugar
- 1 package (3.4 oz.) instant lemon pudding mix
- 1-1/2 tsps. baking soda
- 1 tsp. baking powder
- 1 tsp. salt
- 4 eggs
- 1-1/4 cups milk
- 1 cup canola oil
- 3 tbsps. lemon juice
- 1 tsp. lemon extract
- 2 cups shredded zucchini
- 1/4 cup poppy seeds
- 2 tsps. grated lemon peel

Direction

- In a big bowl, mix the salt, baking powder, baking soda, pudding mix, sugar and flour. Mix the oil, milk, eggs, lemon juice and extract in a separate bowl. Into the dry ingredients, mix till just moistened. Fold in lemon peel, poppy seeds and zucchini.
- Put into 2 greased loaf pans 9x5-inch in size. Bake at 350° for 50 to 55 minutes till a toothpick pricked in the middle comes out clean. Allow to cool for 10 minutes prior to

taking out from pans to wire racks to let cool fully.

Nutrition Information

- Calories: 187 calories
- Total Carbohydrate: 25 g
- Cholesterol: 28 mg
- Total Fat: 8 g
- Fiber: 1 g
- Protein: 3 g
- Sodium: 195 mg

279. Makeover Chocolate Zucchini Bread

"Enjoy the makeover of this recipe."
Serving: 2 loaves (12 slices each). | Prep: 15m | Ready in: 55m

Ingredients

- 1-1/4 cups sugar
- 3 eggs
- 2/3 cup unsweetened applesauce
- 1/3 cup canola oil
- 3 tsps. vanilla extract
- 1-1/2 cups all-purpose flour
- 1 cup cake flour
- 1/2 cup baking cocoa
- 1 tsp. salt
- 1 tsp. baking soda
- 1 tsp. ground cinnamon
- 1/4 tsp. baking powder
- 2 cups shredded peeled zucchini

Direction

- Beat vanilla, oil, applesauce, eggs and sugar until well mixed in a big bowl. Combine baking powder, cinnamon, baking soda, salt, cocoa, and flours. Beat it gradually into the sugar mixture until mixed then mix in zucchini. To 2 loaf pans coated with cooking spray that are 8x4 inches in size, transfer the mixture.

- Bake at 350 degrees until toothpick comes out clean when inserted in the middle or for 40 to 45 minutes. Allow to cool for 10mins in pans. Move onto wire racks from pans to completely cool.

Nutrition Information

- Calories: 137 calories
- Total Carbohydrate: 23 g
- Cholesterol: 26 mg
- Total Fat: 4 g
- Fiber: 1 g
- Protein: 3 g
- Sodium: 165 mg

280. Makeover Pineapple Zucchini Bread

"This lightened-up bread has crunchy crust and delectable taste."
Serving: 2 loaves (12 slices each). | Prep: 20m | Ready in: 01h10m

Ingredients

- 1-1/2 cups sugar
- 2/3 cup unsweetened applesauce
- 1/3 cup canola oil
- 2 egg whites
- 1 egg
- 2 tsps. vanilla extract
- 3 cups all-purpose flour
- 2 tsps. ground cinnamon
- 1-1/2 tsps. baking powder
- 1 tsp. salt
- 3/4 tsp. ground nutmeg
- 1/2 tsp. baking soda
- 2 cups shredded zucchini
- 1 can (8 oz.) unsweetened crushed pineapple, drained
- 1/3 cup chopped walnuts

Direction

- Whisk the vanilla, egg, egg whites, oil, applesauce and sugar in a big bowl till blended thoroughly. Mix the baking soda, nutmeg, salt, baking powder, cinnamon and flour; slowly beat into sugar mixture till mixed. Mix in walnuts, pineapple and zucchini.
- Put into two 8x4-inch loaf pans sprayed with cooking spray. Allow to bake at 350° for 50 minutes to an hour till a toothpick pricked in the middle comes out clean. Allow to cool down for 10 minutes prior to taking off from pans to wire racks to fully cool.

Nutrition Information

- Calories: 159 calories
- Total Carbohydrate: 27 g
- Cholesterol: 9 mg
- Total Fat: 5 g
- Fiber: 1 g
- Protein: 3 g
- Sodium: 158 mg

281. Makeover Zucchini Apple Bread

"This Zucchini Apple Bread Flavored with cinnamon and nutmeg."
Serving: 3 loaves (12 slices each). | Prep: 30m | Ready in: 01h25m

Ingredients

- 4 cups all-purpose flour
- 3 tsps. baking soda
- 1-1/2 tsps. ground cinnamon
- 1/2 tsp. ground nutmeg
- 1/4 tsp. salt
- 2 large eggs
- 3/4 cup canola oil
- 1-1/2 cups unsweetened applesauce
- 1 cup sugar
- 1 cup packed brown sugar

- 1 tsp. vanilla extract
- 2 cups shredded zucchini
- 1 cup grated peeled apples
- 1/2 cup chopped pecans

Direction

- Mix the salt, nutmeg, cinnamon, baking soda and flour in a big bowl. Whisk eggs till foamy in a big bowl. Put in the vanilla, sugars, applesauce and oil; whisk till incorporated. Mix into dry ingredients till just moistened. Fold in pecans, apples and zucchini.
- Transfer to three 8x4-inch loaf pans sprayed with cooking spray. Bake at 350° for 55 to 60 minutes till a toothpick pricked in the middle comes out clean. Allow to cool for 10 minutes prior to taking out from pans to wire racks.

Nutrition Information

- Calories: 160 calories
- Total Carbohydrate: 24 g
- Cholesterol: 12 mg
- Total Fat: 6 g
- Fiber: 1 g
- Protein: 2 g
- Sodium: 128 mg

282. Makeover Zucchini Bread

"The makeover of this recipe has a slimmed down nutritional profile and perfect for an afternoon snack."
Serving: 2 loaves (12 slices each). | Prep: 20m | Ready in: 01h05m

Ingredients

- 1-1/2 cups sugar
- 1/2 cup unsweetened applesauce
- 2 eggs
- 1/3 cup canola oil
- 3 tsps. vanilla extract
- 3 cups all-purpose flour
- 2-1/2 tsps. ground cinnamon
- 2 tsps. baking powder

- 1 tsp. salt
- 1/2 tsp. baking soda
- 2 cups shredded zucchini
- 3/4 cup chopped walnuts

Direction

- Beat vanilla, oil, eggs, applesauce and sugar until blended well in a big bowl. Mix baking soda, salt, baking powder, cinnamon and flour then beat gradually into sugar mixture until blended. Stir in walnuts and zucchini.
- Put into 2 loaf pans that are 8x4 inches in size coated with cooking spray. At 350 degrees, bake until toothpick comes out clean when inserted in the middle or for 45 to 55mins. Allow to cool for 10mins. Move to wire racks from pans.

Nutrition Information

- Calories: 168 calories
- Total Carbohydrate: 26 g
- Cholesterol: 18 mg
- Total Fat: 6 g
- Fiber: 1 g
- Protein: 3 g
- Sodium: 165 mg

283. Mini Zucchini Bread

"This recipe has a rich flavor."
Serving: 2 loaves (6 slices each). | Prep: 10m | Ready in: 50m

Ingredients

- 1-1/2 cups all-purpose flour
- 1 tsp. baking powder
- 1/2 tsp. salt
- 1/2 tsp. ground cinnamon
- 1/4 tsp. baking soda
- 2 large eggs
- 1 cup shredded zucchini
- 3/4 cup sugar
- 1/2 cup canola oil

- 1-1/2 tsps. molasses
- 1-1/2 tsps. vanilla extract
- 1/2 cup chopped pecans

Direction

- Mix the baking soda, cinnamon, salt, baking powder and flour in a big bowl. Whisk the vanilla, molasses, oil, sugar, zucchini and eggs in a small bowl. Combine mixture with the dry ingredients until it becomes moist then the fold nuts in.
- In 2 greased and floured loaf pans that are 5x3&3/4x2 inches big, put the mixture. Bake at 350 degrees until the toothpick comes out clean when inserted in the middle, about 38 to 42 minutes. Before transferring from pans to a wire rack, let it cool for 10 minutes.

Nutrition Information

- Calories: 239 calories
- Total Carbohydrate: 26 g
- Cholesterol: 35 mg
- Total Fat: 14 g
- Fiber: 1 g
- Protein: 3 g
- Sodium: 171 mg

284. Mom's A-to-z Bread

"You can put whatever fruit is in season in this recipe and you'll get a tailor-made treat."
Serving: 2 loaves (12 slices each). | Prep: 20m | Ready in: 01h10m

Ingredients

- 1-1/2 cups sugar
- 1 cup canola oil
- 3 eggs
- 2 cups A to Z ingredients (choose from list below)
- 3 tsps. vanilla extract
- 3 cups all-purpose flour
- 2 tsps. baking powder
- 2 tsps. ground cinnamon
- 1 tsp. baking soda
- 1 tsp. salt
- 1 cup chopped walnuts
- A TO Z INGREDIENTS:
- Apples, peeled and shredded
- Applesauce
- Apricots (dried), chopped
- Banana (ripe), mashed
- Carrot, shredded
- Sweetened shredded coconut
- Dates, pitted and chopped
- Figs (dried), chopped
- Grapes (seedless), chopped
- Oranges, peeled and chopped
- Peaches, peeled and chopped
- Pears, peeled and chopped
- Pineapple (canned), crushed and drained
- Dried plums, pitted and chopped
- Pumpkin, canned
- Raisins
- Raspberries, fresh or frozen
- Rhubarb, chopped fresh or frozen
- Strawberries, fresh or frozen
- Sweet potatoes, cooked and mashed
- Zucchini, peeled and shredded

Direction

- In a big bowl, mix eggs, oil and sugar. Stir in ingredients of your choice from A to Z and the vanilla. Mix salt, baking soda, cinnamon, baking powder and flour. Stir the flour mixture into the liquid ingredients until it becomes moist. Stir the walnuts in then put it into 2 greased loaf pans that are 8x4 inches in size.
- Bake at 350 degrees until toothpick comes out clean when inserted in the middle, about 50 to 55 minutes. Allow to cool for 10 minutes. Move it from the pans to wire racks.

Nutrition Information

- Calories: 239 calories
- Total Carbohydrate: 28 g
- Cholesterol: 23 mg
- Total Fat: 13 g

- Fiber: 1 g
- Protein: 3 g
- Sodium: 200 mg

285. Onion Zucchini Bread

"In two steps this bread ready for the oven."
Serving: 6-8 servings. | Prep: 15m | Ready in: 55m

Ingredients

- 3 cups all-purpose flour
- 3/4 cup chopped onion
- 1/2 cup grated Parmesan cheese, divided
- 5 tsps. baking powder
- 1 tsp. salt
- 1/2 tsp. baking soda
- 1 cup buttermilk
- 1/3 cup vegetable oil
- 2 large eggs, lightly beaten
- 3/4 cup finely shredded zucchini

Direction

- Mix the baking soda, salt, baking powder, 6 tbsps. of Parmesan cheese, onion and flour in a big bowl. Mix the zucchini, eggs, oil and buttermilk in a small bowl; mix into flour mixture just till incorporated.
- Scoop into a greased 9-in. round baking pan. Scatter the rest of Parmesan on top. Bake at 350° for 40 to 45 minutes till a toothpick pricked in the middle comes out clean. Allow to cool for 10 minutes prior to taking out of pan to cool fully on wire rack.

Nutrition Information

- Calories: 281 calories
- Total Carbohydrate: 40 g
- Cholesterol: 4 mg
- Total Fat: 9 g
- Fiber: 2 g
- Protein: 8 g
- Sodium: 448 mg

286. Orange Zucchini Bread

"This recipe won first place at a fair."
Serving: 4 mini loaves. | Prep: 20m | Ready in: 60m

Ingredients

- 3 large eggs
- 3/4 cup vegetable oil
- 1-1/2 cups sugar
- 2 tsps. grated lemon zest
- 2 tsps. grated orange zest
- 1/2 tsp. orange extract
- 1/4 tsp. vanilla extract
- 2 cups shredded unpeeled zucchini
- 2-1/2 cups all-purpose flour
- 2 tsps. baking powder
- 3/4 tsp. salt
- 1/2 tsp. ground ginger
- 1/4 tsp. baking soda
- 1/2 cup chopped walnuts

Direction

- Combine oil and eggs in a big bowl. Put in sugar and combine well. Stir in extracts, orange zest and lemon zest. Put in zucchini then combine well. Combine baking soda, ginger, salt, baking powder and flour. Into the zucchini mixture, mix the flour mixture just until it becomes moist then fold walnuts in.
- Put into 4 greased loaf pans that are 5 3/4x3x2 inches in size. At 350 degrees, bake until golden brown and a toothpick comes out clean when inserted in the middle, about 35 to 40 minutes. Allow to cool for 10mins then move to wire racks from the pans to completely cool.

Nutrition Information

- Calories: 275 calories
- Total Carbohydrate: 35 g
- Cholesterol: 40 mg
- Total Fat: 14 g
- Fiber: 1 g
- Protein: 4 g

- Sodium: 193 mg

287. Orange Zucchini Muffins

"For tender muffins avoid overmixing."
Serving: 10 muffins. | Prep: 15m | Ready in: 35m

Ingredients

- 1 cup shredded zucchini
- 1-1/4 cups all-purpose flour
- 3/4 tsp. ground nutmeg, divided
- 1/2 tsp. baking powder
- 1/2 tsp. baking soda
- 1/2 tsp. ground cinnamon
- 1/4 tsp. salt
- 2 large eggs
- 3/4 cup packed brown sugar
- 1/3 cup canola oil
- 2 tbsps. orange juice
- 1 tsp. grated orange zest
- 1 tsp. vanilla extract
- 1/2 cup raisins
- 1 tbsp. sugar

Direction

- Squeeze zucchini till dehydrated; reserve. Mix the salt, cinnamon, baking soda, baking powder, 1/2 tsp. nutmeg and flour in a big bowl. Mix the vanilla, orange zest, orange juice, oil, brown sugar and eggs in a separate bowl. Mix into dry ingredients till moistened. Fold in the raisins and reserved zucchini.
- Fill muffin cups lined with paper 2/3 full. Mix sugar and the rest of the nutmeg; scatter over batter. Bake at 350° for 18 to 22 minutes till a toothpick pricked in the middle comes out clean. Allow to cool for 5 minutes prior to taking out from pan to a wire rack. Serve while warm.

Nutrition Information

- Calories: 230 calories
- Total Carbohydrate: 36 g

- Cholesterol: 42 mg
- Total Fat: 9 g
- Fiber: 1 g
- Protein: 3 g
- Sodium: 165 mg

288. Parmesan Zucchini Bread

"This loaf has an old fashioned appeal and has a rugged texture."
Serving: 1 loaf (16 slices). | Prep: 10m | Ready in: 01h10m

Ingredients

- 3 cups all-purpose flour
- 3 tbsps. grated Parmesan cheese
- 1 tsp. salt
- 1/2 tsp. baking powder
- 1/2 tsp. baking soda
- 2 large eggs
- 1 cup buttermilk
- 1/3 cup sugar
- 1/3 cup butter, melted
- 1 cup shredded peeled zucchini
- 1 tbsp. grated onion

Direction

- Combine baking soda, baking powder, cheese, salt and flour in a big bowl. Whisk butter, sugar, buttermilk and eggs in a separate bowl then stir into the dry ingredients until just moist. Fold in onion and zucchini.
- Put it into a greased and floured loaf pan that is 9x5 inches in size. Bake at 350 degrees until toothpick comes out clean when inserted in the middle or for an hour. Allow to cool for 10mins. Move to wire rack from the pan.

Nutrition Information

- Calories: 156 calories
- Total Carbohydrate: 23 g
- Cholesterol: 35 mg
- Total Fat: 5 g

- Fiber: 1 g
- Protein: 4 g
- Sodium: 288 mg

289. Pear Zucchini Bread

"This recipe has moist bread."
Serving: 2 loaves. | Prep: 15m | Ready in: 01h10m

Ingredients

- 2 cups chopped peeled pears
- 1 cup shredded zucchini
- 1 cup sugar
- 1 cup packed brown sugar
- 3 eggs, beaten
- 1 cup vegetable oil
- 1 tbsp. vanilla extract
- 2 cups all-purpose flour
- 1 cup rye or whole wheat flour
- 2 tsps. pumpkin pie spice
- 1 tsp. baking soda
- 1/2 tsp. baking powder
- 1/2 tsp. salt
- 1/2 cup chopped pecans

Direction

- Mix the first 7 ingredients in a big bowl. Mix baking powder, salt, baking soda, pie spice and flours. Mix the flour mixture into the pear mixture until combined then fold the nuts in. In 2 greased loaf pans that are 8x4 inches in size, put the mixture. Bake at 350 degrees until the toothpick comes out clean when inserted in the middle, about 55 to 65 minutes. Let it cool for 10 minutes in pans then cool it completely by transferring it to a wire rack.

Nutrition Information

- Calories: 178 calories
- Total Carbohydrate: 23 g
- Cholesterol: 20 mg
- Total Fat: 9 g
- Fiber: 1 g

- Protein: 2 g
- Sodium: 92 mg

290. Pecan Zucchini Bread

"This the best quick bread is a combine flavors of sour cream plenty of chopped pecans and zucchini."
Serving: 2 loaves. | Prep: 15m | Ready in: 01h15m

Ingredients

- 3 cups all-purpose flour
- 2 cups sugar
- 1 tsp. baking soda
- 1 tsp. salt
- 1 tsp. ground cinnamon
- 1/4 tsp. baking powder
- 3 large eggs
- 1/2 cup vegetable oil
- 1/2 cup sour cream
- 1 tsp. vanilla extract
- 2 cups shredded zucchini
- 1 cup chopped pecans

Direction

- Mix the first 6 ingredients in a big bowl. Whisk the vanilla, sour cream, oil and eggs in a separate bowl. Mix into dry ingredients till just moistened. Fold in the nuts and zucchini.
- Put into two greased 9x5-inch loaf pans. Bake at 350° for 60 to 65 minutes till a toothpick pricked in the middle comes out clean. Allow to cool for 15 minutes prior to taking out from pans to wire racks to cool fully.

Nutrition Information

- Calories: 163 calories
- Total Carbohydrate: 22 g
- Cholesterol: 22 mg
- Total Fat: 7 g
- Fiber: 1 g
- Protein: 2 g
- Sodium: 125 mg

291. Pina Colada Zucchini Bread

"You will love the cake like texture of and tropical flavor of this recipe."
Serving: 3 loaves (12 slices each). | Prep: 25m | Ready in: 01h10m

Ingredients

- 4 cups all-purpose flour
- 3 cups sugar
- 2 tsps. baking powder
- 1-1/2 tsps. salt
- 1 tsp. baking soda
- 4 large eggs
- 1-1/2 cups canola oil
- 1 tsp. each coconut, rum and vanilla extracts
- 3 cups shredded zucchini
- 1 cup canned crushed pineapple, drained
- 1/2 cup chopped walnuts or chopped pecans

Direction

- Use waxed paper to line the bottoms of 3 greased and floured loaf pans that are 8x4 inches in size; oil the paper. Put it aside.
- Mix baking soda, salt, baking powder, sugar, and flour in a big bowl. Whisk extracts, oil and eggs in a separate bowl. Mix into the dry ingredients until just moist then fold in the walnuts, pineapple and zucchini.
- Put it into prepared pans. Bake at 350 degrees until toothpick comes out clean when inserted in the middle or for 45 to 55 minutes. Allow to cool for 10mins prior to moving to wire racks from the pans. Remove the waxed paper gently.

Nutrition Information

- Calories: 225 calories
- Total Carbohydrate: 29 g
- Cholesterol: 24 mg
- Total Fat: 11 g
- Fiber: 1 g
- Protein: 3 g

- Sodium: 165 mg

292. Pineapple Zucchini Bread

"A quick and easy bread recipe."
Serving: 12 | Prep: 15m | Ready in: 1h30m

Ingredients

- 1 cup packed brown sugar
- 1/2 cup margarine, softened
- 1 cup grated zucchini
- 1 (8 oz.) can crushed pineapple with juice
- 2 eggs
- 2 cups all-purpose flour
- 1 tsp. baking soda
- 1 tsp. ground cinnamon
- 1/4 tsp. salt
- 1/4 tsp. ground allspice
- 1/2 cup chopped walnuts
- 1/2 cup confectioners' sugar
- 1 tsp. corn syrup
- 1/4 tsp. ground cinnamon

Direction

- Heat the oven to 175°C or 350°F. Oil and flour only the base of a loaf pan 9x5 inch in size.
- Cream margarine and brown sugar in big bowl till fluffy and light. Set aside a tbsp. pineapple juice. Mix in eggs, zucchini and pineapple. Put in allspice, salt, cinnamon, baking soda and flour; mix thoroughly. Fold in the nuts. Scatter equally in prepped pan.
- Allow to bake for 60 to 70 minutes till toothpick pricked in middle comes out clean. Let cool for 10 minutes, and then take out of pan.
- For glaze: Mix together 1/4 tsp. ground cinnamon, corn syrup, reserved pineapple juice and confectioners' sugar. Combine till smooth, and scoop on top of warm loaf. Fully cool on wire rack. Wrap and keep in the refrigerator.

Nutrition Information

- Calories: 291 calories;
- Total Carbohydrate: 43.5 g
- Cholesterol: 31 mg
- Total Fat: 11.9 g
- Protein: 4.2 g
- Sodium: 274 mg

---

293. Pineapple Zucchini Bread With Pecans And Raisins

"A slice of this tender and moist bread is good for breakfast or for coffee."
Serving: 2 loaves (16 slices each). | Prep: 20m | Ready in: 01h10m

Ingredients

- 3 cups all-purpose flour
- 2 tsps. baking soda
- 1/2 tsp. baking powder
- 1/2 tsp. salt
- 3 eggs
- 2 cups sugar
- 1 cup canola oil
- 2 tsps. vanilla extract
- 2 cups shredded zucchini
- 1 can (8 oz.) unsweetened crushed pineapple, undrained
- 1 cup chopped pecans
- 1 cup raisins

Direction

- Mix salt, baking powder, baking soda and flour together in a big bowl. Whisk vanilla, oil, sugar and eggs in a separate bowl. Put in pineapple and zucchini then mix the mixture in the dry ingredients till it becomes moist. Fold in raisins and pecans.
- In 2 greased loaf pans that are 8x4 inches in size, pour the mixture. Bake at 350 degrees until toothpick comes out clean when inserted in the middle, about 50 to 55 minutes. Allow to

cool for 10 mins in pans then transfer from pans to wire racks to complete cooling.

Nutrition Information

- Calories: 205 calories
- Total Carbohydrate: 27 g
- Cholesterol: 20 mg
- Total Fat: 10 g
- Fiber: 1 g
- Protein: 2 g
- Sodium: 130 mg

---

294. Pineapple Zucchini Bread With Walnuts

"A Pineapple Zucchini Bread with slightly crunchy crust."
Serving: 2 loaves (12 slices each). | Prep: 20m | Ready in: 01h10m

Ingredients

- 2 cups sugar
- 1 cup vegetable oil
- 3 eggs
- 2 tsps. vanilla extract
- 3 cups all-purpose flour
- 2 tsps. ground cinnamon
- 1-1/2 tsps. baking powder
- 1 tsp. salt
- 3/4 tsp. ground nutmeg
- 1/2 tsp. baking soda
- 2 cups shredded zucchini
- 1 can (8 oz.) unsweetened crushed pineapple, drained
- 3/4 cup chopped walnuts

Direction

- Whisk the vanilla, eggs, oil and sugar in a big bowl till well incorporated. Mix the baking soda, nutmeg, salt, baking powder, cinnamon and flour; slowly beat into sugar mixture till incorporated. Mix in walnuts, pineapple and zucchini.

- Put into 2 greased 8x4-inch loaf pans. Bake at 350° for 50 to 60 minutes till a toothpick pricked in the middle comes out clean. Allow to cool for 10 minutes prior to taking out from pans to wire racks to cool fully.

Nutrition Information

- Calories: 243 calories
- Total Carbohydrate: 31 g
- Cholesterol: 27 mg
- Total Fat: 12 g
- Fiber: 1 g
- Protein: 4 g
- Sodium: 158 mg

295. Pumpkin Zucchini Bread

"This recipe is one of many ways you can use zucchini."
Serving: 2 loaves. | Prep: 15m | Ready in: 60m

Ingredients

- 3 large eggs, lightly beaten
- 2 cups sugar
- 1 cup canned pumpkin
- 1 cup butter, melted
- 1 tbsp. vanilla extract
- 3 cups all-purpose flour
- 1 tsp. baking soda
- 1/2 tsp. baking powder
- 1/2 tsp. salt
- 1/2 tsp. ground cinnamon
- 1/2 tsp. ground nutmeg
- 1/2 tsp. ground cloves
- 1 cup shredded zucchini
- 1 cup chopped walnuts

Direction

- Combine sugar and eggs in a bowl. Put in vanilla, butter and pumpkin. Mix the dry ingredients; put into pumpkin mixture gradually and combine well. Mix in nuts and zucchini. Put into two 9x5-inch loaf pans that are greased and floured. Bake at 350 degrees

until breads test done or for 45 to 50mins. Allow to cool for 10mins in the pans. Put onto wire rack.

Nutrition Information

- Calories: 176 calories
- Total Carbohydrate: 23 g
- Cholesterol: 35 mg
- Total Fat: 9 g
- Fiber: 1 g
- Protein: 3 g
- Sodium: 147 mg

296. Raisin Banana Bread

"Grated carrots and zucchini added raisins and walnuts, brings great blend of flavors to this banana bread."
Serving: 4 loaves (5 slices each). | Prep: 15m | Ready in: 60m

Ingredients

- 3 cups all-purpose flour
- 2 cups sugar
- 1 tsp. baking powder
- 1 tsp. salt
- 1 tsp. pumpkin pie spice
- 1/2 tsp. baking soda
- 1/2 tsp. ground cinnamon
- 3 eggs
- 1 cup canola oil
- 2 tsps. vanilla extract
- 1 cup grated zucchini
- 1 cup grated carrot
- 1/2 cup mashed ripe banana
- 1/2 cup raisins
- 1/2 cup chopped walnuts

Direction

- Mix the first 7 ingredients in a big bowl. Mix the vanilla, oil and eggs in a separate big bowl; put into dry ingredients and combine thoroughly. Mix in nuts, raisins, banana, carrot and zucchini.

- Put into 4 greased and floured loaf pans 5x3x2-inch in size. Bake at 350° for 45 to 48 minutes till a toothpick pricked in the middle comes out clean. Allow to cool for 10 minutes; take out from pans to wire racks.

Nutrition Information

- Calories: 293 calories
- Total Carbohydrate: 40 g
- Cholesterol: 32 mg
- Total Fat: 14 g
- Fiber: 1 g
- Protein: 4 g
- Sodium: 182 mg

297. Sesame Zucchini Bread

"This zucchini-flecked bread is very healthy."
Serving: 1 loaf (16 slices). | Prep: 15m | Ready in: 01h10m

Ingredients

- 3/4 cup buttermilk
- 1/2 cup sugar
- 1/2 cup packed brown sugar
- 1 egg
- 1 egg white
- 2 tbsps. vegetable oil
- 2 to 3 tsps. maple flavoring
- 1-1/2 cups all-purpose flour
- 1/2 cup whole wheat flour
- 1/4 cup toasted wheat germ
- 1 tsp. baking powder
- 1 tsp. baking soda
- 1/4 tsp. salt
- 1/2 cup raisins
- 1/4 cup chopped walnuts
- 4 tsps. sesame seeds, divided
- 1-1/2 cups shredded zucchini

Direction

- Mix together the first 7 ingredients in a bowl then beat until it becomes smooth. Mix baking soda, salt, baking powder, wheat germ and flours together in a separate bowl. Put in 3 tsps. of sesame seeds, walnuts and raisins. Mix into the sugar mixture just until it becomes moist. Mix the zucchini in then pour the mixture into a loaf pan that is 9x5 inches in size with grease. Use the leftover sesame seeds to sprinkle.
- Bake it at 350 degrees until the toothpick comes out clean when inserted in the middle, about 55 to 60 minutes. Allow to cool for 10 minutes before transferring from pan to wire rack.

Nutrition Information

- Calories: 168 calories
- Total Carbohydrate: 31 g
- Cholesterol: 14 mg
- Total Fat: 4 g
- Fiber: 0 g
- Protein: 4 g
- Sodium: 170 mg

298. Spiced Pear Zucchini Bread

"There is a subtle spin on this traditional zucchini recipe."
Serving: 2 loaves. | Prep: 15m | Ready in: 01h05m

Ingredients

- 2 cups all-purpose flour
- 1 cup whole wheat flour
- 3/4 cup sugar
- 3/4 cup packed brown sugar
- 2 tsps. pumpkin pie spice
- 1 tsp. baking soda
- 1/2 tsp. baking powder
- 1/2 tsp. salt
- 3 eggs
- 3/4 cup vegetable oil
- 3 tsps. vanilla extract
- 2 cups finely chopped peeled ripe pears (about 3 medium)
- 1 cup shredded zucchini
- 1/2 cup chopped pecans or walnuts

Direction

- Mix the first 8 ingredients in a big bowl. Beat vanilla, oil and eggs in a separate bowl. Put in zucchini and pears then stir into dry ingredients just until moist. Fold the nuts in and put into two 9x5-inch loaf pans that are greased.
- At 350 degrees, bake until toothpick comes out clean when inserted in the middle or for 50 to 60 minutes. Allow to cool for 10mins. Move to wire racks from the pans.

299. Three Loaves In One

"You can enjoy this bread anytime you crave a healthy snack."
Serving: 3 mini loaves (6 slices each). | Prep: 25m | Ready in: 60m

Ingredients

- 2 cups all-purpose flour
- 3/4 cup sugar
- 1 tsp. baking powder
- 1/2 tsp. salt
- 1/4 tsp. baking soda
- 1 large egg
- 2/3 cup orange juice
- 2 tbsps. butter, melted
- FOR ZUCCHINI BREAD:
- 1/3 cup shredded zucchini
- 1 tsp. grated orange zest
- 1/4 tsp. ground cinnamon
- FOR BLUEBERRY BREAD:
- 1/3 cup fresh or frozen blueberries
- 2 tsps. all-purpose flour
- 2 tsps. honey
- 2 tsps. orange juice
- FOR CINNAMON BREAD:
- 4-1/2 tsps. sour cream
- 1 tbsp. sugar
- 3/4 tsp. ground cinnamon
- 1 tbsp. confectioners' sugar
- 1/2 tsp. 2% milk

Direction

- Use cooking spray to coat three loaf pans that are 5 3/4x3x2 inches in size; put aside. Combine baking soda, salt, baking powder, sugar and flour in a small bowl. Whisk the butter, orange juice and egg then into the dry ingredients, mix just until it becomes moist.
- In a separate bowl, put 3/4 cup of batter. Mix in the cinnamon, orange zest and zucchini. In one prepared pan, pour the mixture. In the second bowl, put another 3/4 cup of batter. With the flour, toss the blueberries then fold into the batter. Pour into the second pan. Mix orange juice and honey then set aside.
- Into the remaining batter, mix sour cream. In the third pan, spoon half of the batter. Mix cinnamon and sugar and sprinkle on top of batter. Put remaining batter on top and swirl by cutting through using a knife.
- Bake all three loaves at 325 degrees until toothpick comes out clean when inserted in the middle or for 33 to 36 minutes. Over warm blueberry bread, pour preserved honey mixture. Let the loaves cool for 10mins then move to a wire rack from the pans.
- Whisk milk and confectioners' sugar until smooth. Over cooled cinnamon bread, drizzle the mixture.

Nutrition Information

- Calories: 56 calories
- Total Carbohydrate: 10 g
- Cholesterol: 15 mg
- Total Fat: 2 g
- Fiber: 0 g
- Protein: 0 g
- Sodium: 122 mg

300. Yummy Zucchini Coffee Cake

"It was the best thing I ever made."
Serving: 16 servings. | Prep: 25m | Ready in: 60m

Ingredients

- 1/3 cup packed brown sugar
- 1/4 cup all-purpose flour
- 1/4 cup quick-cooking oats
- 2 tbsps. butter, softened
- 1/2 tsp. ground cinnamon
- BATTER:
- 1-1/2 cups quick-cooking oats
- 1 cup all-purpose flour
- 3/4 cup whole wheat flour
- 1-1/4 tsps. ground cinnamon
- 1 tsp. baking powder
- 1 tsp. baking soda
- 1/2 tsp. salt
- 1/4 tsp. ground nutmeg
- 1/3 cup butter, softened
- 1 cup packed light brown sugar
- 1-1/2 tsps. vanilla extract
- 2 large eggs
- 1/3 cup reduced-fat sour cream
- 2-1/2 cups shredded zucchini (about 2 medium)
- Confectioners' sugar

Direction

- Preheat an oven to 350°. Using cooking spray, grease a fluted 10-inch tube pan; slightly flour, patting out extra.
- Using fork, combine the initial 5 ingredients till crumbly. Scatter onto the bottom of the pan.
- For the batter, combine nutmeg, salt, baking soda, baking powder, cinnamon, flours and oats. Whip brown sugar and butter in a separate bowl till crumbly; whip in the vanilla and the eggs, one by one. Put in the oat mixture alternating with the sour cream, whipping thoroughly, batter will turn thick. Fold in the zucchini. Put on top of crumb mixture.
- Bake for 35 to 40 minutes till a toothpick pricked in middle gets out clean. Let cool for 10 minutes prior to transferring to the wire rack. Serve at room temperature or while warm; sprinkle with confectioners' sugar prior to serving.

Nutrition Information

- Calories: 223 calories
- Total Carbohydrate: 37 g
- Cholesterol: 38 mg
- Total Fat: 7 g
- Fiber: 2 g
- Protein: 4 g
- Sodium: 244 mg

301. Yummy Zucchini Fritters

"Change veggie-critics minds with these speedy and delicious snacks."
Serving: 10 servings (3/4 cup sauce). | Prep: 20m | Ready in: 40m

Ingredients

- 1/4 cup buttermilk
- 1/4 cup egg substitute
- 1/2 cup panko (Japanese) bread crumbs
- 1/2 cup seasoned bread crumbs
- 1/4 cup grated Parmesan cheese
- 1-1/2 tsps. taco seasoning
- 1/4 tsp. garlic salt
- 3 medium zucchini, cut into 1/4-inch slices
- 1/4 cup fat-free sour cream
- 1/4 cup fat-free ranch salad dressing
- 1/4 cup salsa

Direction

- Mix egg substitute and buttermilk in a shallow bowl. Mix garlic salt, taco seasoning, cheese and breadcrumbs in a different shallow bowl. Plunge the zucchini into the buttermilk mixture, then the breadcrumb mixture.

- Arrange on baking sheets greased in cooking spray. Bake at 400 degrees and turn once until golden brown, for 20-25 minutes.
- Mix salsa, the ranch dressing, and sour cream in a small bowl. Serve along with zucchini.

Nutrition Information

- Calories: 67 calories
- Total Carbohydrate: 11 g
- Cholesterol: 3 mg
- Total Fat: 1 g
- Fiber: 1 g
- Protein: 3 g
- Sodium: 296 mg

Nutrition Information

- Calories: 142 calories
- Total Carbohydrate: 18 g
- Cholesterol: 21 mg
- Total Fat: 6 g
- Fiber: 1 g
- Protein: 4 g
- Sodium: 341 mg

---

302. Zu-key-ni Dill Muffins

"These light muffins are a favorite menu item."
Serving: about 2 dozen. | Prep: 15m | Ready in: 35m

Ingredients

- 3-1/2 cups all-purpose flour
- 1/3 cup sugar
- 2 tbsps. baking powder
- 1 tbsp. dill weed
- 2 tsps. salt
- 2 cups grated unpeeled zucchini
- 2 eggs
- 1-1/2 cups milk
- 1/2 cup vegetable oil
- 1/2 cup grated Parmesan cheese

Direction

- Mix the first 5 ingredients in a big bowl. Put in zucchini and mix till coated. Mix together the oil, milk and eggs; mix into zucchini mixture just till moistened. Fill paper-lined or oiled muffin cups 2/3 full. Scatter Parmesan cheese on top.
- Let bake at 400° till a toothpick comes out clean, about 18 to 20 minutes. Allow to cool down for 5 minutes prior to taking out from pans to wire racks.

---

303. Zucchini & Cheese Drop Biscuits

"These colorful drop biscuits are so easy make yet loaded with flavors."
Serving: 1 dozen. | Prep: 25m | Ready in: 50m

Ingredients

- 3/4 cup shredded zucchini
- 1-1/4 tsps. salt, divided
- 2-1/2 cups all-purpose flour
- 1 tbsp. baking powder
- 1/2 cup cold butter, cubed
- 1/2 cup shredded cheddar cheese
- 1/4 cup shredded part-skim mozzarella cheese
- 1/4 cup shredded Parmesan cheese
- 2 tbsps. finely chopped oil-packed sun-dried tomatoes, patted dry
- 2 tbsps. minced fresh basil or 2 tsps. dried basil
- 1 cup 2% milk

Direction

- Preheat the oven to 425°. In a colander over a plate, put the zucchini; scatter a quarter tsp. salt on top and toss. Allow to stand for 10 minutes. Wash and drain thoroughly. Squeeze the zucchini to get rid of extra liquid. Pat it dry.
- Mix remaining salt, baking powder and flour in a big bowl. Cut in butter till the mixture resembles coarse crumbs. Mix in basil, tomatoes, cheeses and zucchini. Put in milk; mix just till moistened.

- Into a greased 13x9-inch baking pan, drop by scant 1/3 cupfuls. Bake 22 to 26 minutes till golden brown. Serve while warm.

Nutrition Information

- Calories: 205 calories
- Total Carbohydrate: 22 g
- Cholesterol: 29 mg
- Total Fat: 11 g
- Fiber: 1 g
- Protein: 6 g
- Sodium: 482 mg

304. Zucchini Anise Bread

"The zucchini gives it a moist texture while anise lends a unique licorice-like flavor and fragrance."
Serving: 2 loaves. | Prep: 15m | Ready in: 01h15m

Ingredients

- 3 cups all-purpose flour
- 2 cups sugar
- 2 tbsps. toasted wheat germ
- 1 tsp. baking soda
- 1 tsp. salt
- 1 tsp. ground cinnamon
- 1/2 to 1 tsp. aniseed
- 1/4 tsp. baking powder
- 1 cup vegetable oil
- 1/4 cup buttermilk
- 2 eggs, lightly beaten
- 2 tsps. vanilla extract
- 1-2/3 cups shredded peeled zucchini
- 1 cup chopped walnuts
- 1 cup raisins
- 1/3 cup shredded carrot

Direction

- Mix the first 8 ingredients in a big bowl. Mix vanilla, eggs, buttermilk and oil in a separate bowl. Put into the dry ingredients; mix thoroughly. Mix in carrot, raisins, walnuts and zucchini. Scoop into two greased 8x4-in. loaf

pans. Allow to bake at 350° for an hour till a toothpick pricked in the middle comes out clean. Allow to cool for 10 minutes; take out of pans and allow to fully cool on wire racks.

Nutrition Information

- Calories: 198 calories
- Total Carbohydrate: 26 g
- Cholesterol: 13 mg
- Total Fat: 10 g
- Fiber: 1 g
- Protein: 3 g
- Sodium: 124 mg

305. Zucchini Apple Bread

"This version of zucchini has light and fluffy bread."
Serving: 24 | Prep: 20m | Ready in: 1h20m

Ingredients

- 4 eggs
- 1 cup white sugar
- 1 cup brown sugar
- 1/2 cup vegetable oil
- 1 tsp. vanilla extract
- 3 1/2 cups all-purpose flour
- 1 1/2 tsps. baking soda
- 1/2 tsp. salt
- 2 tsps. ground cinnamon
- 1/2 cup chopped walnuts
- 2 cups peeled, chopped zucchini
- 1 cup chopped, peeled apple

Direction

- Heat the oven beforehand to 175 °C or 350 °F. Grease 2 loaf pans that are 9x5 inches in size.
- Mix vanilla, oil, eggs, white sugar and brown sugar until mixed well in a big bowl. Mix cinnamon, salt, baking soda and flour together in another bowl. Mix the flour mixture into the egg mixture then fold in apple, zucchini and walnuts. In the prepared pans, pour the mixture.

- Bake until top springs back when touched lightly in the middle, about an hour. Cool for 10 mins in pans. Move it to wire rack to let it completely cool.

Nutrition Information

- Calories: 207 calories;
- Total Carbohydrate: 32.9 g
- Cholesterol: 31 mg
- Total Fat: 7.2 g
- Protein: 3.5 g
- Sodium: 143 mg

306. Zucchini Banana Bread

"This wholesome loaf has the right flavor without too much sugar added on it."
Serving: 12 | Prep: 15m | Ready in: 1h15m

Ingredients

- ¾ cup all-purpose flour
- ¾ cup white whole-wheat flour
- 1 tsp. ground cinnamon
- ¾ tsp. baking soda
- ½ tsp. salt
- 2 large eggs
- ¾ cup sugar
- ¼ cup canola oil or melted unsalted butter
- 1½ tsps. vanilla extract
- 1 cup shredded zucchini (about 1 medium)
- 1 cup mashed ripe banana

Direction

- Heat the oven beforehand to 350°F. Use cooking spray to coat a 9x5-inch loaf pan.
- In a big bowl, whisk salt, baking soda, cinnamon, whole wheat flour and all-purpose flour then put aside. In a medium bowl, whisk vanilla, melted butter or oil, sugar and eggs. Mix in banana and zucchini until combined well. Put the wet ingredients into the flour mixture and stir just until combined. In the prepared pan, put the batter. Bake for 50 to 60 minutes until toothpick comes out clean when

inserted in the middle of the loaf. Allow to cool for 10mins in the pan. Move the loaf to rack to completely cool. Serve at room temperature or while warm.

Nutrition Information

- Calories: 178 calories;
- Total Carbohydrate: 29 g
- Cholesterol: 31 mg
- Total Fat: 6 g
- Fiber: 2 g
- Protein: 3 g
- Sodium: 189 mg
- Sugar: 15 g
- Saturated Fat: 1 g

307. Zucchini Bread

"Perfect gifts for holidays, substitute raisins for the chocolate if you desire."
Serving: 24 | Prep: 20m | Ready in: 1h40m

Ingredients

- 3 cups all-purpose flour
- 3 eggs
- 2 cups white sugar
- 1 cup vegetable oil
- 2 cups grated zucchini
- 1 cup semisweet chocolate chips
- 1 tsp. ground cinnamon
- 1 tsp. baking soda
- 1/4 tsp. baking powder
- 1/2 cup sour cream

Direction

- Preheat the oven to 175°C or 350°F. Grease 2 loaf pans 9x5-inch in size.
- Whisk together oil, sugar and eggs. Mix in grated zucchini, and then sour cream. Stir in the cinnamon, baking powder, baking soda and flour. Mix in raisins or chocolate chips. Put batter into prepped pans.

- In prepped oven, bake for 80 minutes till a tester pricked in the middle of every loaf comes out clean. Allow to cool down on wire rack.

Nutrition Information

- Calories: 257 calories;
- Total Carbohydrate: 33.7 g
- Cholesterol: 25 mg
- Total Fat: 13.1 g
- Protein: 3 g
- Sodium: 71 mg

308. Zucchini Carrot Muffins

"I usually serve these muffins for breakfast or lunch together with a bowl of salad or soup. My better half loves them!"
Serving: 18 standard size muffins. | Prep: 15m | Ready in: 35m

Ingredients

- 2 cups shredded carrot
- 1 cup shredded zucchini
- 1 cup chopped peeled apple
- 3/4 cup sweetened shredded coconut
- 1/2 cup chopped almonds
- 2 tsps. grated orange zest
- 2 cups all-purpose flour
- 1-1/4 cups sugar
- 1 tbsp. ground cinnamon
- 2 tsps. baking soda
- 1/2 tsp. salt
- 3 large eggs, lightly beaten
- 3/4 cup canola oil
- 1 tsp. vanilla extract

Direction

- Combine apple, orange zest, almonds, coconut, carrot, and zucchini in a bowl and then put aside.
- Mix salt, flour, cinnamon, baking soda, and sugar in a separate big bowl. Mix eggs, vanilla,

and oil in another bowl. Pour the egg mixture into the dry mixture, whisking well until evenly moistened and thick.
- Add the carrot mixture into the batter. Grease the muffin cups or line each with paper liners. Fill the muffin cups with batter.
- Set the oven to 375°F and bake the muffins for 20-22 minutes until completely done. Allow it to cool in the pan for 10 minutes before transferring the muffins onto wire racks.

Nutrition Information

- Calories: 249 calories
- Total Carbohydrate: 30 g
- Cholesterol: 35 mg
- Total Fat: 13 g
- Fiber: 2 g
- Protein: 4 g
- Sodium: 231 mg

309. Zucchini Cheddar Biscuits

""Your family would enjoy this recipe of biscuits!""
Serving: 16 biscuits. | Prep: 15m | Ready in: 25m

Ingredients

- 1/4 cup butter, cubed
- 1 large onion, chopped
- 2-1/2 cups biscuit/baking mix
- 1 tbsp. minced fresh parsley
- 1/2 tsp. dried basil
- 1/2 tsp. dried thyme
- 3 eggs, lightly beaten
- 1/4 cup 2% milk
- 1-1/2 cups shredded zucchini
- 1 cup shredded cheddar cheese

Direction

- Melt butter in a large skillet. Stir in onion; sauté till gets softened. Mix onion mixture, thyme, basil, parsley, and biscuit mix together in a large bowl. Whisk milk and eggs together in the second bowl. Stirring into biscuit

166

mixture just till mixed. Fold cheese and zucchini in.

- Onto greased baking sheets, drop 1/4 cupfuls of batter, 2 inches apart. Allow to bake for 10-14 minutes at 400 degrees till get golden brown. Serve these biscuits warm. Store leftovers in the fridge.

Nutrition Information

- Calories: 148 calories
- Total Carbohydrate: 13 g
- Cholesterol: 55 mg
- Total Fat: 9 g
- Fiber: 1 g
- Protein: 4 g
- Sodium: 315 mg

310. Zucchini Cheese Bread

"A great recipe for making a zucchini bread without sugar."
Serving: 1 loaf (16 slices). | Prep: 10m | Ready in: 01h05m

Ingredients

- 3 cups all-purpose flour
- 1 tsp. baking powder
- 1 tsp. baking soda
- 1 tsp. salt
- 3 large eggs
- 3/4 cup vegetable oil
- 2-1/2 cups shredded unpeeled zucchini (about 2 medium)
- 1 cup shredded cheddar cheese
- 1/2 cup chopped onion

Direction

- Mix the flour, baking powder, baking soda, and salt in large bowl. Whip oil and eggs in a separate bowl. Mix into the dry ingredients barely till moisten. Fold in onion, cheese and zucchini.
- Transfer to a 9x5-inch greased loaf pan. Bake for 55 to 65 minutes at 375° or till a toothpick

comes out clean when inserted in the center. Allow 10 minutes to cool then remove from pan to a wire rack. Serve while warm. Refrigerate the remaining.

Nutrition Information

- Calories: 219 calories
- Total Carbohydrate: 19 g
- Cholesterol: 47 mg
- Total Fat: 13 g
- Fiber: 1 g
- Protein: 5 g
- Sodium: 307 mg

311. Zucchini Chip Bread

"Zucchini bread with added flavor from shredded orange peel, toasted walnuts, and chocolate chips."
Serving: 24 | Prep: 30m | Ready in: 1h35m

Ingredients

- 3 cups all-purpose flour (see Tips)
- ¾ cup sugar or sugar substitute blend equivalent to ¾ cup sugar (see Tips)
- 1 tsp. baking soda
- 1 tsp. ground nutmeg
- ½ tsp. salt
- ½ tsp. ground cinnamon
- ¼ tsp. baking powder
- ¾ cup refrigerated or frozen egg product, thawed
- ½ cup unsweetened applesauce
- ½ cup canola oil
- 1 tbsp. finely shredded orange peel
- 2 tsps. vanilla
- 2 cups shredded zucchini
- 1 cup chopped walnuts, toasted (see Tips)
- 1 cup semisweet chocolate pieces

Direction

- Preheat the oven to 350°F. Oil the bottom and half an inch up the sides of two 8x4x2-inch loaf pans. Reserve.

- Mix baking powder, cinnamon, salt, nutmeg, baking soda, sugar and flour in a big bowl. Mix vanilla, orange peel, oil, applesauce and egg product in a small bowl; put into flour mixture. Mix till just moistened. Fold in the chocolate pieces, walnuts and zucchini.
- Evenly distribute mixture among 2 prepped pans. Bake for 55 minutes till a toothpick pricked close to the middle comes out clean. Allow to cool in pans on wire rack for 10 minutes. Take bread out of pans and on rack, cool fully. Wrap and keep overnight for easier slicing prior to serving.

Nutrition Information

- Calories: 197 calories;
- Total Carbohydrate: 25 g
- Cholesterol: 0 mg
- Total Fat: 10 g
- Fiber: 1 g
- Protein: 4 g
- Sodium: 120 mg
- Sugar: 11 g
- Saturated Fat: 2 g

312. Zucchini Cornbread

"This is a fun, summer zucchini squash recipe."
Serving: 8 | Prep: 15m | Ready in: 45m

Ingredients

- 1 cup coarsely chopped zucchini
- 1 cup milk
- 1/2 cup chopped onion
- 2 eggs
- 1/4 cup vegetable oil
- 1 1/4 cups cornmeal
- 1 cup all-purpose flour
- 2 tbsps. white sugar
- 4 tsps. baking powder
- 1 tsp. salt
- 1 cup shredded Cheddar cheese

Direction

- Preheat oven to 400 °F / 200 °C. Place a greased 10-in cast-iron pan in the oven while preheating.
- In a blender, put in the onion, vegetable oil, zucchini, eggs, and milk and 5 to 8 times pulse until the mixture has been thoroughly combined. Make sure that the onion and zucchini have been chopped finely in very small pieces.
- In a big bowl, combine the flour, baking powder, cornmeal, sugar, and salt. Add the zucchini mixture to cornmeal mixture and stir together until well combined. Gently add in cheddar cheese.
- Pour the batter carefully in greased hot skillet and use a spoon to smoothen it. Bake the cornbread until golden brown for about 30 minutes. To check for doneness, insert a toothpick at the center and if it comes out clean then the cornbread is ready.

Nutrition Information

- Calories: 307 calories;
- Total Carbohydrate: 36 g
- Cholesterol: 64 mg
- Total Fat: 13.9 g
- Protein: 9.6 g
- Sodium: 656 mg

313. Zucchini Cranberry Bread

"This mini loaf is simply delightful."
Serving: 1 loaf (12 slices). | Prep: 20m | Ready in: 60m

Ingredients

- 2 tbsps. butter, softened
- 1/2 cup sugar
- 1 large egg
- 1-1/2 cups all-purpose flour
- 1-1/2 tsps. baking powder
- 1/4 tsp. salt
- 3/4 cup shredded zucchini

- 2/3 cup whole-berry cranberry sauce
- 1/2 cup chopped walnuts
- 1-1/2 tsps. grated orange zest

Direction

- Cream sugar and butter in a small bowl. Put in egg and mix well. Combine salt, baking powder and flour then put into the creamed mixture. Fold in the orange zest, walnuts, cranberry sauce and zucchini – it will become thick.
- Put into an 8x4-inch loaf pan that is coated with cooking spray. Bake at 350 degrees until a toothpick comes out clean or for 40 to 45mins. Allow to cool for 10mins. Move to a wire rack from the pan.

Nutrition Information

- Calories: 167 calories
- Total Carbohydrate: 27 g
- Cholesterol: 23 mg
- Total Fat: 5 g
- Fiber: 1 g
- Protein: 4 g
- Sodium: 128 mg

314. Zucchini Dinner Rolls

"Golden dinner rolls made with grated squash that makes it amazingly tender."
Serving: 2 dozen. | Prep: 25m | Ready in: 45m

Ingredients

- 1 cup shredded peeled zucchini
- 1 tsp. salt, divided
- 3-1/2 cups all-purpose flour, divided
- 1 package (1/4 oz.) quick-rise yeast
- 5 tbsps. grated Parmesan cheese, divided
- 1 tsp. sugar
- 1 cup warm water (120° to 130°)
- 1/4 cup butter, softened

Direction

- In a small bowl, add zucchini, then sprinkle 1/2 tsp. salt on top. Allow to stand for 5 minutes, then drain.
- In the meantime, mix together leftover salt, sugar, 2 tbsp. cheese, yeast and 3 cups flour in a separate bowl. Add zucchini, then toss to blend. Mix together butter and water, then add to the dry ingredients. Mix in the leftover flour until a soft dough forms.
- Flip out onto a surface dusted with flour and knead for about 6 to 8 minutes until pliable and smooth. Put in a bowl coated with cooking spray, flipping once to grease the top. Put on a cover and allow to rise for about an hour in a warm area until doubled.
- Split the dough in half, then form each part into 12 balls. Put in a greased 13x9-inch baking pan, then sprinkle leftover cheese over. Redo the process. Put on a cover and allow to rise for about 45 minutes in a warm area until doubled.
- Bake for 20 to 25 minutes at 375 degrees or until golden brown. Take out of the pan, then transfer to a wire rack.

Nutrition Information

- Calories: 90 calories
- Total Carbohydrate: 14 g
- Cholesterol: 6 mg
- Total Fat: 2 g
- Fiber: 1 g
- Protein: 3 g
- Sodium: 138 mg

315. Zucchini Fritters

""Carrot cakes, yellow squash, and pan-fried zucchini with tender insides and golden crispy edges. These make perfect dippers for everyone.""
Serving: 4 | Prep: 20m | Ready in: 45m

Ingredients

- 2 cups shredded zucchini

- 1 cup shredded yellow squash
- 1 cup shredded carrots
- 1/2 tsp. salt
- 1 cup corn muffin mix
- 1 tsp. baking powder
- 1/2 tsp. sweet paprika
- 2 large eggs, lightly beaten
- 2 tbsps. vegetable oil, or more as needed

Direction

- In a colander, toss salt, carrots, yellow squash, and zucchini and strain for 15 minutes. Use a clean kitchen towel to wrap vegetables and wring out as much moisture as you can; place the mixture into a bowl.
- In a bowl, mix paprika, baking powder, and corn muffin mix. Mix in eggs and vegetables until well blended.
- In a large skillet, put 2 tbsps. of vegetable oil and heat over medium heat, slanting skillet to scatter oil evenly. Add a tablespoonful of the zucchini batter into the hot oil, using the back of a spoon to flatten each dollop. Pan-fry for 1-2 minutes each side until golden brown. Place fritters onto a plate lined with a paper towel and drain. Let them slightly cool before serving.

Nutrition Information

- Calories: 258 calories;
- Total Carbohydrate: 29.7 g
- Cholesterol: 94 mg
- Total Fat: 12.9 g
- Protein: 7.3 g
- Sodium: 1029 mg

316. Zucchini Fruit Cocktail Loaf

"This bread has fruit cocktail for more flavor and moisture."
Serving: 2 loaves. | Prep: 15m | Ready in: 01h15m

Ingredients

- 3 eggs

- 2 cups sugar
- 1 cup vegetable oil
- 2 tsps. vanilla extract
- 2 cups chopped peeled zucchini
- 1 can (17 oz.) fruit cocktail, drained
- 3 cups all-purpose flour
- 2 tsps. baking soda
- 1-1/2 tsps. ground cinnamon
- 1 tsp. salt
- 3/4 tsp. ground nutmeg
- 1 cup chopped walnuts

Direction

- Beat the eggs in a big bowl. Put in vanilla, oil and sugar; beat thoroughly. Mix in fruit cocktail and zucchini. Mix the dry ingredients; mix into the zucchini mixture. Mix in nuts. Put into 2 greased and floured 8x4-inch loaf pans. Allow to bake at 325° for 60 to 70 minutes till bread tests done. Let cool down for 10 minutes prior to taking off from pans to a wire rack.

Nutrition Information

- Calories: 195 calories
- Total Carbohydrate: 25 g
- Cholesterol: 20 mg
- Total Fat: 10 g
- Fiber: 1 g
- Protein: 3 g
- Sodium: 160 mg

317. Zucchini Muffins

"Low-fat zucchini muffins."
Serving: 12 | Prep: 15m | Ready in: 35m

Ingredients

- 2 cups whole wheat flour
- 1 tbsp. baking powder
- 1/2 tsp. salt
- 1 tsp. ground cinnamon
- 3/4 cup nonfat milk
- 2 egg whites

- 1/4 cup vegetable oil
- 1/4 cup honey
- 1 cup grated zucchini

Direction

- Preheat the oven by setting at 190°C/375°F. Lightly grease with oil/spray nonstick cooking spray on muffin tins.
- Mix ground cinnamon, salt, baking powder and whole wheat flour well.
- Mix shredded zucchini, honey, oil, slightly beaten egg whites and milk. Put in dry ingredients; mix till just barely moist and lumpy. Use batter to fill muffin tips to 2/3 full.
- Bake till lightly browned for 20 minutes at 190°C/375°F.

Nutrition Information

- Calories: 140 calories;
- Total Carbohydrate: 21.9 g
- Cholesterol: < 1 mg
- Total Fat: 5 g
- Protein: 4 g
- Sodium: 237 mg

318. Zucchini Oat Muffins

"People wouldn't notice the vegetable in these treats."
Serving: 1 dozen. | Prep: 10m | Ready in: 35m

Ingredients

- 2-1/2 cups all-purpose flour
- 1-1/2 cups sugar
- 1 cup chopped pecans
- 1/2 cup quick-cooking oats
- 1 tbsp. baking powder
- 1 tsp. salt
- 1 tsp. ground cinnamon
- 4 large eggs
- 1 medium zucchini, shredded (about 3/4 cup)
- 3/4 cup vegetable oil

Direction

- Combine cinnamon, salt, oats, baking powder, pecans, sugar and flour in a big bowl. Beat eggs in a small bowl. Mix with oil and zucchini then mix into dry ingredients. Stir just until it becomes moist – it will become lumpy.
- Put into greased muffin cups to 3/4 full. Bake at 400 degrees until a toothpick comes out clean when inserted in the middle or for 20 to 25mins. Let it cool for 5mins then move to wire rack from the pan.

Nutrition Information

- Calories: 421 calories
- Total Carbohydrate: 49 g
- Cholesterol: 71 mg
- Total Fat: 23 g
- Fiber: 2 g
- Protein: 6 g
- Sodium: 319 mg

319. Zucchini Pineapple Bread

"Without an overpowering pineapple taste, pineapple makes this bread extra moist."
Serving: 18 | Prep: 20m | Ready in: 2h20m

Ingredients

- 3 cups all-purpose flour
- 2 tsps. baking soda
- 1 tsp. salt
- 1/4 tsp. baking powder
- 1 1/2 tsps. ground cinnamon
- 2 cups white sugar
- 1 cup vegetable oil
- 3 eggs
- 3/4 tsp. vanilla extract
- 2 cups shredded zucchini
- 1 (8 oz.) can crushed pineapple, well drained
- 1 cup raisins
- 1 cup chopped walnuts

Direction

- Preheat the oven to 165°C or 325°F. With parchment paper, line the base of 2 loaf pans 9x5-inch in size.
- In a bowl, combine cinnamon, baking powder, salt, baking soda and flour. In a big mixing bowl, whisk vanilla extract, eggs, vegetable oil and sugar together, and mix in pineapple and zucchini. Slowly add the flour mixture, stirring till just combined. Fold in walnuts and raisins, combining to equally incorporate. Distribute batter equally among the 2 prepped loaf pans.
- In the prepped oven, bake for an hour till a toothpick pricked into the middle comes out clean. Working with one loaf at a time, hold pan on its side and softly pat the sides against the counter to let it loosen. Cover pan using a cooling rack, and turn it to tip cake out of pan onto the rack. Remove the parchment paper, and let the bread cool fully.

Nutrition Information

- Calories: 359 calories;
- Total Carbohydrate: 48.1 g
- Cholesterol: 31 mg
- Total Fat: 17.6 g
- Protein: 4.7 g
- Sodium: 290 mg

---

320. Zucchini Pizza Loaves

"Delectable loaves loaded with healthy vegetables. Freeze some of them to bring to winter parties or potlucks."
Serving: 2 loaves (4 servings each). | Prep: 30m | Ready in: 60m

Ingredients

- 2 medium zucchini, thinly sliced
- 1 medium onion, finely chopped
- 1 cup sliced fresh mushrooms
- 2 tsps. olive oil
- 2 garlic cloves, minced
- 1 can (8 oz.) no-salt-added tomato sauce
- 1 medium tomato, seeded and chopped
- 1 can (2-1/4 oz.) sliced ripe olives, drained
- 2 tsps. Italian seasoning
- 2 tubes (11 oz. each) refrigerated crusty French loaf
- 3 slices provolone cheese, chopped
- 1 oz. sliced turkey pepperoni, julienned
- 1 cup shredded part-skim mozzarella cheese

Direction

- Sauté mushrooms, onion, and zucchini in oil in a large skillet until they are tender. Add garlic and cook for 1 more minute. Stir in the Italian seasoning, olives, tomato, and tomato sauce; then retrieve from the heat.
- Beginning with the seam, unroll a loaf of dough. Pat to a 14x12-inch rectangle. Scatter pepperoni and 1/2 of the provolone leaving 1/2 inch border from edges. Scatter 1/2 of the zucchini mixture over; scatter with 1/2 of the mozzarella.
- Beginning at a long side, roll up jelly-roll style; press the seams to seal. Arrange on a baking sheet greased using cooking spray, seam side down. Repeat with the rest of the zucchini mixture, cheeses, pepperoni, and dough.
- Bake at 350 degrees until golden brown, 30-35 minutes. Cut and serve it warm.

Nutrition Information

- Calories: 322 calories
- Total Carbohydrate: 42 g
- Cholesterol: 20 mg
- Total Fat: 10 g
- Fiber: 3 g
- Protein: 15 g
- Sodium: 801 mg

321. Zucchini Raisin Bread

"Moist bread that is made of cinnamon, plump raisins and shredded zucchini. You can experiment slices of it toasted."
Serving: 1 loaf (about 1-1/2 lbs.). | Prep: 10m | Ready in: 03h10m

Ingredients

- 3/4 cup plus 2 tbsps. water (70° to 80°)
- 2 tbsps. butter, softened
- 1 cup shredded zucchini
- 2 tbsps. sugar
- 4-1/2 tsps. nonfat dry milk powder
- 1 tsp. salt
- 1/2 tsp. ground cinnamon
- 3-1/2 cups bread flour
- 2-1/2 tsps. active dry yeast
- 1/2 cup raisins

Direction

- Put the first 9 ingredients in the bread machine pan in the order proposed by machine's maker. Then use the basic bread setting. If available select the loaf size and crust color.
- Bake according to the directions on the bread machine (after five minutes of mixing elapse, you can add one to two tbsps. of flour or water if necessary). Add in raisins just before the last kneading (the machine may signal this audibly).

Nutrition Information

- Calories: 125 calories
- Total Carbohydrate: 25 g
- Cholesterol: 4 mg
- Total Fat: 1 g
- Fiber: 1 g
- Protein: 4 g
- Sodium: 167 mg

322. Zucchini Snack Bread

"This is a very good snack."
Serving: 2 loaves. | Prep: 15m | Ready in: 01h05m

Ingredients

- 3 cups all-purpose flour
- 2-1/4 tsps. ground cinnamon
- 1-1/4 tsps. salt
- 1 tsp. baking soda
- 1/4 tsp. baking powder
- 1/4 tsp. ground nutmeg
- 3 eggs
- 2 cups sugar
- 1 cup canola oil
- 1 tbsp. vanilla extract
- 2 cups shredded zucchini
- 1 cup chopped walnuts

Direction

- Mix the nutmeg, baking powder, baking soda, salt, flour, and cinnamon in a big bowl, then set it aside. Lightly beat eggs in a separate big bowl. Stir in vanilla, oil and sugar. Put in the dry ingredients and stir just until moistened. Fold in nuts and zucchini – it will become stiff.
- Pour mixture into 2 greased and floured loaf pans that are 8x4 inches in size. Bake at 350 degrees until toothpick comes out clean when inserted in the middle or for 50 to 60mins. Allow to cool for 10mins in the pan. Move to a wire rack.

Nutrition Information

- Calories: 184 calories
- Total Carbohydrate: 22 g
- Cholesterol: 20 mg
- Total Fat: 10 g
- Fiber: 1 g
- Protein: 3 g
- Sodium: 141 mg

323. Zucchini Yeast Bread

"A delicious breakfast with a mixture of zucchini bread and sweet dough."
Serving: 1 loaf. | Prep: 20m | Ready in: 60m

Ingredients

- 1 tbsp. active dry yeast
- 1/2 cup warm water (110° to 115°)
- 1/3 cup warm whole milk (110° to 115°)
- 1/3 cup sugar
- 3 tbsps. butter, softened
- 3 tbsps. grated orange zest
- 1/2 tsp. salt
- 1-1/2 cups shredded unpeeled zucchini
- 1/3 cup raisins
- 1-1/2 cups whole wheat flour
- 2 tsps. ground cardamom
- 1-2/3 to 2-1/3 cups all-purpose flour

Direction

- Dissolve the yeast in warm water in a large bowl. Whisk in salt, orange zest, butter, sugar, and milk. Whisk in enough all-purpose flour, cardamom, whole wheat flour, raisins, and zucchini to make a soft dough.
- Transfer on a floured surface and knead for 6-8 minutes until elastic and smooth. Put in a greased bowl and rotate one time to grease the top. Put a cover and allow to rise in a warm place for 1 1/4 hours until it is doubled.
- Punch down the dough and form into a loaf. Arrange into a 9x5-inch greased loaf pan. Put a cover and allow to rise for 45 minutes until it is doubled.
- Bake at 375 degrees until golden brown, for 40-45 minutes. Transfer from the pan onto a wire rack to cool down.

Nutrition Information

- Calories: 138 calories
- Total Carbohydrate: 26 g
- Cholesterol: 6 mg
- Total Fat: 3 g
- Fiber: 2 g
- Protein: 4 g
- Sodium: 100 mg

324. Zucchini-oatmeal Muffins

"Use zucchini in these healthy oatmeal muffins."
Serving: 16 | Ready in: 55m

Ingredients

- ½ cup plus 1 tbsp. rolled oats
- ¼ cup pecan halves
- 1½ cups all-purpose flour
- 1 cup whole-wheat pastry flour
- 1½ cups sugar
- 1 tbsp. baking powder
- 1½ tsps. ground cinnamon
- 1 tsp. salt
- 2 large eggs
- 3 large egg whites
- ½ cup apple butter
- ¼ cup canola oil
- 2 cups grated zucchini, (about 1 medium)

Direction

- Preheat oven at 375 °F. Use paper lines to line 16 muffin cups or use cooking spray to coat them.
- On separate areas of a baking sheet, spread pecans and rolled oats. Bake for 5 to 10 mins until they are toasted lightly. Allow to cool then chop the pecans.
- In a big bowl, mix pecans, 1/2 cup of toasted oats, salt, cinnamon, baking powder, whole wheat flour, sugar and all-purpose flour together. In a medium bowl, whisk oil, apple butter, egg whites and eggs together. Mix the zucchini in. Mix the wet ingredients into the dry ingredients until it becomes moist. Spoon the batter into the prepped muffin cups and fill about 3/4 full. On top, sprinkle the leftover oats.
- Bake for 20 - 25 minutes until tops spring back when lightly pressed and golden.

Nutrition Information

- Calories: 230 calories;
- Total Carbohydrate: 40 g
- Cholesterol: 23 mg
- Total Fat: 6 g
- Fiber: 2 g
- Protein: 4 g
- Sodium: 271 mg
- Sugar: 23 g
- Saturated Fat: 1 g

Chapter 6: Zucchini Cake Recipes

***

325. Blueberry Zucchini Squares

"This hearty dish features fresh blueberries and shredded zucchini."
Serving: 2 dozen. | Prep: 30m | Ready in: 60m

Ingredients

- 2 cups shredded zucchini (do not pack)
- 1/2 cup buttermilk
- 1 tbsp. grated lemon zest
- 3 tbsps. lemon juice
- 1 cup butter, softened
- 2-1/2 cups sugar
- 2 large eggs
- 3-1/4 cups plus 2 tbsps. all-purpose flour, divided
- 1 tsp. baking soda
- 1/2 tsp. salt
- 2 cups fresh or frozen blueberries
- GLAZE:
- 2 cups confectioners' sugar

- 1/4 cup buttermilk
- 1 tbsp. grated lemon zest
- 2 tsps. lemon juice
- 1/8 tsp. salt

Direction

- Set oven to 350° to preheat. Grease a baking pan of 15x10x1 inches.
- Mix lemon juice, lemon zest, buttermilk and zucchini together in a small bowl; toss to combine. In a large bowl, cream sugar and butter until fluffy and light. Beat in eggs, one at a time. Whisk salt, baking soda and 3-1/4 cups flour together in another bowl; slowly put into creamed mixture alternately with zucchini mixture, blending completely after each adding. Toss the blueberries with remaining flour; then fold into batter.
- Remove the batter to the greased pan, evenly spreading, the pan will be full. Bake in the oven until lightly golden brown and a toothpick put in the middle goes out clean, about 30-35 minutes. Allow to completely cool in pan on a wire rack.
- Mix glaze ingredients in a small bowl until smooth; spread on top. Allow to sit until set.

Nutrition Information

- Calories: 270 calories
- Total Carbohydrate: 47 g
- Cholesterol: 36 mg
- Total Fat: 8 g
- Fiber: 1 g
- Protein: 3 g
- Sodium: 197 mg

326. Buttermilk Chocolate Zucchini Cake

"Please others with this moist zucchini cake recipe."
Serving: 12-15 servings. | Prep: 20m | Ready in: 01h05m

Ingredients

- 1 cup packed brown sugar
- 1/2 cup sugar
- 1/2 cup butter, softened
- 1/2 cup vegetable oil
- 3 large eggs
- 1 tsp. vanilla extract
- 1/2 cup buttermilk
- 2-1/2 cups all-purpose flour
- 1/2 tsp. ground allspice
- 1/2 tsp. ground cinnamon
- 1/2 tsp. salt
- 2 tsps. baking soda
- 4 tbsps. baking cocoa
- 3 cups grated zucchini (about 3 medium), drained
- 1/2 to 1 cup semisweet chocolate chips

Direction

- Cream oil, butter, and sugars in a large bowl. Add buttermilk, vanilla, and eggs; combine thoroughly. Sift the dry ingredients together; add into the creamed mixture. Add the zucchini and stir until combined. Pour in a greased and floured 13x9-inch baking pan. Scatter top with chocolate chips. Bake at 325 degrees until the cake tests done, for 45 minutes.

Nutrition Information

- Calories: 328 calories
- Total Carbohydrate: 43 g
- Cholesterol: 59 mg
- Total Fat: 16 g
- Fiber: 2 g
- Protein: 5 g
- Sodium: 337 mg

327. Carrot Blueberry Cupcakes

"An interesting combination with zucchini, pineapple, blueberries, and carrots."
Serving: 16 cupcakes. | Prep: 35m | Ready in: 55m

Ingredients

- 1 cup sugar
- 1/2 cup canola oil
- 2 large eggs
- 1 tsp. vanilla extract
- 1-1/2 cups all-purpose flour
- 1 tsp. baking powder
- 1 tsp. ground cinnamon
- 1/2 tsp. baking soda
- 1/2 tsp. salt
- 1 cup finely shredded carrots
- 3/4 cup grated zucchini
- 1/2 cup unsweetened crushed pineapple, drained
- 1 cup fresh or frozen unsweetened blueberries
- FROSTING:
- 3 oz. cream cheese, softened
- 1/4 cup butter, softened
- 2-1/2 cups confectioners' sugar
- 1 tsp. vanilla extract
- 1/2 cup chopped pecans, optional

Direction

- Beat sugar, vanilla, eggs, and oil in a small bowl. Mix salt, baking soda, cinnamon, baking powder, and flour in another large bowl; beat into the sugar mixture gradually until blended. Stir in the pineapple, zucchini, and carrots. Then fold in blueberries.
- Fill 2/3 full into the paper-lined muffin cups. Then bake for 18-22 minutes at 375°, or until inserting in the center with a toothpick and it comes out clean. Then let it cool for around 10 minutes before transferring from pans to wire racks and let it completely cool.
- To make the frosting: Whisk butter and cream cheese in a large bowl until fluffy. Then add vanilla and confectioners' sugar; continue to beat until smooth. Then frost the cupcakes. If desired, scatter with nuts. Chill the leftovers.

Nutrition Information

- Calories: 294 calories
- Total Carbohydrate: 44 g
- Cholesterol: 40 mg
- Total Fat: 13 g
- Fiber: 1 g
- Protein: 3 g
- Sodium: 189 mg

328. Chocolate Zucchini Cake

"The zucchini makes the cake especially moist."
Serving: Serves 12

Ingredients

- 2 1/4 cups sifted all purpose flour
- 1/2 cup unsweetened cocoa powder
- 1 tsp. baking soda
- 1 tsp. salt
- 1 3/4 cups sugar
- 1/2 cup (1 stick) unsalted butter, room temperature
- 1/2 cup vegetable oil
- 2 large eggs
- 1 tsp. vanilla extract
- 1/2 cup buttermilk
- 2 cups grated unpeeled zucchini (about 2 1/2 medium)
- 1 6-oz. package (about 1 cup) semisweet chocolate chips
- 3/4 cup chopped walnuts

Direction

- Set an oven to 325°F and start preheating. Coat a 13x9x2-inch baking pan with butter and flour. Sift salt, baking soda, cocoa powder and flour into a medium bowl. Whip oil, butter and sugar in large bowl till thoroughly combined. Whisk eggs, 1 by 1, whisking thoroughly after every addition. Whisk in the vanilla extract. Combine in the dry ingredients alternating with buttermilk in 3 additions each. Combine in the grated zucchini. Pour the

batter into the buttered and floured pan. Scatter with nuts and chocolate chips.
- Bake the cake for 50 minutes until a tester comes out clean when inserted in the center. Let the cake cool entirely in the pan.

Nutrition Information

- Calories: 493
- Total Carbohydrate: 60 g
- Cholesterol: 52 mg
- Total Fat: 28 g
- Fiber: 3 g
- Protein: 7 g
- Sodium: 317 mg
- Saturated Fat: 9 g

329. Chocolate Zucchini Cake With Coconut Frosting

"A moist cake with crunchy topping and grated zucchini."
Serving: 12-15 servings. | Prep: 20m | Ready in: 01h10m

Ingredients

- 1/2 cup butter, softened
- 1/2 cup canola oil
- 1-3/4 cups sugar
- 2 large eggs
- 1 tsp. vanilla extract
- 2-1/2 cups all-purpose flour
- 1/4 cup baking cocoa
- 1 tsp. baking soda
- 1/2 tsp. baking powder
- 1/2 tsp. ground cinnamon
- 1/2 tsp. ground cloves
- 1/2 cup buttermilk
- 2 cups shredded zucchini
- FROSTING:
- 1 cup sweetened shredded coconut
- 6 tbsps. butter, softened
- 2/3 cup packed brown sugar
- 1/2 cup chopped walnuts
- 1/4 cup whole milk

Direction

- Whisk sugar, oil, and butter in a large bowl until they are smooth. Add 1 egg at a time and whisk thoroughly after every addition. Whisk in vanilla. Mix cloves, cinnamon, baking powder, baking soda, cocoa, and flour; then add gradually into the batter alternately with buttermilk and whisk thoroughly after every addition. Then fold in the zucchini.
- Pour in a 13x9-inch greased baking pan. Bake at 325 degrees until a toothpick comes out clean when inserted into the center, for 45-50 minutes. Let cool for 10 minutes on a wire rack.
- In the meantime, mix frosting ingredients in a small bowl. Spread on the warm cake. Broil 4-6 inches from the heat source until golden brown, 2-3 minutes. Let cool entirely.

Nutrition Information

- Calories: 440 calories
- Total Carbohydrate: 54 g
- Cholesterol: 58 mg
- Total Fat: 24 g
- Fiber: 2 g
- Protein: 5 g
- Sodium: 246 mg

330. Chocolate Zucchini Cupcakes

""*A nice way to get your grandkids eat veggies happily.*""
Serving: 21 cupcakes. | Prep: 25m | Ready in: 45m

Ingredients

- 1-1/4 cups butter, softened
- 1-1/2 cups sugar
- 2 eggs
- 1 tsp. vanilla extract
- 2-1/2 cups all-purpose flour
- 3/4 cup baking cocoa
- 1 tsp. baking powder
- 1 tsp. baking soda
- 1/2 tsp. salt

- 1/2 cup plain yogurt
- 1 cup grated zucchini
- 1 cup grated carrots
- 1 can (16 oz.) chocolate frosting

Direction

- Cream sugar and butter in a large bowl, till fluffy and light. Include in eggs, one each time, beating well after each increment. Mix in vanilla. Mix salt, baking soda, baking powder, baking cocoa and flour together; put alternating with yogurt into the creamed mixture, beating well after each addition. Fold in carrots and zucchini.
- Fill paper-lined muffin cups two-thirds full. Bake at 350° till a toothpick comes out clean when inserted into the center, 18-22 minutes. Allow to cool for 10 minutes; take out of pans and place on wire racks; cool completely. Frost the cupcakes.

Nutrition Information

- Calories: 326 calories
- Total Carbohydrate: 40 g
- Cholesterol: 50 mg
- Total Fat: 17 g
- Fiber: 1 g
- Protein: 3 g
- Sodium: 288 mg

331. Chocolate Zucchini Roll

"*Just a superb way to have some delicious cake and use remaining garden zucchini.*"
Serving: 10 servings. | Prep: 20m | Ready in: 35m

Ingredients

- 3 large eggs
- 1 tsp. vanilla extract
- 1 cup all-purpose flour
- 3/4 cup sugar
- 1/2 cup baking cocoa
- 1 tsp. baking soda
- 1 tsp. ground cinnamon

- 1/4 tsp. salt
- 1 cup shredded peeled zucchini
- FILLING:
- 1 package (8 oz.) cream cheese, softened
- 1/4 cup butter, softened
- 2 tsps. vanilla extract
- 1 cup confectioners' sugar
- Additional confectioners' sugar

Direction

- Prepare a 15x10x1-inch greased baking pan by lining with waxed paper. Grease the waxed paper and put aside. In a mixing bowl, whisk eggs for 3 minutes, gradually adding sugar. Whisk for additional 2 minutes, making the mixture lemon-colored and thick. Add in vanilla and zucchini. In a separate bowl combine the cocoa, flour, cinnamon, baking soda, and salt; add to the egg mixture to form a thick batter.
- Evenly pour the batter in the prepared pan and bake for 10-15 minutes at 350 degrees Fahrenheit. The cake should spring back when gently touched. Let the cake cool for 5 minutes and then invert onto a cocoa-dusted kitchen towel. Carefully remove the paper. Start with the short side and form a jelly-roll style cake using a kitchen towel. Set on a wire rack and wait for the cake to cool completely.
- Prepare a filling by combining butter, vanilla, and cream cheese in a big bowl. Whisk until filling becomes fluffy. Whisk in the confectioners' sugar until well combined.
- Unroll the cake and evenly spread the filling on the cake, leaving half inch of edges empty. Roll up once more and transfer on a serving platter placing the seam side down. Sprinkle with confectioners' sugar. Cover; refrigerate for one hour.

Nutrition Information

- Calories: 309 calories
- Total Carbohydrate: 40 g
- Cholesterol: 101 mg
- Total Fat: 15 g
- Fiber: 1 g

- Protein: 6 g
- Sodium: 318 mg

332. Chocolate Zucchini Sheet Cake

"This recipe is perfect for Texas sheet cake lovers. It is made like the Texas sheet cake. Make use of your garden-fresh zucchini!"
Serving: 20 servings. | Prep: 15m | Ready in: 40m

Ingredients

- 2 cups sugar
- 1 cup vegetable oil
- 3 large eggs
- 2-1/2 cups all-purpose flour
- 1/4 cup baking cocoa
- 1 tsp. baking soda
- 1/4 tsp. baking powder
- 1/4 tsp. salt
- 1/2 cup whole milk
- 2 cups shredded fresh zucchini
- 1 tbsp. vanilla extract
- FROSTING:
- 1/2 cup butter, softened
- 1/4 cup baking cocoa
- 6 tbsps. evaporated milk
- 1 lb. (4 cups) confectioners' sugar
- 1 tbsp. vanilla extract

Direction

- Mix sugar and oil in a bowl. Add in eggs one at a time beat well after each one. Mix cocoa, flour, baking powder, baking soda, and salt. Add mixture slowly while alternating with milk to the egg mixture. Pour in extract and zucchini. In a greased 15x10x1-in. pan, pour the mixture. Bake for 25 minutes or until when tested it is done at 375 degrees. When baking cake, mix all frosting ingredients until smooth. Spread frosting on while cake is still hot. Let cool on wire rack.

Nutrition Information

- Calories: 395 calories
- Total Carbohydrate: 58 g
- Cholesterol: 46 mg
- Total Fat: 17 g
- Fiber: 1 g
- Protein: 4 g
- Sodium: 162 mg

333. Chocolaty Zucchini Cake

"This chocolate cake that my mom always makes tastes wonderful. They especially come in handy when you need to use up zucchini."
Serving: 14 servings. | Prep: 15m | Ready in: 01h20m

Ingredients

- 4 eggs
- 3 cups sugar
- 1-1/2 cups vegetable oil
- 3 oz. unsweetened chocolate, melted and cooled
- 3 cups all-purpose flour
- 1-1/2 tsps. baking powder
- 1 tsp. baking soda
- 1 tsp. salt
- 3 cups shredded zucchini, squeezed dry
- 1 cup finely chopped nuts

Direction

- Beat eggs in a bowl on high until they turn into a lemon color and thick. Slowly beat in sugar. Put in chocolate and oil then beat thoroughly. Mix together salt, baking soda, baking powder and flour; pour into the beaten mixture. On low, beat the mixture just until incorporated. Mix in nuts and zucchini.
- Transfer batter to a 10-inch fluted tube pan that is already greased and floured. Bake in 350-degree oven until a toothpick is clean when coming out of the middle, or 65 to 75 minutes. Allow to cool for 10 minutes, then transfer to a wire rack and finish cooling.

Nutrition Information

- Calories: 580 calories
- Total Carbohydrate: 68 g
- Cholesterol: 61 mg
- Total Fat: 33 g
- Fiber: 2 g
- Protein: 7 g
- Sodium: 302 mg

334. Cranberry Zucchini Wedges

"The mixture of the tender texture and delicious flavor with zucchini, cranberries, and pineapple in these cake wedges is so amazing."
Serving: 2 cakes (8 wedges each). | Prep: 15m | Ready in: 45m

Ingredients

- 1 can (20 oz.) pineapple chunks
- 3 cups all-purpose flour
- 1-3/4 cups sugar
- 1 tsp. baking powder
- 1 tsp. baking soda
- 1 tsp. salt
- 3 large eggs
- 1 cup canola oil
- 2 tsps. vanilla extract
- 1 cup tightly packed shredded zucchini
- 1 cup fresh or frozen cranberries, halved
- 1/2 cup chopped walnuts
- Confectioners' sugar

Direction

- Drain juice from pineapple and save 1/3 cup (reserve the rest for other use). In a blender, put the saved juice and pineapple; put a cover and pulse until smooth. Then put aside.
- Mix salt, baking soda, baking powder, sugar, and flour in a large bowl. Beat the pineapple mixture, vanilla, oil, and eggs in a small bowl; then add into the dry ingredients and stir until combined. Fold in nuts, cranberries, and zucchini.

- Pour in 2 greased and floured 9-inch round baking pans. Bake at 350 degrees until a toothpick comes out clean when inserted into the center, for 30-35 minutes.
- Let cool for 10 minutes, then transfer from the pans onto wire racks to cool entirely. Sprinkle with the confectioners' sugar just before serving.

Nutrition Information

- Calories: 354 calories
- Total Carbohydrate: 47 g
- Cholesterol: 40 mg
- Total Fat: 17 g
- Fiber: 1 g
- Protein: 5 g
- Sodium: 264 mg

335. Garden Patch Cake

"This is a different moist cake where vegetables like shredded zucchini, beets and carrots are mixed with chocolate chips."
Serving: 12-16 servings. | Prep: 60m | Ready in: 01h35m

Ingredients

- 1 cup canola oil
- 3 large eggs
- 1-1/2 cups sugar
- 1 tsp. vanilla extract
- 2 cups all-purpose flour
- 2 tsps. baking powder
- 1-1/2 tsps. ground cinnamon
- 1/4 tsp. salt
- 1 cup finely shredded carrots
- 1 cup finely shredded zucchini
- 1/2 cup finely shredded beets
- 1-1/2 cups semisweet chocolate chips
- FROSTING:
- 6 oz. cream cheese, softened
- 1/2 cup butter, softened
- 2 tsps. vanilla extract
- 4-1/2 cups confectioners' sugar
- GARDEN PATCH CAKE DECORATING:

- 3/4 cup shortening
- 1 tsp. vanilla extract
- 1/2 tsp. almond extract
- Pinch salt
- 3 to 3-1/2 cups confectioners' sugar
- 2 tbsps. whole milk
- 7 wooden craft or Popsicle sticks (4-1/2 inches)
- 1/2 tsp. baking cocoa
- Red, yellow, orange and green liquid or paste food coloring
- Pastry tips - #5 and #10 round, #67 leaf and #20 star
- 5 pastry bags or small heavy-duty resealable plastic bags

Direction

- Beat eggs, oil, sugar and vanilla in a big bowl. Add in flour, cinnamon, baking powder and salt. Mix well. Then add the vegetables and chocolate chips. Ensure mixture is blended well. Transfer the mixture to a 13x9-inch sized baking pan that is previously greased and floured. Then bake for 35 to 40 minutes or until toothpick comes out clean when inserted at the middle at 350°F. Remove from oven and cool for around 15 minutes. Take out the cake from the pan and cool completely on a wire rack.
- For the frosting, whip butter, cream cheese and vanilla until fluffy and light. Slowly add confectioners' sugar while mixing until smooth and pour over the cake. Chill in refrigerator.
- To decorate, see below for the frosting recipe.
- Garden Patch Cake Decorating: Whip shortening, salt and extracts in a bowl then slowly add in sugar and milk alternately. Continue beating until stiff and smooth. Cover the bowl with damp paper towel and plastic wrap until ready for use.
- For Making Trellis: Arrange 5 popsicle sticks or craft with 1/4 inch distance between stick bottom that are inserted into cake and 1/2 inch distance between tops on waxing paper sheet. Put frosting at the back part of remaining

popsicle sticks then place across the 5 sticks with 1 inch and 2 inch distance from top. Let it dry for an hour then press the stick bottom to upper left side corner of the cake.

- For Garden Patch Preparation: Put a mark at the lower right corner of about 5.5x3.5 inch size using a toothpick. Sprinkle with cocoa powder and lightly press into cake.
- For Vegetables and Border Preparation: Mix red food color and 1/4 cup frosting and fill a plastic bag or pastry bag with round tip #10. Put 8-10 tomatoes in the trellis front by holding the pastry bag up and down. Mix yellow food color and 1/2 cup frosting, and fill in another pastry bag with round tip #5. Repeat the previous procedure to form small dots in a row to pattern 8-10 ears of corn kernel at upper right corner. Mix orange food color and 1/2 cup frosting, and fill in another pastry bag with tip #10. Repeat procedure to form 4 carrots in 3 rows at the garden patch. For the remaining frosting, add some green food color and fill in a pastry bag with leaf tip. Form leaves and stems of tomatoes and carrots by piping from husks on the corn ear edges. Then add some vines to trellis. Fill remaining green icing to a pastry bag with star tip and form a border around upper edge and base of the cake.

Nutrition Information

- Calories: 720 calories
- Total Carbohydrate: 99 g
- Cholesterol: 61 mg
- Total Fat: 36 g
- Fiber: 2 g
- Protein: 4 g
- Sodium: 191 mg

336. Makeover Chocolate Zucchini Cake

"A rich and moist chocolate flavored cake with less sugar, fat and calories."
Serving: 14 servings. | Prep: 15m | Ready in: 01h10m

Ingredients

- 2 eggs
- 2 egg whites
- 1-1/2 cups sugar
- 1/2 cup packed brown sugar
- 1/2 cup unsweetened applesauce
- 1/2 cup canola oil
- 1/4 cup corn syrup
- 3 oz. unsweetened chocolate, melted and cooled
- 3 cups all-purpose flour
- 1-1/2 tsps. baking powder
- 1 tsp. baking soda
- 1 tsp. salt
- 3 cups shredded zucchini, squeezed dry
- 1/2 cup finely chopped nuts
- 1 tsp. confectioners' sugar

Direction

- Beat the initial 8 ingredients in a big bowl until it becomes smooth. Mix together the salt, baking soda, baking powder and flour, then slowly add it to the egg mixture and stir just until blended. Fold in the nuts and zucchini.
- Pour it into a cooking spray and flour coated 10-inch fluted tube pan. Let it bake for 55 to 65 minutes at 350 degrees or until an inserted toothpick in the middle exits clean. Allow it to cool for 10 minutes prior to taking it out from the pan to fully cool on a wire rack. Dust confectioner's sugar on top.

Nutrition Information

- Calories: 373 calories
- Total Carbohydrate: 59 g
- Cholesterol: 30 mg
- Total Fat: 14 g
- Fiber: 2 g

- Protein: 6 g
- Sodium: 311 mg

337. Maple Zucchini Cake

"A super easy recipe to make this luscious pancake for your family throughout the year."
Serving: 16-20 servings. | Prep: 20m | Ready in: 01h05m

Ingredients

- 3 large eggs
- 2 cups all-purpose flour
- 2 cups shredded zucchini
- 1 cup sugar
- 1 cup vegetable oil
- 1 cup maple syrup
- 3 tsps. ground cinnamon
- 2 tsps. vanilla extract
- 2 tsps. baking soda
- 1 tsp. baking powder
- 1 tsp. salt
- 1-1/2 cups chopped walnuts
- 1 cup raisins
- Prepared cream cheese frosting

Direction

- Mix the first 11 ingredients in a large bowl; beat at medium speed until combined thoroughly, 1-2 minutes. Then fold on raisins and walnuts.
- Place into a 13x9-inch greased baking pan. Bake at 350 degrees until a toothpick comes out clean when inserted into the center, for 45-50 minutes. Transfer onto a wire rack and allow to cool entirely. Then frost with the cream cheese frosting.

Nutrition Information

- Calories: 316 calories
- Total Carbohydrate: 38 g
- Cholesterol: 32 mg
- Total Fat: 17 g
- Fiber: 1 g

- Protein: 5 g
- Sodium: 277 mg

338. Orange Zucchini Cake

"A wonderful cake with tasty cream cheese frosting and tangy orange flavor."
Serving: 8-10 servings. | Prep: 25m | Ready in: 55m

Ingredients

- 1/2 cup golden raisins
- 1 cup boiling water
- 3/4 cup sugar
- 1/2 cup vegetable oil
- 2 large eggs
- 1/2 cup All-Bran cereal
- 1-1/2 tsps. grated orange zest
- 1 tsp. vanilla extract
- 1 cup all-purpose flour
- 1 tsp. baking powder
- 1 tsp. ground cinnamon
- 1/2 tsp. baking soda
- 1/2 tsp. ground nutmeg
- 1/4 tsp. salt
- 1 cup thinly shredded zucchini
- FROSTING:
- 3 oz. cream cheese, softened
- 1 tbsp. butter, softened
- 1 tsp. grated orange zest
- 1-1/2 cups confectioners' sugar
- 1/2 to 1 tsp. water

Direction

- In a bowl, put water and raisins; allow to stand for 5 minutes. Drain raisins; put aside. Mix eggs, oil, and sugar in a bowl; combine thoroughly. Stir in vanilla, orange zest, and cereal. Mix the dry ingredients; add into the sugar mixture; combine thoroughly. Stir in raisins and zucchini. Pour in an 11x7-inch greased baking pan. Bake at 325 degrees until a toothpick comes out clean when inserted into the center, for 30-35 minutes. Let cool.

- Whisk orange zest, butter, and cream cheese in a bowl until they are fluffy and light. Add water and sugar gradually; whisk until smooth. Then frost the cooled cake. Store the leftovers in the fridge.

Nutrition Information

- Calories: 358 calories
- Total Carbohydrate: 52 g
- Cholesterol: 55 mg
- Total Fat: 16 g
- Fiber: 2 g
- Protein: 4 g
- Sodium: 221 mg

339. Raisin-zucchini Spice Cupcakes

"Impress others with these zucchini muffins."
Serving: 2 dozen. | Prep: 30m | Ready in: 50m

Ingredients

- 1 package spice cake mix (regular size)
- 1-1/3 cups water
- 1/4 cup canola oil
- 3 large eggs
- 2 cups shredded zucchini
- 1/2 cup raisins
- CINNAMON FROSTING:
- 1/4 cup butter, softened
- 1-3/4 cups confectioners' sugar
- 1 tsp. vanilla extract
- 1/2 tsp. ground cinnamon
- 1/8 tsp. ground nutmeg
- 1 to 2 tbsps. 2% milk

Direction

- Mix eggs, oil, water, and cake mix in a large bowl; whisk for half a minute at low speed. Whisk for 2 minutes at medium speed. Stir in raisins and zucchini. Pour in paper-lined muffin cups to 2/3 full.

- Bake at 350 degrees until a toothpick comes out clean when inserted into the center, for 18-22 minutes. Let cool for 10 minutes, then transfer onto wire racks and cool entirely.
- To make the frosting: Whisk butter until it is fluffy and light in a small bowl. Whisk in enough milk, nutmeg, cinnamon, vanilla, and confectioners' sugar to reach spreading consistency. Then frost the cupcakes.

Nutrition Information

- Calories: 183 calories
- Total Carbohydrate: 28 g
- Cholesterol: 37 mg
- Total Fat: 7 g
- Fiber: 0 g
- Protein: 2 g
- Sodium: 188 mg

340. Zucchini Cake

"An old-styled recipe for a tasty cake."
Serving: 10-12 servings. | Prep: 30m | Ready in: 60m

Ingredients

- 3 cups all-purpose flour
- 3 cups sugar
- 2-1/2 tsps. ground cinnamon
- 1-1/2 tsps. baking soda
- 1 tsp. salt
- 1-1/2 cups vegetable oil
- 4 large eggs, lightly beaten
- 1 tsp. vanilla extract
- 3 cups shredded zucchini
- 1 cup chopped walnuts
- FROSTING:
- 1 package (8 oz.) cream cheese, softened
- 1/2 cup butter, softened
- 3-3/4 to 4 cups confectioners' sugar
- 1 tsp. vanilla extract

Direction

- Mix salt, baking soda, cinnamon, sugar, and flour in a bowl. Combine vanilla, eggs, and oil in another bowl; add into the flour mixture and whisk. Add zucchini; combine thoroughly. Then fold in nuts. Pour in three 9-inch well-greased round baking pans.
- Bake at 325 degrees until a toothpick comes out clean when inserted into the center, for 30 to 40 minutes. Let cool for 10 minutes, then transfer from the pans onto wire racks to cool entirely.
- To make the frosting: Whisk butter and cream cheese; combine in vanilla and sugar. Whisk until they are smooth. Frost sides and top and between the layers of the cake.

Nutrition Information

- Calories: 931 calories
- Total Carbohydrate: 117 g
- Cholesterol: 112 mg
- Total Fat: 49 g
- Fiber: 2 g
- Protein: 10 g
- Sodium: 511 mg

---

341. Zucchini Cake With Cream Cheese Frosting

"A tasty moist snack cake with sweet cream cheese frosting on top."
Serving: about 24 servings. | Prep: 30m | Ready in: 50m

Ingredients

- 3 large eggs
- 3/4 cup canola oil
- 2 cups all-purpose flour
- 2 cups sugar
- 2 tsps. baking powder
- 1-1/2 tsps. salt
- 1 tsp. ground cinnamon
- 2 cups shredded zucchini
- FROSTING:

- 3 oz. cream cheese, softened
- 2 tbsps. butter, softened
- 1 tsp. vanilla extract
- 3 cups confectioners' sugar
- 2 to 3 tbsps. milk

Direction

- Whisk oil and eggs in a large bowl. Mix cinnamon, salt, baking powder, sugar, and flour; add into the egg mixture and combine thoroughly. Add in zucchini and stir. Scatter in a 15x10x1-inch greased baking pan.
- Bake at 350 degrees until a toothpick comes out clean when inserted into the center, for 20-25 minutes. Place on a wire rack to cool entirely.
- Whisk vanilla, butter, and cream cheese in a small bowl until they are smooth. Whisk in the confectioners' sugar gradually. Add milk, enough to reach spreading consistency. Then frost the cake and slice into squares. Keep the leftovers in the fridge.

Nutrition Information

- Calories: 254 calories
- Total Carbohydrate: 40 g
- Cholesterol: 33 mg
- Total Fat: 10 g
- Fiber: 0 g
- Protein: 2 g
- Sodium: 210 mg

---

342. Zucchini Carrot Cake

"My husband wants this cake on his birthday."
Serving: 12-14 servings. | Prep: 35m | Ready in: 01h10m

Ingredients

- 4 large eggs
- 2 cups sugar
- 1-1/3 cups vegetable oil
- 2-1/2 cups all-purpose flour
- 2 tsps. baking soda

- 2 tsps. baking powder
- 2 tsps. ground cinnamon
- 1 tsp. ground cloves
- 1 tsp. ground allspice
- 1 tsp. ground ginger
- 1/2 tsp. ground nutmeg
- 1 tsp. salt
- 2 cups finely shredded carrots
- 2 cups finely shredded zucchini
- 1 cup coarsely chopped pecans or walnuts
- FROSTING:
- 1 package (8 oz.) cream cheese, softened
- 1/2 cup butter, softened
- 5 cups confectioners' sugar
- 2 tsps. vanilla extract
- Whole or chopped pecans or walnuts for garnish, optional

Direction

- Beat sugar and eggs until frothy in a large bowl. Beat in oil gradually. Mix dry ingredients; add to batter. Whisk for 4 minutes. Stir in nuts, zucchini and carrots. Transfer into 3 greased 9-in. round baking pans. Bake at 350° until top springs back when touched lightly or for about 35 minutes. Cool 5 minutes before taking out of pans. Allow to thoroughly cool on a wire rack.
- For frosting: Beat cream cheese and butter until smooth in a large bowl. Add vanilla and sugar. Keep whisking until sugar dissolves. Spread between layers and over sides and tops of the cake. Decorate with chopped or whole nuts if preferred.

Nutrition Information

- Calories: 749 calories
- Total Carbohydrate: 93 g
- Cholesterol: 96 mg
- Total Fat: 41 g
- Fiber: 2 g
- Protein: 7 g
- Sodium: 545 mg

343. Zucchini Carrot Spice Cake

"This cake with just enough spice and a marshmallow topping to satisfy your craving for sweets."
Serving: 12 servings. | Prep: 20m | Ready in: 50m

Ingredients

- 1 cup whole wheat flour
- 1 cup all-purpose flour
- 2-1/2 tsps. ground cinnamon
- 2 tsps. baking soda
- 3/4 tsp. ground nutmeg
- 1/4 tsp. ground cloves
- 1/2 cup buttermilk
- 1 cup unsweetened applesauce
- 1-1/2 cups shredded carrots
- 1/2 cup shredded zucchini
- 1 tsp. vanilla extract
- 6 egg whites
- 1-1/3 cups sugar
- FROSTING:
- 1 carton (8 oz.) reduced-fat cream cheese
- 1 jar (7-1/2 oz.) marshmallow creme
- 1 tsp. orange juice
- 1/2 tsp. vanilla extract

Direction

- Mix the first 6 ingredients in a large bowl. Add vanilla, zucchini, carrots, applesauce, and buttermilk gradually. Whisk egg whites in a small bowl until soft peaks form; slowly whisk in a tbsp. of sugar at a time until stiff peaks form. Fold gently into the batter.
- Pour in a 13x9-inch baking dish greased in cooking spray. Bake at 350 degrees until a toothpick comes out clean when inserted into the center, 30-40 minutes. Transfer onto a wire rack to cool.
- To make the frosting: Whisk vanilla, orange juice, marshmallow creme, and cream cheese in a large bowl until just mixed. Frost the cake.

Nutrition Information

- Calories: 291 calories
- Total Carbohydrate: 59 g

- Cholesterol: 11 mg
- Total Fat: 4 g
- Fiber: 3 g
- Protein: 7 g
- Sodium: 325 mg

344. Zucchini Chip Chocolate Cake

"Serve this chocolatey and moist cake alongside fresh berries or individually."
Serving: 15 servings. | Prep: 25m | Ready in: 01h10m

Ingredients

- 1/2 cup butter, softened
- 1-3/4 cups sugar
- 1/2 cup canola oil
- 2 eggs
- 1 tsp. vanilla extract
- 1 cup 2% milk
- 1/2 cup buttermilk
- 2-1/2 cups all-purpose flour
- 1/4 cup baking cocoa
- 1 tsp. baking soda
- 1/2 tsp. baking powder
- 1/2 tsp. salt
- 2 cups shredded zucchini
- 1/2 cup semisweet chocolate chips
- Confectioners' sugar

Direction

- Set an oven to 325 degrees and start preheating. Whisk oil, sugar, and butter in a large bowl until they are smooth. Add 1 egg at a time and whisk thoroughly after every addition. Whisk in vanilla. Mix buttermilk and milk. Mix salt, baking powder, baking soda, cocoa, and flour; then add into the batter alternately with milk mixture and whisk thoroughly after every addition. Then fold in the zucchini.
- Place into a 13x9-inch greased baking pan. Scatter with chocolate chips. Bake until a toothpick comes out clean when into the

center, for 45-50 minutes. Let cool on a wire rack. Sprinkle with confectioners' sugar.

Nutrition Information

- Calories: 341 calories
- Total Carbohydrate: 45 g
- Cholesterol: 46 mg
- Total Fat: 17 g
- Fiber: 1 g
- Protein: 5 g
- Sodium: 248 mg

345. Zucchini Chip Cupcakes

"A wonderful recipe for moist, nut-topped cupcakes without frosting to use up zucchini and serve as a quick snack."
Serving: about 2 dozen. | Prep: 15m | Ready in: 35m

Ingredients

- 1/2 cup butter, softened
- 1/2 cup canola oil
- 1-3/4 cups sugar
- 2 eggs
- 1/2 cup milk
- 1 tsp. vanilla extract
- 2-1/2 cups all-purpose flour
- 1/4 cup baking cocoa
- 1 tsp. baking soda
- 1/2 tsp. salt
- 1/2 tsp. ground cinnamon
- 2 cups shredded zucchini
- 1/4 cup miniature semisweet chocolate chips
- 1/4 cup chopped pecans

Direction

- Cream sugar, oil, and butter in a large bowl until they are fluffy and light. Whisk in vanilla, milk, and eggs. Mix cinnamon, salt, baking soda, cocoa, and flour; add into the creamed mixture gradually Fold in chocolate chips and zucchini.

- Add into paper-lined or greased muffin cups to 2/3 full. Place pecans on top. Bake at 375 degrees until a toothpick comes out clean, for 20-25 minutes. Let cool for 10 minutes, then transfer from the pans onto wire racks to cool entirely

Nutrition Information

- Calories: 208 calories
- Total Carbohydrate: 27 g
- Cholesterol: 29 mg
- Total Fat: 11 g
- Fiber: 1 g
- Protein: 3 g
- Sodium: 149 mg

346. Zucchini Chip Snack Cake

"This rich dessert moisten by the shredded zucchini will make your mouth watering."
Serving: 12-15 servings. | Prep: 15m | Ready in: 60m

Ingredients

- 1/2 cup butter, softened
- 1-3/4 cups sugar
- 2 large eggs
- 1/2 cup canola oil
- 1 tsp. vanilla extract
- 2-1/2 cups all-purpose flour
- 2 tbsps. baking cocoa
- 1 tsp. baking soda
- 1/2 tsp. baking powder
- 1/2 tsp. ground cinnamon
- 1/2 tsp. ground cloves
- 1/2 cup buttermilk
- 2 cups shredded peeled zucchini
- 2 cups (12 oz.) semisweet chocolate chips

Direction

- Cream sugar and butter in a large bowl until they are fluffy and light. Add 1 egg at a time and whisk thoroughly after every addition. Whisk in vanilla and oil. Mix the dry

ingredients and add into the creamed mixture alternately with buttermilk, whisk thoroughly after every addition. Add in zucchini and stir.
- Pour in a 13x9-inch greased baking pan. Scatter with chocolate chips. Bake at 350 degrees until a toothpick comes out clean when inserted into the center, for 45-50 minutes. Place on a wire rack to cool.

Nutrition Information

- Calories: 410 calories
- Total Carbohydrate: 55 g
- Cholesterol: 45 mg
- Total Fat: 21 g
- Fiber: 2 g
- Protein: 5 g
- Sodium: 180 mg

347. Zucchini Chocolate Cake

"Enjoy every bite of chocolate in this slightly sweet cake."
Serving: 12-15 servings. | Prep: 15m | Ready in: 55m

Ingredients

- 1/2 cup butter, softened
- 1/2 cup canola oil
- 1-3/4 cups sugar
- 2 eggs
- 1 tsp. vanilla extract
- 2-1/2 cups all-purpose flour
- 1/4 cup baking cocoa
- 1 tsp. baking soda
- 1/2 tsp. baking powder
- 1/2 tsp. ground cinnamon
- 1/4 to 1/2 tsp. ground cloves
- 1/2 cup buttermilk
- 2 cups shredded peeled zucchini
- 1/2 cup semisweet chocolate chips

Direction

- Cream sugar, oil, and butter in a bowl. Whisk in vanilla and eggs. Mix the dry ingredients; then add into the creamed mixture alternately with the buttermilk. Combine thoroughly. Add in the zucchini and stir. Pour in a 13x9-inch greased baking dish. Scatter with chocolate chips.

- Bake at 350 degrees until a toothpick comes out clean when inserted into the center, for 40-45 minutes. Transfer onto a wire rack and let cool.

Nutrition Information

- Calories: 333 calories
- Total Carbohydrate: 45 g
- Cholesterol: 46 mg
- Total Fat: 16 g
- Fiber: 1 g
- Protein: 4 g
- Sodium: 173 mg

348. Zucchini Chocolate Cake With Orange Glaze

"A delicious moist cake filled with nuts and zucchini, a touch of orange, and rich chocolate flavor."
Serving: 16 servings. | Prep: 20m | Ready in: 01h10m

Ingredients

- 1/2 cup butter, softened
- 1-1/2 cups sugar
- 2 large eggs
- 1/4 cup unsweetened applesauce
- 1 tsp. vanilla extract
- 2-1/2 cups all-purpose flour
- 1/2 cup baking cocoa
- 1-1/4 tsps. baking powder
- 1 tsp. salt
- 1 tsp. ground cinnamon
- 1/2 tsp. baking soda
- 1/2 cup fat-free milk
- 3 cups shredded zucchini
- 1/2 cup chopped walnuts
- 1 tbsp. grated orange zest
- GLAZE:
- 1-1/4 cups confectioners' sugar

- 2 tbsps. orange juice
- 1 tsp. vanilla extract

Direction

- Grease a 10-inch fluted tube pan using cooking spray and dust with flour.
- Cream sugar and butter in a large bowl until they are fluffy and light. Add 1 egg at a time and whisk thoroughly after every addition. Whisk in vanilla and applesauce.
- Mix soda, cinnamon, salt, baking powder, cocoa, and flour; then add into the creamed mixture alternately with milk and whisk thoroughly after every addition. Fold in orange zest, walnuts, and zucchini.
- Place into the prepared pan. Bake at 350 degrees until a toothpick comes out clean when inserted into the center, 50-60 minutes.
- Let cool for 10 minutes, then transfer from the pan onto a wire rack to cool entirely. Mix the glaze ingredients; sprinkle on the cake.

Nutrition Information

- Calories: 282 calories
- Total Carbohydrate: 47 g
- Cholesterol: 42 mg
- Total Fat: 9 g
- Fiber: 2 g
- Protein: 4 g
- Sodium: 273 mg

349. Zucchini Fudge Cake

"A succulent cake with baked zucchini inside."
Serving: 12-14 servings. | Prep: 20m | Ready in: 45m

Ingredients

- 1 cup butter, softened
- 2-1/2 cups sugar
- 4 eggs
- 2 tsps. vanilla extract
- 3 cups all-purpose flour
- 1/2 cup baking cocoa

- 2 tsps. baking powder
- 1 tsp. baking soda
- 3/4 tsp. salt
- 1 cup buttermilk
- 3 cups shredded zucchini
- 3-1/2 cups prepared chocolate frosting

Direction

- Cream sugar and butter in a large bowl until they are fluffy and light. Add 1 egg at a time and whisk thoroughly after every addition. Whisk in vanilla. Mix salt, baking soda, baking powder, cocoa, and flour; add into the creamed mixture alternately with buttermilk. Add in zucchini and stir.
- Pour in 3 greased and floured 9-inch round baking pans. Bake at 350 degrees until a toothpick comes out clean when inserted into the center, 25-30 minutes. Let cool for 10 minutes, then transfer from the pans onto wire racks to cool entirely. Spread over sides and tops and between layers of the cake with the frosting.

Nutrition Information

- Calories: 672 calories
- Total Carbohydrate: 102 g
- Cholesterol: 96 mg
- Total Fat: 27 g
- Fiber: 2 g
- Protein: 6 g
- Sodium: 604 mg

350. Zucchini Walnut Cake

"Shred and freeze a generous amount of zucchini to bake a moist sheet cake along with a tasty cream cheese frosting for a speedy dish for potlucks or picnics."
Serving: 20-24 servings. | Prep: 20m | Ready in: 55m

Ingredients

- 2 cups shredded zucchini
- 2 cups sugar
- 1 cup canola oil

- 4 large eggs
- 2-1/2 cups all-purpose flour
- 1-1/2 tsps. ground cinnamon
- 1 tsp. salt
- 1/2 tsp. baking powder
- 1/2 tsp. baking soda
- 1/2 cup chopped walnuts, optional
- FROSTING:
- 3 oz. cream cheese, softened
- 1/4 cup butter, softened
- 1 tbsp. 2% milk
- 1 tsp. vanilla extract
- 2 cups confectioners' sugar
- Additional chopped walnuts, optional

Direction

- Whisk eggs, oil, sugar, and zucchini in a large bowl until combined thoroughly. Mix baking soda, baking powder, salt, cinnamon, and flour; whisk gradually into the zucchini mixture until combined. If desired, fold in walnuts.
- Pour in a 13x9-inch greased baking pan. Bake at 350 degrees until a toothpick comes out clean when inserted into the center, for 35-40 minutes. Let cool.
- To make the frosting: Whisk vanilla, milk, butter, and cream cheese in a small bowl until they are smooth. Add the confectioners' sugar and combine thoroughly. Then frost the cake. If desired, scatter with nuts. Keep in the fridge.

Nutrition Information

- Calories: 275 calories
- Total Carbohydrate: 37 g
- Cholesterol: 45 mg
- Total Fat: 13 g
- Fiber: 1 g
- Protein: 3 g
- Sodium: 174 mg

351. Zucchini Walnut Chip Chocolate Cake

"Shredded zucchini will give great moisture."
Serving: 12-15 servings. | Prep: 15m | Ready in: 45m

Ingredients

- 1/2 cup butter, softened
- 1-1/2 cups sugar
- 3 eggs
- 1/2 cup vegetable oil
- 3 tsps. vanilla extract
- 1-3/4 cups all-purpose flour
- 1/4 cup baking cocoa
- 2 tsps. baking soda
- 1 tsp. baking powder
- 1/2 tsp. ground cinnamon
- 2 cups shredded zucchini
- 1 cup chopped walnuts, optional
- 1/2 cup semisweet chocolate chips

Direction

- In a bowl, cream together sugar and butter. Add in one egg at a time, beating well after each. Beat in vanilla and oil. Combine the cinnamon, cocoa, baking soda, baking powder and flour; add them into the creamed mixture gradually. Fold in walnuts and zucchini if you wish.
- Spread into a 13x9-in. greased baking pan. Sprinkle chocolate chips on top. Bake until inserted toothpick in the middle comes out clean, at 350° for 30-35 minutes. Cool down on a wire rack.

Nutrition Information

- Calories: 298 calories
- Total Carbohydrate: 36 g
- Cholesterol: 59 mg
- Total Fat: 16 g
- Fiber: 1 g
- Protein: 4 g
- Sodium: 270 mg

Chapter 7: Amazing Zucchini Recipes

***

352. Cheesy Shrimp And Zucchini Casserole

"Low-carb casserole recipe."
Serving: 6 | Prep: 20m | Ready in: 1h

Ingredients

- 1 tbsp. olive oil
- 3 zucchini, sliced
- 2 yellow squash, sliced
- salt and freshly ground black pepper to taste
- 1 tbsp. butter
- 1 1/2 lbs. uncooked medium shrimp, peeled and deveined
- 3 tbsps. minced garlic
- 1/4 cup chopped green onions (optional)
- 2 tsps. seafood seasoning (such as Old Bay®)
- 1 cup shredded Cheddar cheese
- 1 cup shredded mozzarella cheese
- 1 cup shredded habanero-flavored cheese

Direction

- Preheat an oven to 190°C/375°F.
- In a skillet, heat olive oil on medium heat. Cook squash and zucchini for 5-10 minutes till tender. Season with pepper and salt.
- In another skillet, melt butter on medium heat. Add garlic and shrimp; cook, 2 minutes per side, till meat is opaque and shrimp are bright pink outside. Add seafood seasoning and green onions; mix to combine. Take off heat.
- Put 1/2 zucchini-squash mixture in 9x13-in. baking dish with slotted spoon. Add skillet drippings and shrimp. Sprinkle 1/2 cup of

habanero pepper cheese, 1/2 cup mozzarella cheese and 1/2 cup cheddar cheese on top. Add leftover squash and zucchini mixture. Top with leftover cheeses.

- In preheated oven, bake for 30 minutes till bubbly and gooey.

Nutrition Information

- Calories: 366 calories;
- Total Carbohydrate: 7.2 g
- Cholesterol: 233 mg
- Total Fat: 21.8 g
- Protein: 35.5 g
- Sodium: 806 mg

353. Chicken Stir-fry With Thai Peanut Sauce

""This homemade peanut sauce is creamy and spicy. Serve this wonderful sauce with rice or rice noodles and a sweet-and-sour cucumber salad and voila you've got a fantastic meal for the day!""
Serving: 6 | Prep: 40m | Ready in: 55m

Ingredients

- 2/3 cup creamy, low-salt peanut butter
- 1 cup hot water, divided
- 1/4 cup brown sugar
- 2 tbsps. low-sodium soy sauce
- 2 tbsps. rice vinegar
- 1 tbsp. red curry paste, or more to taste
- 1/4 cup canola oil, divided
- 1 1/2 lbs. boneless chicken breasts, cut into 1/2-inch cubes
- 1 tbsp. minced fresh ginger
- 1 tbsp. minced garlic, or more to taste
- 1 cup broccoli florets
- 1 large carrot, cut into thick strips
- 1/2 cup halved green beans
- 1/2 cup sliced zucchini
- 1 small onion, sliced
- 1/2 sweet red pepper, thinly sliced
- 3 scallions, sliced
- 1/2 cup unsalted, dry-roasted peanuts, divided
- 1/2 cup chopped fresh cilantro, divided
- 1 lime, cut into wedges
- 1 pinch red pepper flakes, or to taste (optional)

Direction

- In a bowl, mix soy sauce, 1/3 cup of hot water, rice vinegar, curry paste, peanut butter and brown sugar. Put the peanut sauce aside.
- Heat a deep skillet or a big wok with 2 tbsps. of oil over medium-high heat. Put in the garlic, chicken and ginger. Cook and continuously stir the chicken for 5-7 minutes or until the chicken is no longer pink inside and the juices are running clear. Remove the cooked chicken from the wok and put aside.
- Put 2/3 cup of hot water into the same wok. Put in the green beans, broccoli and carrots. Cover and steam for 2 minutes. Remove the cooked vegetables from the wok and put the steaming liquid in a bowl.
- Put 1 tbsp. of oil into the same wok. Put in the onion, red pepper and zucchini and stir-fry for 4 minutes. Put the steamed green beans, broccoli and carrots back into the wok. Put in the remaining oil if needed. Continue cooking for 3-5 more minutes until the vegetables are tender-crisp. Lower the heat setting to medium-low.
- Put the cooked chicken back into the wok. Mix in 1/3 cup of cilantro, scallions, 1/3 cup of peanuts and peanut sauce. Mix well for 1-3 minutes until heated through. If needed, mix in the steaming liquid to make the consistency of the sauce thin.
- Top off with cilantro and the remaining peanuts and put lime wedge on one side. Put a sprinkle of red pepper flakes on top.

Nutrition Information

- Calories: 527 calories;
- Total Carbohydrate: 26.4 g
- Cholesterol: 65 mg
- Total Fat: 34.8 g
- Protein: 36.4 g

- Sodium: 308 mg

354. Fresh Zucchini Pasta Sauce

"This pasta dish is not only tasty but also simple to make! The pasta cooks the zucchini in its bowl."
Serving: 4 | Prep: 15m | Ready in: 1h15m

Ingredients

- 2 zucchini, grated
- 3 cloves garlic, minced
- 2 tbsps. olive oil
- salt to taste
- 1 (8 oz.) package angel hair pasta

Direction

- In a big bowl, mix together garlic and zucchini, stirring with salt and olive oil. Set the mixture aside for 1 hour until flavors blend.
- Boil a big pot of lightly salted water and cook angel hair, occasionally stirring, for 4-5 minutes until cooked through and firm to the bite. Drain then add with the zucchini mixture, tossing to blend and to cook the zucchini slightly.

Nutrition Information

- Calories: 239 calories;
- Total Carbohydrate: 35.1 g
- Cholesterol: 0 mg
- Total Fat: 8.4 g
- Protein: 7.3 g
- Sodium: 125 mg

355. Garlic Vegetable Saute

"A tasty combination of spices and fresh veggies pan-fried with olive oil and butter."
Serving: 4 | Prep: 20m | Ready in: 30m

Ingredients

- 1 tbsp. olive oil
- 1 tbsp. butter
- 3 cloves garlic, finely minced
- 1 jalapeno pepper, seeds and ribs removed, minced
- 2 zucchini, halved lengthwise and sliced
- 1 yellow bell pepper, cut into chunks
- 1 red bell pepper, cut into chunks
- 1 shallot, sliced
- 1/4 tsp. salt
- freshly ground black pepper to taste
- 1 pinch paprika

Direction

- In a large skillet, heat butter and olive oil; stir and cook jalapeno and garlic in the hot skillet for 5 minutes until they soften. Add shallot, red bell pepper, yellow bell pepper, and zucchini; carry on stirring and cooking for 5 more minutes until tender. Flavor with paprika, pepper, and salt.

Nutrition Information

- Calories: 103 calories;
- Total Carbohydrate: 10.3 g
- Cholesterol: 8 mg
- Total Fat: 6.7 g
- Protein: 2.4 g
- Sodium: 180 mg

356. Mexican Zucchini Cheese Soup

"If you have many squash and zucchini in your garden, this recipe is the right one to make."
Serving: 6 | Prep: 20m | Ready in: 45m

Ingredients

- 1 tbsp. olive oil
- 1 cup chopped onion
- 2 cloves garlic, minced
- 1/2 tsp. dried oregano
- 2 (14.5 oz.) cans chicken broth
- 1 (14.5 oz.) can Mexican-style stewed tomatoes
- 2 medium zucchini, halved lengthwise and cut in 1/4 inch slices
- 2 medium yellow squash, halved lengthwise and cut in 1/4 inch slices
- 1 (8.75 oz.) can whole kernel corn, drained
- 1 (4.5 oz.) can diced green chile peppers
- 12 oz. processed cheese food, cubed
- 1/2 tsp. freshly ground black pepper
- 1/4 cup chopped fresh cilantro

Direction

- In a big pot, heat olive oil, and sauté garlic and onion until soft. Use oregano to season.
- Stir in tomatoes and chicken broth. Boil it. Stir in chile peppers, corn, yellow squash, and zucchini. Lower the heat to low, and simmer until the squash is soft, about 10 minutes.
- Stir cubed processed cheese into the soup. Keep stirring and cooking until the cheese melts. Use pepper to season. Stir in cilantro right before eating.

Nutrition Information

- Calories: 307 calories;
- Total Carbohydrate: 26.2 g
- Cholesterol: 48 mg
- Total Fat: 17.5 g
- Protein: 14.7 g
- Sodium: 1829 mg

357. Shrimp Florentine With Zoodles

"This shrimp dinner uses zoodles in place of pasta."
Serving: 4 | Prep: 10m | Ready in: 25m

Ingredients

- 1 tbsp. butter
- 1 tbsp. extra-virgin olive oil
- 2 zucchini, cut into noodle-shape strands
- 1/2 large yellow onion, minced
- 1 tbsp. chopped garlic
- 1/2 tsp. kosher salt
- 2 tbsps. butter
- 1 lb. large shrimp, peeled and deveined
- 1 tsp. minced garlic
- 1 (6 oz.) bag baby spinach
- 1 tbsp. fresh lemon juice
- 1 tsp. red pepper flakes
- 1/2 tsp. kosher salt
- 1/2 tsp. freshly ground black pepper

Direction

- In a big frying pan, heat olive oil and 1 tbsp. butter on medium; stir and cook onion, 1/2 tsp. salt, zoodles (zucchini noodles), and chopped garlic until onion is translucent and zoodles are tender, 5 minutes. Put the zoodle mixture in a bowl.
- In the same pan, heat 2 tbsps. butter; add minced garlic and shrimp, cook, and stir until shrimp turns pink, 3-4 minutes. Add pepper, red pepper flakes, spinach, 1/2 tsp. salt, and lemon juice; stir and cook for 3-4 minutes until spinach starts wilting. Add the zoodle mixture; stir and cook for 2-3 minutes or until cooked through.

Nutrition Information

- Calories: 229 calories;
- Total Carbohydrate: 7.1 g
- Cholesterol: 195 mg
- Total Fat: 13.4 g
- Protein: 21 g
- Sodium: 781 mg

- Sodium: 1189 mg

358. Southwest Stuffed Zucchini

"Hearty main dish made with zucchini."
Serving: 4 | Prep: 30m | Ready in: 1h15m

Ingredients

- 2 large zucchini, halved and quartered
- 1 1/4 lbs. lean ground turkey
- 1/2 small green bell pepper, finely chopped
- 1/4 onion, finely chopped
- 1 egg
- 1/4 cup bread crumbs
- 1 jalapeno pepper, seeded and minced
- 2 tbsps. chopped fresh cilantro
- 2 cloves garlic, minced
- 2 tsps. steak seasoning (such as Montreal Steak Seasoning®)
- 2 tsps. ground cumin
- 1 tsp. dried thyme
- 1 cup salsa
- 1 cup shredded sharp Cheddar cheese

Direction

- Set an oven to preheat to 200°C (400°F).
- Use a spoon to scoop out the flesh from the zucchini, then create boats.
- In a big bowl, mix the thyme, cumin, steak seasoning, garlic, cilantro, jalapeno pepper, breadcrumbs, egg, onion, green bell pepper and turkey. Fill turkey mixture on the zucchini boats, then cover it with Cheddar cheese and salsa.
- Let it bake for about 45 minutes in the preheated oven, until the zucchini becomes very tender and the turkey has no visible pink color in the middle.

Nutrition Information

- Calories: 427 calories;
- Total Carbohydrate: 18.3 g
- Cholesterol: 181 mg
- Total Fat: 22.4 g
- Protein: 41.2 g

359. Squash And Zucchini Casserole

"A vegetable casserole for summer meals."
Serving: 5 | Prep: 20m | Ready in: 50m

Ingredients

- 2 medium yellow squash
- 2 large zucchini
- 1 Vidalia onions, thinly sliced
- 2 large tomatoes, sliced
- 2 cups grated Romano cheese
- 1/2 cup butter, divided
- salt and pepper to taste

Direction

- Start preheating the oven to 375°F (190°C).
- Slice the squash and zucchini into long, thin layers. Lightly oil a 7x11-inch baking dish and arrange tomatoes, onion, zucchini, and squash in layer onto the baking dish. Spread with cheese and include in pats of butter between each layer of vegetables, and flavor each layer to taste with ground black pepper and salt.
- Keep layering process until every vegetable are used and top with leftover cheese and butter.
- Bake, with cover, for 20 to 30 minutes at 375°F (190°C), until vegetables reach the desired tenderness and cheese melts and bubbles.

Nutrition Information

- Calories: 407 calories;
- Total Carbohydrate: 14.6 g
- Cholesterol: 98 mg
- Total Fat: 31.9 g
- Protein: 18.6 g
- Sodium: 721 mg

360. Summerly Squash

"This recipe will make you like squash even if you don't like it."
Serving: 6 | Prep: 15m | Ready in: 45m

Ingredients

- 2 tbsps. vegetable oil
- 1 small onion, sliced
- 2 medium tomatoes, coarsely chopped
- 1 tsp. salt
- 1/4 tsp. pepper
- 2 small zucchini, cut into 1/2 inch slices
- 2 small yellow summer squash, cut into 1/2-inch slices
- 1 bay leaf
- 1/2 tsp. dried basil

Direction

- In a big skillet, heat the oil over medium heat. Cook and mix the onion until it becomes tender, about 5 minutes. Stir in tomatoes. Use pepper and salt to season. Keep on cooking and stirring for about 5 minutes more. Stir in basil, bay leaf, yellow squash and zucchini. Cover the mixture and then turn the heat down to low. Let simmer for another 20 minutes, occasionally stirring it. Before serving, take the bay leaf out.

Nutrition Information

- Calories: 65 calories;
- Total Carbohydrate: 5.4 g
- Cholesterol: 0 mg
- Total Fat: 4.8 g
- Protein: 1.5 g
- Sodium: 395 mg

361. Vegetarian Farro Skillet

"An all-in-one-skillet dish with tomatoes, farro and zucchini."
Serving: 6 | Prep: 10m | Ready in: 47m

Ingredients

- 1 1/2 cups farro, uncooked
- 1 (14 oz.) can vegetable broth
- 1 (14.5 oz.) can Hunt's® Fire Roasted Diced Tomatoes, undrained
- 2 tbsps. Pure Wesson® Canola Oil, divided
- 2 cups quartered lengthwise, sliced zucchini
- 1 tsp. ground cumin
- 1/2 tsp. salt
- 1/2 cup diced green bell pepper
- 1/2 cup chopped yellow onion
- 1/2 cup fresh corn kernels
- 1 tsp. finely chopped garlic
- 1 (15 oz.) can black beans, drained, rinsed
- 3 tbsps. chopped fresh cilantro

Direction

- In a medium saucepan, combine 1 tbsp. of oil, undrained tomatoes, broth and farro. Boil on medium-high heat. Lower the heat and simmer, covered, until mixture absorbs all the liquid, 25 minutes.
- In a big skillet, heat the rest of oil (1 tbsp.) on medium-high heat. Put in zucchini and top with 1/2 of salt and cumin; cook, while stirring sometimes, until soft and browned, 5-7 minutes. Take out of the skillet, then put aside and keep it warm.
- Put in garlic, corn, onion and bell pepper; top with the rest of salt and cumin. Cook and stir sometimes for 5 minutes. Mix in beans and heat for another 2 minutes. Return zucchini into the skillet to cook with the cooked farro; mix to incorporate. Add cilantro on top, then serve.

Nutrition Information

- Calories: 307 calories;
- Total Carbohydrate: 56.5 g

- Cholesterol: 0 mg
- Total Fat: 6.6 g
- Protein: 11.1 g
- Sodium: 773 mg

362. Zucchini And Rice Casserole

"A great zucchini recipe."
Serving: 10 | Prep: 30m | Ready in: 1h20m

Ingredients

- 1 1/2 cups water
- 1/2 cup uncooked white rice
- 2 lbs. zucchini
- 1/4 cup butter
- 1/4 cup vegetable oil
- 1/2 cup grated Parmesan cheese
- 1/2 cup shredded Cheddar cheese
- salt and pepper to taste
- 2 eggs, beaten
- 1 cup bread crumbs
- 2 tbsps. butter, melted

Direction

- Boil water; put rice. When water boils, lower temperature to low. Cover rice. Cook till rice is tender.
- Preheat an oven broiler then grease a 9x13-in. baking dish.
- Cut zucchini ends; steam till tender. Keep 2 zucchini for a garnish. Dice leftover zucchini.
- In a Dutch oven, mix oil and butter. Heat till butter melts. Add diced zucchini and rice. Sauté, frequently mixing, till golden. Mix cheese in till melted. Put pepper and salt to taste. Slightly cool; quickly mix eggs in. Put into prepped baking dish. Generously sprinkle on breadcrumbs.
- Cut leftover zucchini. Put around diced mixture. Drizzle melted butter on top.
- Broil 6-in. away from heat source till bubbly and lightly browned.

Nutrition Information

- Calories: 262 calories;
- Total Carbohydrate: 19 g
- Cholesterol: 66 mg
- Total Fat: 17.5 g
- Protein: 7.9 g
- Sodium: 263 mg

363. Zucchini Bread Vi

"A lighter version of zucchini bread with nice lemon flavor and lots of pecans."
Serving: 12 | Prep: 15m | Ready in: 1h15m

Ingredients

- 2 cups all-purpose flour
- 3/4 tsp. baking powder
- 3/4 tsp. baking soda
- 3/4 tsp. salt
- 3/4 tsp. ground cinnamon
- 3 eggs
- 1 cup white sugar
- 2/3 cup vegetable oil
- 1 1/3 cups grated zucchini
- 3/4 tsp. lemon extract
- 2/3 cup chopped pecans

Direction

- Preheat the oven to 175°C or 350°F. Grease a 9x5 inch loaf pan lightly. Sift together cinnamon, salt, baking powder, baking soda and flour.
- Whisk eggs with sugar in a big bowl for 10 minutes. Slowly put in oil and mix for 2 minutes longer. Stir in pecans, zucchini and lemon extract. Fold in flour mixture till equally moistened; avoid overmixing. Put batter into prepped pan.
- In prepped oven, bake for an hour till a toothpick pricked into middle of the loaf comes out clean.

Nutrition Information

- Calories: 312 calories;
- Total Carbohydrate: 34.2 g
- Cholesterol: 46 mg
- Total Fat: 18.1 g
- Protein: 4.5 g
- Sodium: 274 mg

364. Zucchini Jelly

"My Grandmother gave me this zucchini recipe many years ago and my family and friends love it. You can try any flavor gelatin you like, but I think strawberry and apricot are best."
Serving: 192 | Prep: 15m | Ready in: 45m

Ingredients

- 6 cups peeled, seeded, and shredded zucchini
- 6 cups white sugar
- 1 (15.25 oz.) can crushed pineapple, drained
- 1/2 cup lemon juice
- 1 (6 oz.) package strawberry flavored Jell-O® mix

Direction

- In a big pot, mix together lemon juice, pineapple, sugar and zucchini over medium heat. Boil the mixture until the zucchini is clear, take away from heat. Add gelatin mix and whisk until fully dissolved.
- Ladle into hot, sterilized jars, leaving approximately 1/4-in. headspace. Close the jars and put into boiling water canner to process, about 5 minutes.

Nutrition Information

- Calories: 30 calories;
- Total Carbohydrate: 7.6 g
- Cholesterol: 0 mg
- Total Fat: 0 g
- Protein: 0.1 g
- Sodium: 3 mg

365. Zucchini Noodle Casserole

"A great low-calorie recipe to replace pasta."
Serving: 4 | Prep: 20m | Ready in: 1h

Ingredients

- 3 tbsps. olive oil, divided, or as needed
- 5 zucchini squash, cut into 'noodles' using a spiral slicer or vegetable peeler
- 1/4 cup minced garlic
- 1 (16 oz.) jar marinara sauce, or to taste
- 1 (7 oz.) container 2% Greek yogurt
- 1 pinch Italian seasoning, or to taste
- salt and ground black pepper to taste
- 1/2 cup shredded mozzarella cheese

Direction

- Set an oven to 220°C (425°F) and start preheating.
- In a large skillet, heat a tbsp. of oil on medium-high heat. Sauté zucchini in batches, enough to fit in the skillet with a tsp. of garlic for 3-6 minutes until the zucchini soften and browns slightly. Repeat with the rest of the garlic, zucchini, and olive oil. Place the cooked zucchini mixture into a 9x13-inch baking dish.
- In a saucepan, beat together black pepper, salt, Italian seasoning, yogurt, and marinara sauce on low heat; stir and cook for 5-10 minutes until the sauce is warmed throughout. Pour the sauce on the zucchini mixture in the baking dish. Dust the top with a pinch of the Italian seasoning and mozzarella cheese.
- In the prepared oven, bake for 20-30 minutes until the cheese is bubbly.

Nutrition Information

- Calories: 292 calories;
- Total Carbohydrate: 25.7 g
- Cholesterol: 14 mg
- Total Fat: 16.7 g
- Protein: 12 g
- Sodium: 618 mg

Index

Turkey, 3, 5, 17, 21, 103–104, 122–123, 127–129, 134, 172, 195

Turnip, 118

V

Vanilla extract, 12–13, 138–139, 141, 143–147, 149–160, 162, 164–166, 170–173,

176–181, 183–191

Vegan, 92

Vegetable oil, 28, 40, 43, 45, 52, 55, 62–63, 65, 69, 72–73, 78, 90, 118, 139–143,

146–147, 154, 156, 158, 160, 163–165, 167–168, 170–172, 176–177, 179–180, 183–185, 191,

196–197

Vegetable stock, 93

Vegetables, 8–10, 15, 18, 21–26, 29–30, 32, 34–35, 37–40, 42–43, 46–47, 50, 55–56,

58–59, 61–64, 66, 69, 71, 75, 79–83, 85–86, 88–89, 91, 94–107, 111–112, 114, 117–125,

128–129, 131–134, 136, 170, 172, 181–182, 192, 195

Vegetarian, 5, 7, 90, 95, 131, 134, 196

Vinegar, 22–24, 27–33, 35–38, 40–43, 45, 47, 49–57, 59–76, 78, 84, 86, 101, 105–106,

119–120, 129, 192

W

Walnut, 4, 6–7, 12, 25–26, 37, 57–58, 72, 74, 131, 138, 141–144, 146–147, 149, 151–154,

157–160, 164, 167–173, 177, 180, 183–184, 186, 189–191

Water chestnut, 33–34, 76

Watercress, 8

Whipping cream, 116

White pepper, 19, 30, 99

White sugar, 12–13, 51, 55, 108, 141, 143, 164–165, 168, 171, 197–198

White wine, 24, 29–30, 32, 38, 41, 49, 52, 54, 56–57, 62–63, 69–70, 73, 84

White wine vinegar, 24, 29–30, 32, 38, 41, 49, 52, 54, 56–57, 62–63, 69–70, 73, 84

Wild rice, 4, 64

Wine, 22, 24, 29–32, 36–38, 40–41, 43, 47, 49–50, 52, 54–58, 61–63, 69–73, 78, 84, 94,

105–107, 109, 119

Worcestershire sauce, 86

Y

Yeast, 6, 148, 169, 173–174

Z

Zest, 13, 28, 50, 96, 142, 154–155, 161, 166, 169, 174–175, 183–184, 189

Conclusion

Thank you again for downloading this book!

I hope you enjoyed reading about my book!

If you enjoyed this book, please take the time to share your thoughts and post a review on Amazon. It'd be greatly appreciated!

Write me an honest review about the book – I truly value your opinion and thoughts and I will incorporate them into my next book, which is already underway.

Thank you!

If you have any questions, **feel free to contact at:** *msfruit@mrandmscooking.com*

Ms. Fruit

www.MrandMsCooking.com

Made in the USA
Middletown, DE
19 April 2022